THE MOUNTAIN LEADER

Mike Raine

First published 2023

Published in Great Britain 2023 by Pesda Press
Tan y Coed Canol
Ceunant
Caernarfon
Gwynedd
LL55 4RN

© Copyright 2023 Mike Raine

ISBN: 9781906095802

The author has asserted his rights under the Copyright, Designs and Patents Act, 1988, to be identified as Author of this Work. All rights reserved. No part of this publication may be reproduced, stored in a retrieval system, or transmitted, in any form or by any means, electronic, mechanical, photocopying, recording or otherwise, without the prior written permission of the publisher.

Printed and bound in Poland. www.lfbookservices.co.uk

To the 3rd Spen Valley Scouts for getting me started, thank you.

FOREWORD

When Mike first mentioned the context of this book to me, I must admit to a little scepticism. Where was this book going to sit with the official Mountain Leader Handbook? A quick scan of the first few pages certainly changed my mind. This book gets as far away as possible from the technical skills we have to gain on training and assessment courses in order to reach the standard required to pass the awards. What the ML handbooks don't do so well is demonstrate what is required to be a good and effective leader after attaining the award. In fact, much of the content is also valid for the Hill and Moorland Leader and Lowland Leader holders.

The Mountain Training qualifications have undergone seismic shifts since they came into being in the mid-sixties, and rightly so. It has long since been unnecessary to be a full-blown meteorologist to pass the weather paper, and some of the rope work / security on steep ground taught and assessed in the 70s was more akin to the MIC! However, in the past 20 years or so more radical changes have taken place, not so much in the skill set required to attain the qualifications, but in the change of emphasis on environmental issues, conservation, leaders' responsibilities, and many other areas. The amount of time a candidate will spend with their head buried in a map and compass on assessment is vastly disproportionate to time they will spend navigating once they are qualified. This book addresses these issues, and many others, and in so much more detail than training or assessment courses ever could.

There is no such thing as *"you can't teach an old dog new tricks"*. The more recently qualified, or even those considering signing up to one of the schemes, should take advantage of Mike's vast experience of the Mountain Training Schemes, he has a wealth of knowledge to draw on.

Mal Creasey
WMRCI (retired)
BMG (retired)

ACKNOWLEDGEMENTS

I have had enormous help and the following people have held my hand, advised, persuaded and inspired me – none more so than my wife Sally Hancox. I thank the staff and students of Plas y Brenin with whom I worked for fifteen years and the volunteer Scout leaders and teachers who gave their time to get me started in the hills such a long time ago. It would be rude not to mention Franco Ferrero who keeps believing in my projects, not only that, he makes sense of them, edits and publishes them – thank you Franco.

Thank you to the following who have all provided input, photographs, stories, top tips or opinions that have helped to create this book: Wasim 'drBackpack' Ahmed, Rusty Bale, Adam Betts, Jez Brown, Tim Cain, Katie Cannell, Derek Clarke, Graham Cole, Malcolm Creasey, Gareth Davies, Jimbob Derry, Dave Evans, Carlo Forte, Tom Fury, Steve Goodrum, Rob Goodsell, Richard Hale, Stuart Halford, Mike Hammill, Mark Hardy, Adam Harmer, Graham Hassall, Patrick Hickie, Albert Hinton, Helen and Steve Howe, Keith Hulse, Claire Iley, Kath James, Merfyn 'Smyrff' Jones, Shahin Karimi, Alice Kerr, Dan Lane, Helen Lawless, John Mainwaring, Alan Manouch, Gareth Martin, Branwen McBride, Andy Merrick, Katie Merrick, Gereldene Nee, Andy Newton, Rob Nicholson, Alistair Othen, Darren Parkinson, Iona Pawson, Gary Peasland, Mark Reid, Mark 'Baggy' Richards, Nick Rowe, Adrian Sancroft, Paul Sanderson, Kamala Sen, David Tainton, Al Topping, Lou Tully, Graham Uney, Bren Whelan, Bryn Williams, Nigel Williams, Kevin Woods, Kate Worthington, Ross Worthington and Belal Younis.

I would also like to mention the participants in my Nature of Snowdonia workshops. Thank you, your feedback and enthusiasm has been essential.

Photographs

All photographs are by Mike Raine except where acknowledged in the captions.

ABOUT THE AUTHOR

Mike Raine is a Geography graduate and a former teacher and senior manager in secondary schools. He worked at Plas y Brenin, the National Outdoor Centre, for fifteen years mostly as a Senior Instructor. He is a Winter Mountaineering and Climbing Instructor and an International Mountain Leader. Mike has directed a range of Mountain Training courses in a range of locations and has been involved as a trainer and assessor of the Mountain Leader Qualification and the Mountaineering Instructor Qualification.

Mike now runs a small business in Eryri (Snowdonia) offering continuing professional development and further training workshops to mountain leaders and mountaineering instructors. He offers eLearning modules, is the author of the popular *Nature of Snowdonia* (Pesda Press 2020) and posts regularly on his Facebook blog *Notes from the Hill*.

You can find out more about Mike at www.mikeraine.co.uk. where there are links to his shop, his blogs and further resources such as his Podcast *Outdoor Lives* and his patreon.com/mikeraine channel. Here you can sign up to his newsletter and this is where to go to book on to his workshops and first aid courses.

INTRODUCTION

There aren't many better feelings than getting to the summit of a mountain or a hill. It's a magical moment that never diminishes. To look down on the world below, be it clear or even partly obscured by cloud, is a truly wondrous experience. It is one that you have enjoyed, described and celebrated. Maybe you've shared it with friends, maybe you just told your family, maybe you just did it to share on social media. If you remain untouched by summit fever, then this book is probably not for you. When the mist is around us, when the rain is driving in horizontally, and even when the wind tries to pluck you off your feet, the summit experience is immensely rewarding. It's rewarding because it takes physical effort to get there and because on our journey we find head space. There's a satisfaction, an inner satisfaction, that only we who have experienced it can fully grasp. Why wouldn't you want to share that? Why would you not want to introduce people to the mountains? Why would anyone not want to be a mountain leader and what's more, be the best mountain leader they can be? The aim of this book is to encourage you to think, to inform and to help you to be the best mountain leader you can be.

"When I went for my ML, I had been an active walker on the hills and mountains for over thirty years and during that time I had taken several courses on navigation as to me that was the most important aspect of being out there, how wrong I was!

Why did you want to become an ML? This was the question asked to all of us, by Andy Newton, on our ML training first day. If I recall correctly, the answers varied from; Taking DoE groups, guiding people (for money), improving navigation and confidence on the hill; not much mention of conservation, land management or wildlife etc!

Things changed for me pretty quickly. I was active with Cymdeithas Eryri / the Snowdonia Society, joined the Yr Wyddfa Volunteer Warden team and then joined the likes of Mike Raine, Jim Langley, Paul Gannon and more for educational days out on the hills. I now think that I have a reasonably good broad knowledge of many things relating to our outdoors and of course I have in-depth knowledge in specific areas.

So although I had my ML, most of my learning was done afterwards, it's a bit like passing your driving test and then learning to drive over the following years!"

Keith Hulse

Contents

FOREWORD	4
ACKNOWLEDGEMENTS	5
ABOUT THE AUTHOR	6
INTRODUCTION	7
CONTENTS	8
BEING A MOUNTAIN LEADER	10

SECTION A – TO BE A MOUNTAIN LEADER

Clothing and Equipment — 17

SOCKS AND BOOTS	18
CLOTHING	20
EQUIPMENT	31
GROUP CLOTHING AND KIT	33
THE LEADER'S SACK	34

Navigation — 35

HOW WE APPROACH NAVIGATION	36
HANDRAILING	41
MAP-READING	44
TIMING	48
CONTOUR INTERPRETATION	51
USING THE COMPASS	55
TOOLBOX OF NAVIGATION TOOLS	62
ROUTE PLANNING	67

Weather — 69

SOURCES OF WEATHER INFORMATION	70
WHY IS IT COLDER ON THE HILL?	73
WHY IS IT WETTER ON THE HILL?	74
WHY IS IT WINDIER ON THE HILL?	75
WHAT DOES THE SYNOPTIC CHART INDICATE?	76
WHEN IS IT SUMMER?	82

Access, Environment and Conservation — 85

MOUNTAIN LEADERS AND THE ENVIRONMENT	89
HOW DO MOUNTAIN LEADERS LEARN MORE ABOUT THE ENVIRONMENT?	90
NICE TO KNOW, NEED TO KNOW	93
INFORMING AND INSPIRING OTHERS	95
WHERE ARE WE ALLOWED TO WALK?	100
UP TO DATE INFORMATION ABOUT ACCESS	104
THE COUNTRYSIDE CODE	105
WHY OUR HILLS LOOK THE WAY THEY DO	109
THE SPREAD OF BRACKEN	118
REWILDING OR NATURE FRIENDLY FARMING	120
FURTHER PRESSURE ON THE UPLANDS	122
CONSERVATION	124

SECTION B – BEING A MOUNTAIN LEADER

Leadership — 135

WHAT ARE THE CHARACTERISTICS OF A MOUNTAIN LEADER?	136
BEFORE THE DAY	**138**
RESPONSIBILITIES	138
DOES EVERYBODY KNOW WHAT THEY SHOULD HAVE?	139
RESPONSIBILITIES TO PARENTS, GUARDIANS AND NEXT OF KIN	143
RESPONSIBILITY TO ORGANISING ORGANISATIONS	145
PRE TRIP RISK ASSESSMENT	146
RESPONSIBILITIES TO THE WIDER, UPLAND COMMUNITY	147
ON THE DAY	**150**
THE BRIEFING	151
THE IMPORTANCE OF LEARNING NAMES AND GETTING TO KNOW YOUR GROUP	152
WALKING SKILLS	158
GENDER	165
WORKING WITH MINORITY ETHNIC GROUPS	166
MENTAL HEALTH ISSUES	167
WORKING WITH VULNERABLE PEOPLE	169
REFLECTIVE PRACTICE	170

FURTHER CONSIDERATIONS	**171**
OTHER UNFORESEEN CIRCUMSTANCES	174
MEDICAL MATTERS	175
REMOTE SUPERVISION	183
LOOKING AFTER YOURSELF	185
WORKING OR VOLUNTEERING FOR LARGE-SCALE EVENTS	188
WORKING AS A FREELANCER	194
STYLES AND MODELS	**197**
LEADERSHIP STYLES	197
LEADERSHIP MODELS	198
THE LEGAL BIT	**205**
A CHECKLIST FOR LEADERS	**209**

Hazards and Emergencies — 211

WHAT IS A HAZARD?	212
HAZARD MANAGEMENT	213
ENVIRONMENTAL HAZARDS	216
MANAGING STEEP GROUND	219
ATMOSPHERIC HAZARDS	223
HAZARDS UNDER FOOT	224
WATER HAZARDS INCLUDING RIVER CROSSINGS	227
HAZARDOUS ANIMALS	233
HAZARDS CREATED BY PEOPLE	240
ROPEWORK FOR MOUNTAIN LEADERS	**243**
UNPLANNED USE OF THE ROPE	243
WHICH ROPE	245
TO PUT IT IN CONTEXT	246
HOW TO CARRY THE ROPE	247
APPROPRIATE KNOTS	248
SELECTING ANCHORS AND BELAYING	248
USING THE ROPE ON ITS OWN	251
MANAGING A GROUP ON A SHORT ROCK STEP IN ASCENT OR DESCENT	251
TYPES OF ABSEIL	253
CONFIDENCE ROPING	254
EMERGENCY PROCEDURES AND FIRST AID	**257**
DEALING WITH AN INCIDENT	257
THE FIRST AID KIT	261
IMPROVISED CARRIES	265
EMERGENCY BIVOUAC SKILLS	267
POST SCENARIO	267
A FINAL REFLECTION	268

Expedition Skills — 271

WILD CAMPING	273
EQUIPMENT FOR CAMPING	276
USING CAMP STOVES	284
WATER	289
CAMP FOOD – WHAT SHOULD WE EAT?	292
WHERE TO CAMP	293
WASHING	295
TOILETS	296
DRESSING FOR DINNER	297
USE OF HUTS, BOTHIES AND OTHER SHELTERS	299
ENTERTAINMENT	301
ON REFLECTION	302

The Development of Hillwalking and its Representative Bodies — 305

A POTTED HISTORY OF THE DEVELOPMENT OF HILLWALKING AS A RECREATIONAL ACTIVITY	306
WALKING ETHICS	308
REPRESENTATIVE BODIES	310
REPRESENTATIVE BODIES FOR MOUNTAIN LEADERS AND OTHER LEADERS WORKING IN THE BRITISH HILLS	312
OTHER MOUNTAIN TRAINING WALK LEADER QUALIFICATIONS	314

Appendices — 318

APPENDIX A – TEACHING AND LEARNING SKILLS	318
APPENDIX B – RUNNING FOR MOUNTAIN LEADERS	322
APPENDIX C – GAELIC, IRISH AND WELSH FOR MOUNTAIN LEADERS	324
APPENDIX D – NOTES FOR TRAINEES	335
APPENDIX E – GOOD LEADERS	342
BIBLIOGRAPHY AND FURTHER READING	**343**
INDEX	**348**

The mountains are calling, looking north from Rhinog Fawr.

Being a Mountain Leader

There seems to be, to some people, a gap between what we train and assess on the Mountain Leader qualification and what people do as Mountain Leaders. It is not quite that simple. One of the areas walkers tend to need to develop to become a Mountain Leader is their navigation. The fact is, that before we enter the scheme, we tend to follow footpaths and then, once we qualify, we go back to following footpaths, so why the intense focus on navigation?

We justify it by pointing out that a Mountain Leader needs to know exactly where they are all of the time, well at least, most of the time. There may be a requirement to adjust your route for the day in order to respond to the needs of the group. Maybe low cloud is rolling in and knowledge of location is required as visibility starts to disappear. Maybe, just maybe, you come across someone in trouble. So, the need to be able to relocate with pinpoint accuracy is a very important skill for the Mountain Leader. It is true modern technology is aiding this process and it will be interesting to see to what degree GPS technology becomes part of the expected skill set of Mountain Leaders.

The Mountain Leader line

One of the motivations for writing this book is best explained by the Mountain Leader line. I noticed that whenever anyone was asking for advice, particularly in online forums, about what they needed to focus on for a

Being a Mountain Leader

Navigation is important but in this book I will advocate that there is so much more to being a Mountain Leader.

successful Mountain Leader assessment the answer would come back, navigation, navigation, navigation and some ropework. Yet, when we lead groups we barely look at a map and we hope never to use the rope.

In the illustration, the Mountain Leader line, you can see that technical skills such as micro-navigation and ropework play a disproportionately large role in a typical Mountain Leader training course. On the other hand, areas such as leadership are probably less obvious. There are no Mountain Leader trainers in the country who do not cover leadership and environment on training courses (they'd soon be found out by Mountain Training's moderators if they didn't) but it is hard to push the importance of these aspects of the qualification when new and quite tricky technical skills need to be learnt, practised and consolidated. Inevitably any training course is dominated timewise by the process of acquiring new skills, and action planning will often emphasise the need to practise these skills.

As your navigation skills and your ability to use the rope appropriately develop and become practised, then you will see and feel the 'softer' areas of the qualification take on more importance. Indeed, leadership and the environment will, as time goes by, become one of the main features of working as a Mountain Leader.

The Mountain Leader needs to be able to walk, to talk, to navigate, to lead, to motivate, to be a friend, to be an inspiration, to care, to inform, to know what to do if things go wrong, to know about kit, and not get lost. Is this you?

The Mountain Leader line

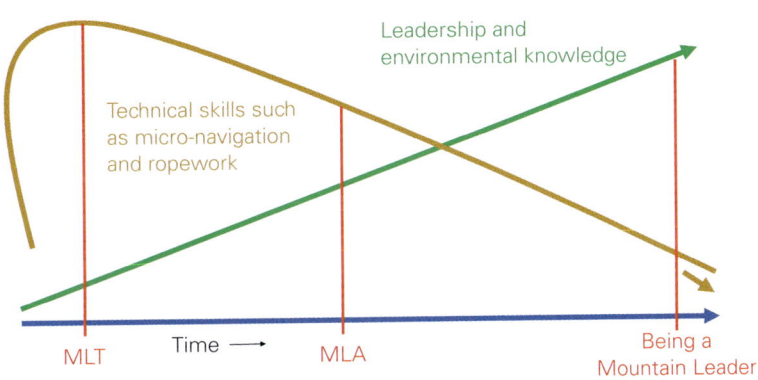

What do Mountain Leaders do?

Mountain Leaders work in many different ways. Once it was all about taking youngsters walking from outdoor centres, The Duke of Edinburgh Award Scheme has been around for some time now, while Scouting and Guiding have also been important organisations for introducing members to the hills. The military are fully in line with Mountain Training qualifications too.

THE MOUNTAIN LEADER

Many Mountain Leaders guide walks, volunteer at walking festivals or use their qualification to take people out on geography field work, photography trips or on hunts for artic-alpine flowers. Some runners become Mountain Leaders so that they can lead and coach on the hill, others are on the journey to becoming International Mountain Leaders. There are many reasons for attaining the Mountain Leader qualification and you do need to be mindful of this as you progress through the scheme. You should also be aware that it is a UK and Ireland based qualification.

Walking is proven to be a good form of exercise. It is gentle on the body and is something most can do for their entire lives. We now know that it is also good for mental health. Physical exercise in natural places takes us back to our anthropological roots and takes us away from our stressed, urban lives and everyone should try it. If people are out walking they start to see nature, they start to ask questions and enquire about our environment. It is well-known that we are more likely to want to conserve that with which we are familiar and that which we know something of. The role of Mountain Leaders as inspirational people who can lead others in healthy exercise is a growing one.

Is hillwalking safe?

Hillwalking is safe. In 2018 the BMC, which represents walkers and climbers in England and Wales, reported from a Sport England 'Active Lives Survey' that 2.8 million people claimed to go hillwalking regularly. Statistics from mountain rescue, as reported in the Mountain Rescue for England and Wales report released in 2018, confirmed that, compared to the number of people going hillwalking, the number of rescue call outs was tiny. In 2017 mountain rescue teams were deployed just over 2,000 times, 1,722 people were assisted, of those 1,081 were unhurt or had minor injuries. It's shame that the media takes so much pleasure in reporting every mountain rescue call out – lazy journalism some might say. It also really nice to know that we do have such a wonderful group of selfless volunteers who have formed themselves into mountain rescue teams and are on standby to help us, should we ever need them.

You need to know

This book is a moment in time and will be out of date as soon as you read it. The key area for change at the moment is how we use our mobile phones to navigate. I think their use as a convenient way to carry the map is growing, but new walkers are increasingly being guided by phone apps, it will be interesting to see how areas like this develop. The scheme syllabus could change. It changes slowly and has been established and tried and tested over many years. I don't think we'll see any major revision, although as I write, the leadership section has been developed so that it is clearer and teaching and learning skills have been brought into the syllabus. These topics were already incorporated into the plan for this book. What I also know, is that the key principals of looking after people and the environment in the uplands will change not one jot.

I'm caught in a glorious mix of imperial and metric measurements, I think that's partly my age and partly a British anomaly. As we become more influenced by 'Americanisms', our pastime is becoming more commonly known as hiking, rather than hillwalking. To be fair, it was hiking when I started, but I'll stick to hillwalking in the first edition of this book. I'm also going to call 'rucksacks' rucksacks not backpacks. I might refer to paths as trails, but I'll steadfastly hang on to the English name for a bum bag!

I don't intend to mention manufacturers by name, there has been no product placement or sponsorship in the creation of this book. However, there are exceptions to this, you'll find them and I make no apologies for singing the praises of Blizzard, everyone should carry a Blizzard blanket.

I use the term 'on the hill' a lot. Again, sorry, it's just what we say. It might be a mountain, we might be scrambling, but we just say, 'on the hill'. We might need to explain this to new walkers (or hikers).

Once qualified as a Mountain Leader you may be lucky enough to get to work on training and assessment courses. To help you, I've included some notes for trainers and assessors. Not comprehensive notes, just a few things to think about.

Remember, the final arbitrators of what is OK and what is not OK, will always be the officers of Mountain Training. This book, despite wide canvassing of views, perceptions and practice, is my opinion and I take sole responsibility for its contents.

This is a world of experts and 'experts'. 'Experts' may have done one training course and one assessment course and may be good social media creators. Experts run the training and assessment courses as well as continuing to lead groups. Be mindful of advice from 'experts' and, instead, try to seek opinion from experts. It maybe that your expert doesn't agree with everything in this book, you could almost say it would be odd if they did. I'm glad to argue, debate and discuss, as that is how we'll reach a mutual way forward together or in parallel. Nothing here is absolute and opinion can be discussed and debated, there will always be some grey areas. If in doubt seek advice from your trainer or assessor.

I hope this book will act as an aide memoir of your training and assessment. It might also touch on some aspects of the course that weren't covered on your journey to becoming a Mountain Leader. We only have the experience of our own journey so it's good to be able to learn from that of others' too.

The layout of this book does not match up exactly with the content of the syllabus. I have arranged it, broadly speaking, in the way I approach a Mountain Leader training course, or indeed any hillwalking course.

THE MOUNTAIN LEADER

The mountains are calling, looking towards Great Gable from Haystacks.

To be a Mountain Leader

- Have we got the right kit?

- Do we know where we are going?

- What is the weather doing?

- What will we see on our journey and what issues are there in our uplands?

Being a Mountain Leader

- How do we look after people in the hills?

- What sort of things could go wrong?

- How do we deal with things if they do go wrong?

- How we lead overnight trips?

- What else do we need to know?

Opposite page
Heading into
the Carneddau
from Ogwen.

SECTION A
TO BE A MOUNTAIN LEADER

Mountain Leaders enjoying fine weather on a CPD workshop.

Walking in Ireland
Photo: Bren Whelan

Have we got the right kit?

Clothing and Equipment

"There's no such thing as bad weather, just unsuitable clothing."

Alfred Wainwright 1973

When I meet a group for the first time, be it for a day walk or a course, even a Mountain Leader course, I need to know if they are adequately clothed and equipped for the forthcoming venture. As a Mountain Leader you need to be comfortable yourself and you need to project a professional image as first impressions are important. You need to understand the principles of clothing designed for the hills and you need to help others make sensible choices about what to wear, what to carry and how to carry it.

Top tips from Mountain Leaders

Looking after yourself and dressing for the conditions, means you can look after your group. Don't neglect your own self-care on a wet, windy day. It will make it so much harder to look after others if you are cold and damp.

Kath James

THE MOUNTAIN LEADER

What to wear and what to carry on the hill are quite personal matters and there is a vast array of fantastic clothing and equipment available today to help us deal with the vagaries of our upland climate. We can experience four seasons in one day at any time of year and we can be too hot, we can be too cold, it can be incredibly wet and there is almost always a wind to cool us down. Being able to operate comfortably in the hills and still be able to look after other people is the hallmark of a good Mountain Leader. The Mountain Leader needs to make wise decisions about what to carry, what spares might be needed and also what emergency equipment to carry. Too much results in a very heavy load, which is probably as bad as not having enough kit to deal with whatever incident may come your way.

You need to be able to advise other people on the kit required to go hillwalking. What do they need to think about first, how should they prioritise their spending and what can they repurpose that they already own?

You should have, by now, established your own favourite kit for hillwalking. It does, however, always seem to be a topic of interest for a lot of Mountain Leaders. Bear with me as I share some thoughts on outdoor kit. Then we'll consider the group kit and any extras a leader might think about carrying.

Well-dressed Mountain Leaders

Socks and boots

Simple, buy the best. I go for any sock that contains a good proportion of merino wool. It's warm, feels dry even when wet and is very comfortable, do not cut corners on socks. Most modern boots can be worn from the box. Breaking boots in is much easier than it used to be. Most boots are comfortable from the very start provided they fit properly. You should only need a handful of walks to get the feeling that you've had them for ages. Fabric or leather is an often debated topic. For me, it's leather every time. You can always keep a leather boot topped up with waterproofing by applying the recommended products. Whereas, once fabric boots let in water you can never really make them waterproof again. Fabric boots rose to prominence as lighter, more colourful, alternatives to leather boots and, it's fair to say, they can be a joy to wear in dry conditions.

> **Looking after your boots**
>
> The great attraction of fabric boots is the ease of care. You just let them dry out, brush the dirt off and as long as the waterproof, breathable liner works then you're all set to go. Modern leather boots are pretty easy to look after too as many of them have layers of various technical linings as well. However, what has changed is how you treat the leather. We used to use petroleum based waxes and all credit is due to the manufacturers, in particular Nikwax and Grangers, who have shifted away from harmful products. This is a great story of them taking the environmental lead and asking us not to use some of their old products. Hats off to them for their leadership. Today you'll get a water based or beeswax product to rub into your boots. One of the things emphasised by the manufacturers is that it's always best to dry your boots naturally. While it would be lovely to leave them in the hot baking sun at the end of a wet walking day this is an unlikely scenario. On the other hand do you really need to put them into a dehumidifying, drying room, or will they dry just as well in well ventilated warm part of your home?
>
> Some people swear by stuffing newspaper into boots to dry the insides. Apart from the obvious fact that newspapers aren't as commonly purchased anymore, this only works if you take out the wet paper and put in more dry paper frequently. Leaving them empty will help air move around and dry them quicker. If you have insoles remove them as well.

A well worn, comfortable looking, nicely waxed pair of boots – lovely.

Sole stiffness may have been something you needed to revise your view on as you went through the Mountain Leader qualification. Most of us do prefer a lighter bendier boot or even a walking shoe. When walking on man-made paths such as those on Yr Wyddfa or Ben Nevis, or on well travelled ground such as on Helvellyn, walking shoes or light boots can be a perfectly reasonable choice. They are actually more comfortable than boots on well-constructed, modern paths. But as you move on to steeper, more mountainous terrain off the path, then extra sole stiffness becomes really useful. For a more secure footing on terrain such as, steep, wet grass, scree and rocky ground (in both ascent and descent) whatever the weather, a stiffer boot, particularly laterally is a wise choice. Do remember that whatever you wear, you'll be role modelling and setting an example to those you lead, make it a good example, not an eccentric one.

A selection of footwear for walking in the mountains. Make sure you choose the right footwear for the right day and set a good example to those you lead.

Top tips from Mountain Leaders

When lacing up your boots, put an extra turn in the first simple knot. This will stop the lace slipping. When you've tied the bow put a simple knot in the bow and it will be far less likely to come undone.

Derek Clarke

Clothing

The current norm is base layer, one or two fleeces and a breathable outer layer that is windproof and waterproof.

Bucking the trend

An alternative is to go for the 'directional fabric' garments produced by companies like Buffalo and Paramo. These are usually worn as one layer with lots of ventilation for when it's warm (bare flesh exposed) and can be on the warm side when moving. For slower moving or when stationary, they are clearly very good. The fans of these garments claim they are better than the standard layering system at keeping you dry. They work by moving water as a liquid away from your body rather than using your body heat to drive water vapour out through a breathable layer. The claim is that they will keep you cooler when it's hot and warmer when it's wet. They are designed to be water repellent and they work in a similar way to the capillary process found in your wicking base layer.

Base layer

The most important layer is your base layer. This layer, which may or may not be insulating, wicks moisture away from your body and is paramount to your comfort. Moisture (sweat) is generated by you working hard, walking up hill for example. If you were wearing cotton next to your skin this moisture would collect in the cotton fabric, then cool down and cool you down at the same time. On a hot summer day this can be a good thing, but for most of the time in our hills it is not. A wicking base layer takes moisture away from your skin and transfers it to the mid layers and out through your breathable outer layer. The wicking base layer will also deal with penetrating moisture and move it away from your skin. However good your outer layer waterproofs are, moisture does seem to get in, particularly in the front by your chin. The wicking base layer will keep you feeling warm, dry and snug. Base layers come in many different types and although the pricey ones are nice, some of the bargain ones will do the job just as well. That is, if you think of the job as wicking, rather than insulating, the insulation can easily be added in the mid layers. Be sure to wash them as recommended by the manufacturer. Ordinary washing detergents, particularly those with fabric conditioner, are not so good for this type of garment.

Wicking fabrics weren't actually designed as wicking fabrics. Fabric manufacturers, in the 1970's, were looking for ways of using some of the newly developed synthetic materials. Damart would have been one of the first to put it into clothing that might be worn by mountaineers. It was good, I remember having some. I wore them in the mountains, my Gran wore hers at home (not the same garment I hasten to add). A good friend of mine had a bit of an epic in the Scottish mountains in winter once, ending up alone and benighted. He worried about falling asleep as, in the films, climbers in such situations don't tend to wake up. However, he couldn't help nodding off as he was so tired but he did wake up in the morning, surprised to do so, but very relieved – his Damart underwear had kept him warm and, more importantly, dry all night. He made a few quid selling his story and the rest of us took to the delights of wicking underwear. It's everywhere now, even sports players use it and many manufacturers claim that they have produced the best wicking fabrics.

What is wicking fabric?

The actual fabric is a polyester, which, unlike cotton, absorbs very little water. Wicking polyester has a special cross-section and a large surface area. The fibres can be hollow or trilobal (triangular) and they pick up moisture and carry it away from your body, spreading it out, to evaporate easily on the outside of the fabric. Capillary action, like paint moving up a paint brush or a sponge collecting water, is the main force responsible for the movement of moisture through the fabric. Merino wool is a wool which has hollow strands and works in a similar fashion.

Mid layer

I've had some excellent fleece jackets, pullovers and modern, technical mid layer garments, including some with windproof coverings and I've liked them all. Those with a windproof outer can be incredibly light and comfortable and can often make more sense than a softshell layer in UK conditions. One of the great things about these super-lightweight, warm layers is that they are not a burden to carry. If you decide you don't need to wear them, then carrying them doesn't add greatly to your load. They can be quite expensive however and many cheap fleeces will do a pretty good job for you, particularly if worn under a hard shell and over a base layer. Fleece itself has come to be a given in the world of hillwalking wear. It has also become a common piece of clothing in all walks of life, it works, it's light and it's easy to wash. There is a vast range of quality and price, but most people will simply go on appearance. Your main choice is whether you go for two thinner ones or one thicker one. We should also, perhaps, start to question the environmental impact of our fleeces (and other technical attire) which are made from oil, but can be made from recycled products.

Environment and fleece

Fleece was invented as a light-weight replacement for wool in the late 1970s. Typically it is made from a type of polyester called polyethylene terephthalate (PET). (Yes, this is the same stuff that is used to make plastic bottles of the type we would never consider buying these days).

Unfortunately, when we wash fleece, microfibres, which will not break down, are released into the environment. It's estimated that more than one-third of the microplastics in the ocean come from synthetic clothing, though this is not solely from fleece. Plastic microfibres have been found in food, water, and air. Cheaper fleeces will release more of these fibres. Wool is a good alternative, but it is heavier, retains moisture longer and is harder to wash, it does stay warm when wet though, just like fleece. You could also keep your fleece for longer and try to resist the fashion swings and marketing blurb.

Clothing and Equipment

If you wash your fleece at lower temperatures this will help to release fewer fibres, avoid long washes and don't use a dryer. Maybe even consider handwashing?

Clothes pollute more the first few times we wash them, so consider buying less new clothing and keep your old garments for as long as possible. Try to get someone else to reuse your old fleece and look for recycling initiatives. Unfortunately, the cheaper fleeces are the worst offenders.

Typical fleeces and one lambswool jumper

Top tips from Mountain Leaders

Don't let your mid layers get damp before putting on waterproofs. Some are very difficult to get on over damp clothing and damp hands.

Mike Hammill

The outer layer

A lot has been said and written about the importance of breathability in outdoor clothing. If you are involved in fast moving, hardworking pastimes like riding a mountain bike then breathability really aids your comfort. The very breathable, yet windproof properties of softshell garments are ideally suited to mountain biking. There are hillwalking days when they are really nice garments to wear, but I'd venture to suggest they're in the minority. In the UK your hard shell layer will be with you most of the time, this layer is waterproof as well as windproof.

Hard shells come in a range of prices and qualities. If you are not using it every day for days on end it might be more appropriate to buy something more affordable and invest more in those less visible but very important base and mid layers.

With a wicking base layer and a layer of fleece under your waterproof, breathability is not as important on a day walk as you might think. Condensation won't penetrate your fleece and base layers. Yes, it'll be clammy inside your jacket, but you'll be warm and dry, and even the cheapest non-breathable waterproof jackets often have a mesh lining on the inside. Remember, breathable fabric breathes, this means they cool you down. Yes, a breathable outer layer is colder than a non-breathable one. Mountain leaders will be happier and more comfortable in a breathable hard shell. However, if cost is an issue for people you are leading or advising, a lowly priced, less breathable or even non-breathable hard shell will keep them warm, and will keep the rain out. Even the mountain leader will experience some conditions in which the breathable layer will not function as well as it could due to a lack of internal and external temperature variation. This creates a clammy interior.

Breathable fabrics need to be clean. They must be washed regularly and there are special washing agents designed for this purpose. Washing your hard shell layers will make sure they continue to work.

Hard shell trousers can be frustrating as they do let in water at the bottom, knees and groin. It's because you create a pumping action as you walk, and this reverses the process of moisture exhalation and changes it to one of inhalation.

A selection of waterproofs showing a heavier, more breathable all-year-round model, a slightly less breathable, lighter model and a non-breathable model. The price range is enormous.

Clothing and Equipment

When advising new walkers or people heading into the hills occasionally, it is advisable to impress upon them the importance of good base layers, fleece and intermediate layers rather than a very expensive set of waterproofs.

> **Leadership behaviours 'on the hill'**
>
> Waterproofs? Shall I shan't I and when to put them on are always tricky questions. Typically, it's best to do it when you are not in an exposed place. Think ahead, where are you going to be soon, is the weather forecast for a deterioration in conditions? Better to put them on, in a sheltered spot, sooner rather than later. Better to all put them on at the same time to minimise stops.

Extra layer – the belay jacket

One of the issues with wearing a breathable, outer layer is the loss of heat. You don't have to stand around for long to start to feel a bit clammy inside your jacket and start to cool down. The answer to this is to carry an extra layer, a synthetic duvet jacket, often known as a belay jacket. This is a fabulous bit of kit that has developed alongside the breathable, outer shells and if you are stopping for any period of time, even just for a bite to eat, having one handy in the top of your rucksack will be a sound move. The best ones are designed to just pull on over your waterproofs, the hardest thing to do is take it off again! They do come in different weights, as in: a summer weight, three-season weight or a four-season weight. The all-year-round ones are actually quite heavy and bulky and wouldn't be a normal piece of kit to carry. A three-season one however, will get lots of use. Look for one that will pack down small, maybe even into one of its own pockets. In the

A range of synthetic-filled jackets for different times of the year.

UK, down is less useful for this layer as it doesn't work when wet. You need a garment which is able to keep you warm even when it is wet. There are several very good synthetic fillings around to choose from now. This is one of those pieces of kit I am never without. Even if I make that scary decision to leave my outer hard shell at home because I trust the weather forecast, it's incredibly unusual for me to go without this layer.

Pockets

It's things like this that really matter. Most of the garments on sale today, for walking in, are pretty good. There is, in truth, little to choose between the manufacturers and reputable stores will all have garments that do the job. So, don't be obsessed with the label, look at the practicalities. How good are the pockets? Can you put your hands in them? Can you put a map in them or will you just be using a mobile phone so a smaller pocket will do? Can you tie your compass into one of them? Do you need an inner pocket? Can you access your pocket without unzipping the jacket? Take your time with pockets, make sure they do what you need them to do. When you are trying jackets on, checking that you can get what you want in the pockets is important, be it hands, a map, a pair of gloves or just a mobile phone.

> **I remember ... how to carry the map**
>
> I was out with a group once on a Mountain Leader course and the weather was fine. I noticed, they were all keeping their waterproofs on, while I'd got rid of mine fairly early on. Given that they all had breathable waterproofs on it wasn't a problem, but I wondered why they continued to wear them. So, I asked them. What it boiled down to was pockets. Each had developed good systems for carrying map and compass with the pockets on their waterproofs. So, however good your pockets are for carrying maps and compasses, can you carry them elsewhere too? What happens when you take off your jacket, where will your map and compass be carried then?

With experience and familiarity it's actually true that both your map and compass might well stay in your rucksack, but I still think you need the map handy, even if it is just to show your group, where you are and how it works. An outside leg pocket on your trousers works well for some people, it certainly does for a mobile phone. Whatever you do, a cut down, laminated, map, that will easily go into a pocket is typically better than having a map case around your neck, there will, however, be (many) exceptions to that rule. Indeed, that day when we use our phone for most navigation and leave the map in the rucksack all the time, is already here for some. Dare you buy a jacket with a pocket designed to take a mobile phone rather than a map?

Clothing and Equipment

A lightweight zip gone wrong.

Zips

If one bit of kit is designed to drive you mad it's zips. Before launching into an anti-zip tirade, I need to point out that I'm not sure if there is an alternative. The ability to zip and unzip your jacket is a fantastic luxury. A pullover the head smock is all well and good, but getting it over your head isn't always the easiest and you can't unzip to improve ventilation, so in actual fact zips are brilliant; it's just that sometimes they're not.

Big zips tend to be easier to work than little zips. Little zips tend to be easier to waterproof than big zips. For me, the real catch seems to be how big the baffle is behind the zip. Some zips seem to have a baffle which is designed to purposely catch in the zip and interrupt its smooth action. Look for a big, thick baffle. Yes, they'll add weight, but not much and they will be much harder to catch in your zip in. Outer baffles were once the norm and these worked better at waterproofing the zip and they would not get caught in the zip.

Hoods

I found myself out walking in the hills a few years ago and I was wearing a woolly hat, it was a blustery day. There was certain amount of bulky discomfort and unrequired, extra warmth around my neck. I realised that my fleece had a hood, my intermediate layer had a hood and of course my outer layer had a hood, I had three hoods and was wearing a woolly hat! Why do we do this?

When rock climbing, I tend not to carry a woolly hat so a hooded fleece is great for pulling over your head, either over or under the helmet for warmth. When I'm walking, I want as clear and unobstructed a view as possible, I want to be able to see all round and look at people, particularly when leading a group. I don't need hoods on my base and mid layers. I'm happy with a woolly hat and with a hard shell hood. If it rains then I'll need the waterproof hood, if it's not raining, but it is cold, then a woolly hat is my choice. You can make your own choice.

Hoods can be large enough to fit over a helmet, useful if you are wearing a helmet, but this volume, despite good volume reduction systems, will encourage the hood to slide backwards off your head in any sort of wind. It's like your woolly hat and hood are designed to repel each other. Consider smaller hoods that aren't designed to go over a helmet when buying a waterproof for walking in rather than climbing in.

THE MOUNTAIN LEADER

A hood that works well with goggles, but without the goggles the cheeks are left exposed.

Neck gaiters, commonly known as Buffs®, including a fleece one.

One other thing about hoods is the fashion to cut them to wear with goggles. The older full-face hoods, that you could pull tight so just your eyes were showing seem rare now. Most hoods, when tightened leave your cheeks exposed. This is a design feature to accommodate goggles. Now, I don't know about you, but it's not often that I wear goggles. I always think it's proper winter if you need your goggles on. Hoods designed for goggles are a bit of a pain in my book and a neck gaiter or 'buff' is the only way to solve this issue, though a buff will get wet.

Neck gaiter, or multifunctional head wear, the Buff®.

One piece of kit that I have found to be very versatile is the neck gaiter. It can be used to keep your neck warm and this makes a real difference on proper cold days. It can be used to keep your head warm if you lose your hat. It can be used as a blindfold when camping (those short nights can be so wearing!) and I've used it as a scarf to keep the sun off my neck. Dipped in water they are brilliant for cooling you down on the hottest of days. They are small, and dry quickly; pop one in your pocket and experiment with it.

Hats

The woolly hat has long been a standard piece of kit for mountain leaders. We need to keep our heads warm. We know that's where we lose a lot of body heat from. A hat needs to cover your ears, but whether it's thick or thin, wool or synthetic, with or without bobble, will be down to the choice of the user. Make sure you have a spare one as well.

Sun hats on the other hand are a little less commonly used and not always understood well. A baseball style hat is good for keeping the sun out of your eyes, but it doesn't keep the sun off your ears and neck. If it is properly sunny and hot you'll need a hat that offers more protection such as a large brimmed one.

A selection of hats that might be worn or carried.

A selection of gloves that might be worn or carried.

Gloves

I usually have at least two pairs of gloves with me all year round. I carry a spare pair, along with a spare hat, in a waterproof bag in the bottom of my rucksack. I use them frequently and I have always been grateful I had them. The warmest of sunny days can evaporate instantly with a cold breeze on the tops. In winter, I can have three or four pairs of gloves, especially when it gets wet.

Buying gloves is, I'm sorry to say, a bit of a lottery. Some of the most unlikely looking gloves I've used have turned out to be amazing, while some of the smartest looking ones have proven unreliable. Just get into the mindset that you'll need several pairs. Have you tried the 'can you put the gloves on when your hands are wet' test? Pile gloves tend to be easier to put on when wet, but do try this test with the various pairs of gloves you own. Some gloves are still warm when wet, others are not. For reliability you might include a pair of shrunken, wool gloves, such as the Dachstein ones, in your spares bag as they will be warm when wet and you can put them on with wet hands.

Gaiters

Gaiters were originally known as snow gaiters and were worn to keep snow out of the tops of your boots. They became standardised at knee length to match up with the breeches that were usually worn by mountaineers up until around the 1980s.

Over time, the manufacturers dropped the word snow and gaiters have become a standard year-round piece of kit. They keep heather out of your boots, they minimise water seeping into the tops of your boots and they will minimise grit getting in and, to some degree, protect your boots. You can get shorter gaiters known as scree or debris gaiters, these are a good compromise for those who dislike knee length gaiters. Gaiters also reduce the chance of ticks getting into your sock band too.

The gaiter is, however, another piece of kit to carry. They can be hot around your calves and there are always issues with the strap, or lace, under your boot getting worn or coming loose. They have a tendency to ride up the back of your boots and, unless fitted well will soon fail to do what they are supposed to do. If out for the day, many leaders won't bother wearing gaiters, unless they are venturing off the path into heather, bracken or into boggy areas

Spare clothes

You should always have the minimum of another pair of dry gloves, a dry hat and a belay jacket. I carry these in my 'always bag'. It is one of the first things put into my rucksack and I'm never without it whether leading or just on the hill for fun.

This is my 'always bag'. I'm never without a spare pair of gloves, a spare hat and a belay jacket in a waterproof bag in my rucksack.

Equipment

There is, of course, a little bit more which requires carrying. You'll need a rucksack to carry your lunch, water and few spares. Here are a few other things to consider.

Rucksacks

A rucksack will long be one of your favourite bits of kit, most of us a have a favourite or mourn the passing of the 'best ever' rucksack we owned. I could say backpack as we seem to be Americanising the name of this piece of kit along with so many others, but I'll stick with rucksack for the time being. If you have one rucksack, make it a good one as it will last a long time. If you have more than one then you'll start to need an exponential number of rucksacks and then you'll be craving the exact, right model for any particular day's activity. You have been warned!

It's amazing how many rucksacks are designed for activities other than just going for a walk. They might have straps for skis, they might have had pockets removed for climbing purposes, they might have fancy, drinking systems for trail running. They will also have a range of fathomless straps and seemingly pointless additions. Rucksacks designed for walkers are usually too small for leaders. Yes, of course you want the smallest sack you can get away with, but you also need space, and over-stuffed rucksacks are difficult to get things out of and re-pack, they have no flexibility should you need to take an extra layer off or you find something you want to bring off the hill. Typically, for the mountain leader, a larger rucksack with a bit of space works best. Look for a simple, clean-cut rucksack. It's better to get everything inside your rucksack, including poles. This makes the rucksack easier to handle, in and out of vehicles, on and off your back and it prevents eye-poking-out episodes with things like poles randomly attached to the side of your bag. I always have everything in my sack in waterproof bags so unpacking and repacking isn't very difficult.

> **Top tips from Mountain Leaders**
>
> I put my kit in different coloured, waterproof bags so I know what is where in my rucksack. I try to pack my bag in the order that I think I will need it.
>
> Kath James

I do quite like those side netting pockets you can get as they are ideal for stashing any litter you collect from the hill. I struggle with fiddly buckles, over-fancy waist belts, buckles that break easily and sloping bottoms that mean you can't just put your rucksack down without it falling over.

Fashionable roll-tops and zip closures are very limiting in that you can't stuff discarded layers under your lid. Pear shaped rucksacks that are wider at the bottom than they at the top are more designed for skiing than walking. Of course, it's all down to personal choice, but don't rush to follow fashion.

Walking poles

Walking poles are an increasingly popular item to carry. In the interests of looking after your own longevity you should consider using poles as a matter of course. A word of warning though; I have met people with wrist and elbow problems from overuse of poles, so do be careful. If the track is good then having your hands in the wrist loops helps you to use the poles efficiently without having to grip them too tightly. If the ground is uneven I suggest you remove your wrists from the loops as a slip could result in injury to your wrist. Poles can be used as a bit of group kit too. They could help someone with a minor injury off the hill. I've seen someone given confidence by using poles. They also could be used as a splint or to aid a river crossing.

Sunglasses and sun cream

Using sunglasses will protect your eyes. Being out in the sun, or at least out in bright light, all day for many years can contribute to deterioration of your eyesight. Try to use good quality ones but lift them away from your eyes when talking to people. Sun cream will be mainly for personal use, but being able to offer it to someone who has none might well be wise option to have.

Headtorch

I aways have a small headtorch in my first aid kit and I carry a spare one during the winter months.

Global positioning system (GPS)

You'll have a pretty good GPS on your mobile phone, but many mountain leaders like to carry a separate GPS device as well. All I can say is that I have carried one in the past, but don't currently. I found the battery life poor and the screen is so small compared to your phone that I just didn't use it. Given the speed we walk, keeping map contact is rarely a problem, so a GPS unit will be superfluous for most of us. You should, however, be used to using one as you will be asked about them by people you are leading. They are more accurate for location than your phone and they will be robust and weatherproof.

A small, neat, compact GPS unit that is waterproof and robust. A mobile phone in a waterproof case and a PLB.

Personal locator beacon (PLB)

A PLB is not currently a standard part of a mountain leader's kit, but given the size and weight of them, the robustness and relative low cost this is another piece of kit you should consider carrying. It can pinpoint your position to rescue services when you are far from any mobile phone signal. See; calling 999.

> **Note for Trainers – what are they wearing?**
>
> Be kind. You may have people turning up on your training course who have never really tested their kit like you have. They will potentially be at the stage where they think that a very expensive pair of waterproof overtrousers are the bee's knees, but they haven't worn them on consecutive wet days with a wild camp in between. They may use a 70 litre rucksack for the expedition. Yes, you can get your camp kit into a 45 litre rucksack, but you've been doing this for years and you've got all the latest, lightweight kit. Yes, you need to reduce the contents of the 70 litre rucksack, but reducing to 45 litres in one go is a big ask. They may swear by wearing shorts all year round, they'll learn. They may insist on carrying a solid fuel stove for use at lunchtime, they'll learn. They may turn up in cotton camouflage trousers, they'll learn. You are here to teach them, this will be more effective if you lead by example, discuss and consider rather than admonish and belittle.

Group clothing and kit

When I meet a group, I'm keen to see that they have the right kit with them, so sending out a kit list in advance is wise. Think about key principles with the list and make it achievable. Think as much about windproof as waterproof, think about comfortable rather than unfamiliar clothing, think about layering rather than big coats. Embrace technical sports shirts, regardless of team colours! Don't be too snooty about footwear, if you are going to be on paths, comfort will be paramount. Clearly flip-flops and high heels are less than ideal, but good trainers can work well on man-made, mountain paths.

Hats and gloves

I'll always have some extra hats and gloves and these can be worth their weight in gold. They don't have to be expensive (you can often collect them on the hill). The fleece lined, wool gloves you can buy from garages are perfect for this purpose, dirt cheap, but very effective. It still surprises me that people are not always aware of the fact that it will be colder, windier and potentially wetter the higher you go up a hill. It seems mad having to tell people this, but even when we do, they never quite believe us. Having three or four pairs of gloves and a similar number of wool hats can really save a day.

Spare clothes

This will vary with the group you are leading. Ideally they'll be well equipped and self-contained. You might carry an extra, thin fleece, but carrying any more than this for your group will soon start to be rather onerous.

The leader's sack

What else do you need to carry? There is no definitive list as it will vary depending on the route planned, the time of year, the experience and preparedness of your group. The contents of your sack may need to compensate for the inadequacies of the kit that your team bring with them. You might choose to carry a rope, a spare map and compass, a penknife maybe even a water filter. You should have a Blizzard blanket, group shelter, sweets, spare food and a first aid kit. Most leaders will have a repair kit comprising duct tape, cable ties and a spare lace or two. Everything should be in dry bags. I do not carry spare socks, or spare trousers. I might have an extra thin fleece, but never a stove (unless on expedition), a flask or two could be handy though.

Could you repair a boot that has lost its sole well enough to get the walker down to the valley?

Top tips from Mountain Leaders

Typically, if you wrap some duct tape around a walking pole or your water bottle there will be less tape than you think. It's worth carrying a roll of part used duct tape, so it's not full size but still has a quarter or third of its tape.

Steve Howe

Note for Assessors – extra kit clues

There will always be clues about people in the kit they wear and the kit they carry. First impressions are important and Mountain Leaders should look like Mountain Leaders – role modelling and leading by example are important. If they've got to assessment then everything they should be wearing and carrying should be fit for purpose, look at the rucksack that they are carrying, it can be worryingly small or worryingly big.

You could defer someone for poor leadership if you felt they were not adequately prepared for leading in the hills. Take particular note of the leader's sack. Is it too heavy? Too light? Have they got the spares that matter: laces, hats, group shelter, a Blizzard blanket or similar? Is what they are carrying based on experience? Could they 'fix a boot'?

A team enjoying some off the beaten track map work.

Do we know where we are going?

Navigation

Where shall we go today? It's one of my favourite questions and I will constantly be wanting to go to places which I have never been before. That said, for teaching purposes, a Mountain Leader needs to have a few reliable venues where they know they can teach navigation skills.

One of the slightly odd things about becoming a Mountain Leader is that, while you are doing your training and assessment, navigation seems to completely dominate. You might have the feeling that this is a navigation qualification. Some people do and they are wrong. It's frustrating for trainers and assessors when, despite them constantly reminding people it's a leadership qualification, advice pops up on social media suggesting success will revolve around navigation, navigation and more navigation. The bare facts are that once you are qualified, navigation recedes significantly in terms of importance. Though I, for one, still spend hours poring over maps and mapping apps!

How we approach navigation

A key skill of a Mountain Leader has always been the need to be able to locate themselves at any time. This is necessary so that you can judge your progress during a day. For example, you may be going more quickly than expected so you might want to extend your route. On the other hand, you may be going at a slower pace and feel the need to shorten your route. You may notice cloud descending and you're about to be swallowed up by the 'white room', in which case it's a good idea to locate your position while you have full visibility. You may also come across someone who needs help or someone who has had an accident. It may even be yourself, or someone in your group who you need to support and evacuate from the mountain.

This ability to relocate yourself has been a key part of the Mountain Leader qualification since its inception. On a typical training or assessment course you had to constantly find your location, in different ways, in different landscapes and were required to practise it constantly. You probably came to dread being asked again and again, "where are we now?" However nicely your assessor asked, you probably felt a cold sweat and the stress levels begin to rise. You needed to be a very confident person to assert your location with complete certainty time after time for five consecutive days, especially when the only thanks you got was a non-committal, monotone, "thank you". I suspect things will remain this way for some time, but there is another way.

A group relocating as the cloud drifts in and visibility reduces.

The development of GPS technology is an enormous help in terms of finding your position. Most of us now have a smart phone and with tools such as OS Locate, and other mapping apps such as OS Maps, Outdoor Active or FATMAP. Your phone will identify your location with good, and improving accuracy, time after time. You may still need to keep a wary eye on battery life, weather-proofness and temperature. The questions about how you do this should probably be taking a larger part in the development of the Mountain Leader qualification. Consequently, dare I say, the assessment might then be able to move away from the constant question of 'where are we now?'. Indeed, we should be beginning to embrace this exceptional

Navigation

handheld tool and using newly created time to look more carefully at our leadership qualities and our environmental knowledge. How we navigate is changing, changing slowly and being modernised. We will always need to be able to read a map, and indeed, we need to be able to do that to use the phone apps that use the Harvey maps, Ordnance Survey maps or even the open source maps available online. GPS will be the choice of some people, but most of us will tend to use our mobile phones now, even if it's just as an easy way to carry the map. Knowing your location is a great bonus, but you still need a map and your eyes to match the ground to the map, and the map to the ground, then work out the best way to get to your destination. You still need a love of maps to be a successful Mountain Leader and you may find you need to spend even more time teaching and introducing map-reading as new walkers come along more used to matching dots with lines on one of the many mobile phone mapping systems.

Top tips from Mountain Leaders

Although I'm in my 50's I like gadgets and having GPS and maps downloaded on my mobile is acceptable. I don't get hung up, like some, on using tech – it's there so let's use it to our benefit to learn from and help us.

Gary Peasland

Note for Trainers

There is no getting away from the fact that we all still need to be able to map read to a high standard. You may find new entrants to the scheme have relied too heavily on mobile technology and actually need more input on map-reading. But the time has come to look at other tools. Get your group to show you what they have. Get them to use it and practise with it to see if it really works. Can it be managed in the great outdoors and all that it can throw at you?

Note for Assessors

Of course you must be absolutely convinced that the people you are assessing can work out their position using the map alone, can follow bearings when appropriate and that they can interpret contours, but try easing off sooner rather than later. Try to get as much of this covered early on in the week then start to look at some of the other navigation tools. Get people learning about modern tools, evaluating them and developing their skills with them. Send them away looking forward and able to positively influence others; welcome the modern technology, it isn't going away.

THE MOUNTAIN LEADER

A leader points out the current location of the group.

Navigation tools; maps, map-case, GPS, compass, phone.

I remember ... excuse me please, where are we?

While out on the hill I've been asked by strangers, several times over the years, "Where are we please?". Twenty years ago, I might have been approached by someone random who was a bit lost. Very often they'd pull out a map and compass and say, "do you know where we are?". You could then have a conversation with them about their map and compass, and features on the map, and point them in the right direction. Maybe tell them to follow the ridge north until it steepens and then turn west and descend to the valley. All this would make sense to them. They just weren't sure exactly where they were.

Fast forward to today, and I might be approached by someone who will pull out a smartphone, pre-loaded with a GPX file they are following. They say something like "Is this the path?" Their GPS shows them exactly where they are but they have no concept of what's around them. To these folks, navigation is the art of walking such that a blue dot (your location) doesn't deviate from a red line (the downloaded route).

Patrick Hickie

Navigation

It can be tricky managing your map when the weather is poor.

Map management

I think most people appreciate the ease of use a laminated, Ordnance Survey map will give them. The Harvey, waterproof, paper maps are lighter and nice to use as well. Neither of these maps will, unfortunately, stand up to constant tough use, they'll soon get damaged on the folds. You can use a permanent marker (on a wet day), a non-permanent marker (on a dry day) or a chinagraph pencil on the laminated maps. Be careful with the Harvey version though, if you use a permanent marker, then try cleaning the map with meths or similar, you'll lose the printing on the map. Cutting up a laminated map or cutting up a paper map and laminating it yourself are good options. Be careful of printing maps out at home as you need a really good quality printer. Map cases are a bit of a pain, but they do have their place. Carrying one round your neck is fraught with problems, particularly when it's windy; they just get in the way. It's also difficult to mark locations on a map case too.

I remember ... a map lost to the wind

We were out on the Carneddau in some pretty poor weather and one of my group had their map blown away. It was a Mountain Leader assessment course so I was disappointed that this had been allowed to happen, but it is the sort of thing that can happen to the best of us (as I found out later). For now, I suggested he just carry on with his spare map, he didn't have one. I had to lend him mine. Then the worst thing happened, my map blew away, this had never happened to me before – how embarrassing. The candidate who'd already lost his map seemed to think this was funny. Well, he did until I took back my spare map, and asked him to continue his navigation leg ...

Mark 'Baggy' Richards

Top tips from Mountain Leaders

Print and laminate large-scale maps of your day. They can be folded and stuffed into a pocket more easily than a full, folded map and a lot easier to use.

Mike Hammill

Note for Trainers and Assessors

Writing on maps is really useful as it removes ambiguity about locations. There are a few things to watch out for though. Make sure that if you mark a location on a map, you don't obliterate any details. Make sure the candidate double checks the location with you should the mark wash off the map. It's best to use the non-permanent pens as the marks can be wiped off easily after use (but you don't want it to disappear during use!). If you mark a map with a permanent pen, covering up details could lead to problems; though permanent pen will work better in wet weather. Try using dots or circles, if you use circles, make it clear you want them to take you to the middle of the circle.

Note for Assessors

It's not a bad ploy to get candidates to put a dot on the map when they show you their position. You can then see exactly where they mean with no ambiguity. You might record these dots on your own map, particularly when a candidate gives an incorrect location, it might help with your debrief later.

Two hillwalkers working out their location.
Photo: Bren Whelan

Handrailing

When we are out on the hill, the key navigation skill is actually handrailing. When leading groups, we handrail for the vast majority of the time. We handrail paths, both good ones and intermittent ones. We handrail ridges, valleys, streams, walls, fences and contour features. Progressing your handrailing skills is real navigation. When teaching navigation, check the basics first, start off with a hierarchical list of handrailing progressions.

Handrailing is following linear features. When you are walking on a path you are handrailing that path. It's what we do most of the time, and most of the time, when we are actually leading a group, it's easy. When is it not easy? Well, it's not easy when the path is indistinct and it's not easy when the path doesn't go where you think it should go. So, we need to progress our handrailing skills to enable trickier features to be followed. An old drystone wall or fence might be a good example but we must be mindful that these are features that are prone to change. Fences come and go, new fences don't always follow the exact, same line on the map as old fences and a fence might replace a wall, and again, might not follow the exact line shown. Walls are usually pretty good as they have to be pretty old and broken-down before they escape the sharp eye of the airborne cartographer.

Watercourses might be the next thing to follow on a progression of difficulty. They can be great features to handrail, but in the mountains, you need to be wary of waterfalls and gorges. There are many times when following a stream is not the best plan. If this is the case, it might be that you can still walk near the watercourse, as long as you can hear it and see where it is.

Woodland edges can provide good, linear features to follow. Though it can be surprising how indistinct they are on occasion. This is also a feature that may or may not be present when you arrive. In the UK new areas of forestry are not common whereas ones which have been felled usually leave significant trace of their presence. They are mostly fenced in anyway and you'll actually be following a fence as well as a woodland edge.

You can handrail along contour features. Ridges are the best example of this, following ridges is usually easy, although there are of course some famous exceptions to that. When handrailing ridges, don't forget the maxim that 'crest is best'. You may need to skirt some steeper bits, but always get back to the ridge as soon as is practicable. It's too easy to stray off route along the side of a ridge so repeated visits to the crest will help to keep you on track.

Following edges can be fun. Following the edge of a plateau generally works well. Break of slope points provide interest and challenge for the developing Mountain Leader. Look for places where a slope rears up with widely spaced contours leading into closer ones, here is a definite line, a break of slope that you can either ascend to, descend from or contour across. It's worth noting that handrailing isn't necessarily like literally holding a handrail, it's just walking along with whatever you are handrailing in sight, or at least in ear shot.

> **Note for Trainers**
>
> Try to plan early routes along linear features. Road, then bridleway, then clear path, then less clear path. Look for a fence that has been moved and is in one place on the map and another on the ground. Look for ragged, woodland edges and maybe think about a watercourse which could be followed through a bog, or over a cliff! This is the type of navigation we do most of the time, though it's not without its challenges, particularly around areas of settlement where we wouldn't want to upset anyone by going the wrong side of buildings or through the wrong gate. You might have a footpath junction with one path well marked and the other less so. You might find some confusingly closed gates or have to search for an old, well camouflaged stone stile. Even when handrailing you are decision making all the time and you need to spend time on this when teaching navigation rather than jumping ahead to more technical skills. It leads nicely into working with contours too, certainly along ridges and break of slope points.

A list of features

Here's a list of features you might be handrailing. They are not in any particular order. You could put them in an order of ease to follow. You might wish to make some cards and discuss a hierarchy of handrailing with the groups you are leading or coaching:

- Following a well signposted, and clear on the ground, footpath
- Following a stream
- Following a path with any signposts
- Following a boundary
- Following an intermittent path
- Following a leat
- Following a ridge
- Following a dry valley or re-entrant
- Following a woodland edge

Navigation

Handrailing a fence line.

This group are handrailing a contour feature.

- Following a forestry track
- Following the rim of a cwm / corrie
- Following a break of slope point
- Following a public right of way
- Following a road
- Following a fence
- Following a wall
- Following a series of ring contours
- Contouring

Note for Trainers

Make sure candidates have a good grasp of real navigation before moving on to the fancy stuff. This is the stuff we do day in day out, and should form a large part of teaching navigation. Look for progression in handrailing, try making your own card exercises.

Note for Assessors

It's a tricky balance as you need to be happy that people can get themselves off the hill if it all goes wrong in any weather. You need to be satisfied that they know where they are all the time, but, remember, maintain that balance. Most of the time they'll be handrailing, this skill is key and so should carry more weight in the judgements you make about their abilities as a navigator.

Map-reading

If we spend most of our time handrailing, what else is there to navigation in the hills? We shouldn't neglect some basic map-reading skills: symbols, grid references and scale are all fundamental parts of a bigger picture.

Symbols

Symbols are usually pretty obvious and anyway, the key to them is printed on the maps (I bet you don't know all your different boundary lines though!).

Grid references

This isn't the place to teach grid references, but my approach is usually to start with a four-figure reference then make it a six-figure reference. I never use the terms eastings or northings as they are just confusing given that eastings run north to south and northings run east to west. You can check your grid references against an app like OS Locate. Grid references shouldn't be neglected and are still the best way of identifying a particular location in the British Isles.

Taking a closer look at the map.

Navigation

Methods of identifying a location

We are so lucky here in the UK to have the Ordnance Survey Grid Reference system. The system divides our islands into 100km squares each of which are given a discreet two letter code. Most of Eryri is in SH while Skye is in NG. This is important as the six-figure reference reoccurs in each of these squares.

However, the emergency services, if you have the misfortune to need to contact them, will ask you for your postcode. This can be quite alarming if you are halfway up a mountain. Your phone will tell you your postcode, but you may be better informing the call handler at this point that you really need to talk to mountain rescue. In some places you will be transferred straight through to mountain rescue and they will take over the call, but in other places, you'll be put through to the police, who'll get mountain rescue to ring you back.

At sea, latitude and longitude are normally used, while your phone will give you this information it isn't as useful as a grid reference on the hill.

Much has been made of a new system; What3words. As a geographer I love it. The whole world has been divided into three metre squares and each square given a unique three word code. As I write I'm dreaming of heading to my local pub at frocks.flush.butterfly better known as SH 781 632, or pedantically, using my phone SH 78128 63237. However, there have been some issues, as it isn't as easy to use as it might sound. Words have been misheard or mis-spoken leading to some wild variations in locality, not helpful for a mountain rescue team looking for a casualty. So, while in some parts of the world, or even in urban settings, it may well have a lot of potential, for us, on the hill, the OS grid reference remains our primary means of identifying a location

Scale

The scale of maps used tends to be the 1:25,000 in England and Wales and 1:50,000 in Scotland, traditionally using the Ordnance Survey Maps. Mountain Leader courses have generally stuck to using these two scales with maybe the odd flirtation with the BMC's 1:40,000 scale and 15m contour intervals seems to confuse most people who are used to the afore mentioned scales. It is actually easier to switch between maps these days and the apps can do this quite well, though perhaps not as easily they might and they are expensive. Having maps on a phone app does however mean you can have range of maps, on a range of scales in your pocket. Many people really like the Harvey maps. These are typically in scales of 1:25,000 and 1:40,000, though in Ireland they use a 1:30,000 scale. There's no doubt that these are lovely maps and as a Mountain Leader you should be able to switch between maps with ease. The only reason these maps are not used more, is because the trainers know that you'll be mostly assessed on your use of the Ordnance Survey mapping. A good assessor will encourage you to use other maps, hopefully without intimidating you at the same time. Buying a Harvey map as well as the OS maps is an added expense and they also have edges, by that I mean, with an OS map, you just go onto the next sheet, but the Harvey map may end without a continuing sheet.

Note for Trainers

In England and Wales the OS maps are brilliant! The Harvey ones are too, but it doesn't seem right to ask people to buy more maps than they need. Using the 1:50,000 map in England and Wales is a pain as you miss so much detail on them. Conversely in Scotland the rock markings often obliterate the contour detail and not having all those pesky dry stone walls and fences, you don't really need the 1:25,000. If you're in Scotland you need to seek out places where the 1:25,000 map works well, and in England or Wales you need to seek out places where the 1:50,000 is a good map to use. So, train in England and Wales with a mindset that candidates might be assessed in Scotland, and train in Scotland as though they might be assessed in Wales or England. In Ireland, you can take your pick, although I'm deliberately choosing to ignore 1:30,000.

Note for Assessors

Inevitably you will focus on the best map for the area you are in. Once you are sure that your candidates are comfortable and competent with this map, do use some of the others. Be generous though, deferral for not being particularly good on one map or the other isn't great. Can you help them to be better?

The use of handheld internet-enabled devices, or mobile phones, increases the opportunity for using other maps. If you can have the OS and Harvey map to hand on your phone then switching should become easier, try using the open street mapping (OSM) too as this is what many of the newer apps are using. I can't quite bring myself to work with Google maps yet, though their way of sharing a location definitely has potential. FATMAP are a brand that is catching on and there are open source maps with varying degrees of information on them out there. You should experiment with these, there's a huge variety of apps vying for supremacy at the moment. Personally, I can't really see beyond the excellent maps produced by the Ordnance Survey, though for my own use I'll often grab a Harvey map (especially when I visit Skye). Watch this space and keep an open mind.

Navigation

The world of hiking apps

Some of you will be experimenting with apps. There are some really good apps out there and it is an important and developing field. As I write, some of the smaller apps are being taken over by larger companies. There is battle between the mapping hardware and the location and route planning software; the marrying of these two in favourable ways for walkers is the quest. Have a look at hiking apps in your app store; there are many and it's hard to know which ones to pick. It's pointless giving you an overview of the current trends in a book as it will be out of date before the book is printed. It's areas like this where your association, its magazine and online forums should be a real help. I encourage you to experiment, be critical and share your findings. It might well be something you discussed on your ML training course, but as it's ever changing, keep an open dialogue with other leaders about their favourite apps of the moment

Orientating the map just using contours.

Orientation

One of the ways I illustrate progression in map-reading is to think about orientating the map. It's generally fairly easy to orientate the map in the valleys as roads, buildings, lakes and the valley itself all aid this process. If you are struggling, just popping a compass on the map, and lining up north on your compass with the top of the map will help. A Mountain Leader will be able to orientate the map with fewer features and typically just using the contour features. This is a satisfying skill which takes time to develop and perfect, but once you can do it, you are the complete map reader – you can navigate with map alone.

Top tips from Mountain Leaders

Mark the top of the map with red tape so you can see the map orientated north at a glance.

Nick Rowe

I remember ... the worst ever navigation mistake

It was on day two of an assessment. We'd swopped teams from day one as one of the candidates had been wrong on nearly all of his navigation legs and the other assessor wanted my opinion. I remember we'd wandered up through Cwm Glas looking at steep ground management and route finding, along with the usual navigational legs and environmental discussions. We were stood just to the west of the top of Gryn Las having picked a route up from Cwm Glas, Llyn Bach, and I asked the group for our position. Three of the team were spot on, but the fourth one, the one who'd had a poor day on day one, put us in Cwm Uchaf. He was so far out I asked him to take another look. After a few minutes of looking around he placed us on the lip of Cwm Glas, below Llyn Bach. As he was pointing to where he thought we were on the map, the Snowdon Mountain Railway train steamed up the hill behind us, giving us a helpful toot as it passed us by, a mere 100m away. So, I asked: "If we are where you say we are, what was that?"

The origin of the phrase

Why is it called orientating the map? How did orienteering get its name? Spot the commonality, Orient. The Orient is the holy land, the land to the east, the Middle East. Originally maps were drawn with the Holy Land at the top i.e. the east, not the north, so orientating the map, is holding it with the east (now the north) at the top.

Timing

A knowledge of timing calculations is probably the next most important aspect of navigation after handrailing. I rarely use timing as a tool of precision but it helps to understand if a proposed walk is achievable in the time available. If, for example, I'm leading a group up Yr Wyddfa, they really don't need any ability to navigate. I might show them the map so they can see the journey, but it may not mean a lot to them. If available, I'll show them a picture topo too. The national park has produced a Yr Wyddfa app which is also a great tool for showing people where they are going, they can follow their own progress if they download this app. However, the key with these groups is to work through timings so that they have an idea of how long the walk will take. It's really difficult to come up with a precise time, we all know that the speed at which a group can travel comfortably will vary and fluctuate. It can be quicker, or slower, than expected.

I usually start with 4km an hour and add on a minute per 10 metres of ascent, or if using a typical OS map, for every contour line crossed. I'll be conservative with my estimate and I'll add in breaks. It can be demotivating for a group if they are falling behind the schedule early on. It can be adjusted of course and you can have a chat with the group and tell them you are now moving at 3km an hour not 4km an hour. I find it easier to adjust the km / per hour bit rather than the height gain. With practise it's fairly easy to feel your speed and work out whether you are moving along at 2, 3, 4 or 5 km an hour. The point here however, is that the first thing I'm teaching a group of new walkers is Naismith's rule and not grid references, orientating the map and certainly little to do with the use of a compass.

Naismith's rule

Scottish Mountaineer William Naismith coined his eponymous rule in 1892. Originally set at 3 miles per hour and an additional 30 minutes for every 1000' feet of hight gained. Naismith's rule is a best time, for the 'average, brisk walker on reasonable terrain'. It came to be seen as a fairly fast time so the translation to metric of 4.8km per mile has never really taken off, some might say round up to 5km an hour, most would work on 4km an hour, this is much more of a typical pace on any given hill day. Why convert to kilometres? Well, the grid squares, whichever map you are using, are 1km square, so measure in kilometres, then convert to time. This is a much better way of saying how long a walk might be. Simple miles or kilometres covered on the ground is a bit misleading, hard walks often being shorter than easy walks.

At 4km an hour you'll be doing a kilometre every 15 minutes, 500m every 7.5 minutes and that's accurate enough really. People do tend to get a little too hung up on timing, it's a rough estimate and that's all. Timing less than 500m is a bit pointless really. Do it while you are learning, while you are playing with your numbers and while you are developing a feel for your walking pace. Some people make a little ready-reckoner card which is fine, but you might just be over thinking it.

I've said above, start with 4km an hour and get used to the feel of it but remember to take a look at your group. Look at their loads, are they heavy? Look at the terrain, is it rough or steep? How fit is the group? You might find yourself looking at an expedition for young people and making your plans at 2km an hour. You might be ascending Scafell and work on 3km an hour. Of course, out on your own you might be walking at 5km an hour.

When you add some time on for ascending, the Ordnance Survey have made it easy for us as most of their maps use a 10 metre contour interval. Every time you cross one of these, on ascent, add a minute. On the big climbs look for the index contours, the slightly thicker ones every 50 metres. Be mindful that not all maps have a 10 metre contour interval. There are some OS maps with a 5 metre interval and some of the maps which Harvey produced for the BMC have 15 metre contour intervals.

THE MOUNTAIN LEADER

Teaching navigation in Eryri.

Essentially, you are using timing to help a group understand how far they have travelled or to see if a proposed route is achievable in the time given. People you lead will tend to want to know how far a route is in miles. The trouble with this, as we know, is that the harder the route the shorter the mileage. So, a walk of six or eight miles might not sound too bad, but if it's over the Aonach Eagach Ridge, or the Yr Wyddfa Horseshoe it might feel a bit epic. There are some interesting variations to cope with these factors, but if numbers are your thing, one of the most fun is Scarf's variation. Just for fun, you could also experiment with the Tranter, Aitken and Langmuir corrections for carrying loads, fatigue, rough ground and descent.

Naismith – Scarf's Variation

To compare short hard walks, with long easy walks you could use Scarf's variation. Professor Scarf, a senior statistician at the University of Salford, after all sorts of weird and wonderful maths, worked out a magic, Naismith number of 7.92. This involves working with Naismith's height gain rule verses his horizontal travel rule. If we round up 7.92 to 8 it is easier to work with. The upshot of all this is that 1km of ascent is equivalent to 8km horizontal. So, if you walk 11 kilometres but ascend 700 metres you would add your 11km to 0.7km x 8, to give 11+5.6 or 16.6km. Fell runners do use the formula to get a feel for how far their runs might feel. For example, the Bob Graham Round becomes 102 miles rather than the measured 63, the Marathon Eryri, instead of being 26.2 miles works out at 30.4 and the 23.2 miles of the Yorkshire Peaks is more like 31.2 miles, which I can confirm is what it feels like!

Navigation

Contour interpretation

It wouldn't be unreasonable to suggest that contour interpretation has been the crux of navigation for Mountain Leaders. It is hard to say exactly how good you need to be; as near to perfect as is possible is what I suggest. You need to be able to visualise the land after glancing at the map and, you need to be able to orientate the map in a location which has only contour features. It wasn't always like this. Maps used to have the contour lines drawn in by hand between the measured points, marked by trig points and spot heights. It was only in the 1970s when OS maps were redrawn after aerial surveys that contours came to be as perfect as they are today. They are, in fact, the only thing that is perfectly accurate on the map. Most other things are either exaggerated in size e.g. the width of roads, or subject to change e.g. fences, woodlands and built up areas.

The Mountain Leader has to learn to feel the contours through their legs. Imagine walking on a night navigation leg, as you go up a hill, or down one, you need to be able to feel the changes of angle through your legs. This helps you enormously when reading the terrain in the dark.

Contour interpretation isn't difficult for most people to learn, it just needs a careful, but practical introduction. This will involve walking up and down some steep, rough ground in good and poor visibility. With structured practise, you soon get the hang of it and start to enjoy the micro-navigation games. See them simply as that for now – games to be enjoyed.

You can get people to measure the gap between the contour lines and this will tell them the angle of the slope in degrees. For example, on the 1:25,000 map if the index contours, the thick ones, are 1cm apart then the slope angle is 10°. If they are 2mm apart the angle of the slope is 45°. This figure is usually less than you'd expect it to be so has little use for the summer Mountain Leader. In winter, when the angle of slopes is a part of your avalanche considerations, this figure is of much more interest.

A pair of walkers working hard to improve their contour only navigation.

The best way to fully grasp contours lines is by walking up and down them and learning to feel them in your legs (and your lungs).

THE MOUNTAIN LEADER

I do come across people who are a little blank regarding contour interpretation. It's a bit like some people getting phased by numbers or letters, a sort of contour dyslexia, you might say. This doesn't make these people stupid, what it does mean, is that their brains are working in different ways and we might need to tap into other ways of explaining contours. For some a smooth, rounded pebble from the beach might help. For others a pile of sand, or loose soil, with lines drawn around might do the trick and for some it'll be a cardboard model. All these great techniques can however fall down, if they are not related to real hills and can be of more use filling up time in a teaching navigation workshop than for actually teaching navigation. You could take a rope and lay it out along the line of a contour or, a more logistically simple way of doing this, is to just to get your group to stand in a line along the chosen contour. I'll often just get the group tracing out the contour line with a finger just by pointing.

Pebbles can be a useful way of illustrating how contours join up points of equal height.

I'm occasionally asked how accurate we need to be when navigating, particularly in contour only terrain. It isn't possible, or helpful, to suggest a set distance i.e. within 10 metres, 5%, or anything like that. It is much more important to look at the features being selected. It is entirely possible that it may be perfectly satisfactory to relocate on to the right type of feature e.g. a knoll, even if it is not the actual feature you were supposed to be going to. Whereas relocating to the wrong type of feature e.g. a col rather than a knoll maybe considered a less redeemable mistake even if it is nearer the target location. Clearly candidates can't keep doing this, but you should give credit if they can distinguish between a col and a knoll, even if it's not the right knoll.

In this picture our destination is the left-hand, skyline knoll. If we'd gone to the central knoll, that would have been a more understandable mistake, despite it being further away from the target point, than going to the bwlch between the two knolls. The right-hand knoll, being lakeside, should be fairly easy to dismiss as not being the correct feature.

Navigation

Sea level

Have you ever wondered where sea level is? To have consistent heights across the UK for our contours and spot heights there must be a continuous sea level line. Sea level is half-way between the lowest and the highest tides, but this varies around the country so after experimenting with several locations for tidal measuring stations it was decided to have one. The UK Ordnance Survey Datum Newlyn is UK sea level, or mean sea level. A modest, concrete hut, now a Grade II listed building, is found on the end of the south pier of Newlyn Harbour in Cornwall. In the floor of this hut is a hole, the hole is connected to the sea by a short tunnel. As the tide rises and falls in the hole, its range is measured. Sea level is midway between these two points. A bolt on the floor of the hut is slightly more than fifteen feet, or 4.751 metres, above the mean sea level mark and it is from this bolt, on this floor, in this shed, on this pier that all UK heights are calculated. The summit of Ben Nevis is, for example, 1,345 metres, or 4.413 feet, above a bolt, on a floor in a shed in Newlyn, Cornwall!

Sometimes it appears that a contour feature is missing, or it appears as a ridge rather than a knoll. You have to allow for the ten metre gap between contours. Ten metres is quite lot, 32 feet and 9.7 inches. Most two-story houses in the UK are around 5 or 6 metres tall while a double decker bus is just shy of 5 metres tall. Hence you could have a knoll as big as a house or at least as tall as a bus that doesn't appear on the map. It's highly likely to be consumed within the curve of a ridge contour line, and it all depends how high it is above the UK Ordnance Survey Datum in Newlyn as to whether or not it gets its own contour line. You could be ascending, or descending, steeply for 19 metres and only crossing one contour line; it's rarely like this, but don't be caught out when it is. Sometimes people are caught out when they see a steep slope and expect to see lots of close contours on the map. You need to think about how high this hill actually is, it might not be as big as it looks or it could be up to 30 metres, 100ft, and just have two close contours. You could also have a small protuberance that pops up, just a metre or two above the contour line, to be shown as a contour feature such as a ring contour.

Top tips from Mountain Leaders

When looking at a map, focus on the contour lines and make them pop out in your mind, so you can visualise the terrain on the map. This will make it easier to understand where you are on the map, thus making it easier to know where it is that you need to go.

Belal Younis

THE MOUNTAIN LEADER

I remember ... lost on Siabod

Every now and then something goes completely wrong. A few years back I found myself in a rather awkward position on day one of an ML assessment, when one unfortunate candidate got every navigation leg completely wrong on the first morning. On day one it is traditional to focus on navigation. People have practised, it's what they are expecting and if you can nail competence in micro-navigation early on then the candidate should be nicely set up to show a more all-round performance as the week goes on. Unfortunately, on this particular week, this particular candidate had a particularly bad start. It soon became apparent to the group as well and that puts them in an awkward position, as through a typical assessment week, they will form a bond and support each other as best they can.

I had to sit her down at lunch, away from the group and present the facts that she hadn't known where she was for the majority of the morning. It turned out she simply wasn't ready for the assessment. She hadn't had the opportunity to practise beforehand, her logbook was marginal and spread over a long period of time, she'd had some personal issues and work had encouraged her to go for the assessment when she knew she wasn't ready.

I suppose the moral of the story is that no one should be pressurised by anyone else into going for assessment if they don't believe they are ready. It is a high-pressure week and they will need to have confidence in their skills. The assessors will do everything they possibly can to put candidates at ease and they are pretty good at this. Remember people have to prepare while normal life carries on.

Two walkers relating the map to the ground.

Teaching navigation and decision making

When we are teaching navigation, we are providing students with a set of tools that require application. During the course of this application, choices have to be made. When we navigate we are constantly making decisions about route choice; route choice from maps, route choice from apps and route choice on the ground. There are large-scale decisions to be made about which is the best route for any particular day. There are smaller scale decisions about which way to turn, which track to follow and how far to follow it. Decision making can be as simple as considering whether or not a path really goes through an unmarked gate and through a garden, to decisions around whether a linear feature such as a fence has changed, or is following a different route to that marked on the map. Decisions must be made about contour features, whether or not they are big enough to show on the map, whether or not a knoll is part of a ridge or, maybe, where the actual summit is on a hill-top plateau. There are also a set of decisions to be made around which particular navigation tool is to be used at any particular time, and which one will be the most reliable. For example, can you handrail? Should you handrail? Can you go on a direct bearing? Should you aim off? How far should you aim off? How much should you adjust your pacing for the terrain being crossed?

Decision making, as a topic, should run through your teaching of navigation with the ability to evaluate the usefulness of each navigation tool and its application in different circumstances being paramount.

Using the compass

An assessor will have had to ascertain, at some stage of the assessment, whether or not the candidates can navigate with 'the map alone'. If any of them followed a bearing, and paced, in broad daylight the assessor will have been concerned. This method of navigation should be restricted to poor visibility as it changes the way you interact with your group, making it autocratic, rather than interactive. So, what is appropriate use of the compass in good visibility?

Top tips from Mountain Leaders

Put a long cord on your compass so it can be used at arm's length and placed on the map without having to be detached from your pocket. I've seen the cord far too short on clients, and it certainly is if they carry their compass around their neck.

Nick Rowe

Using the compass: part one, good visibility

When I ask a group to orientate the map, the majority look at the features around them and line the map up with those, however, a minority, often people who've done some orienteering, will just pop the compass on the map and turn the map until it faces north. Both these methods are perfectly valid, but the Mountain Leader should be practising relating the map to the ground and the ground to the map constantly. You need to be really good at orientating the map without a compass. This is the best way to get better at visualising the 3D world that has been drawn in 2D on your map.

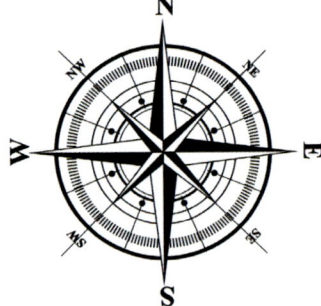

The cardinal and inter cardinal points on a compass
Credit: favpng.com

It is quite possible to get a little disorientated during a summit break, especially if there is some cloud blowing around. This is the perfect time to take a rough bearing just to make sure you are leaving the summit in the right direction, and by rough, I just mean a cardinal or intercardinal (also known as ordinal) direction.

If the visibility is good, having established you are going in the correct direction, your compass should be put away. You should be able to use the features around you to maintain your direction and proceed to the target location.

So, the compass should be used sparingly, if at all, in good visibility. It can be used as a measuring device, to measure distance on the map using the Romer, but even this is only really required when we are measuring a distance to pace along in poor visibility. Most of the time you can use the grid squares, 1km squares, on your map to estimate distance as required.

Sometimes you might use the compass to confirm something i.e. if you take a bearing along a path or a fence, then you may want to be completely sure that it is the one you hoped it was. I've also done this in areas of confusing, bumpy ground. Take a bearing on the bump, or knoll, you are

Using the compass to identify the correct bump on a ridge knoll. Note; I'm talking about the foreground knolls!

heading for just to check you are going to the right one. This is very helpful, but you don't then walk on the bearing. You have identified the correct destination, you can now look at the land and choose your route, typically walking around the bogs between the bumps.

> **Theoretical percentage of time using compass**
>
> - 80% of time – compass not used at all. (Good visibility, map related to ground etc).
>
> - 10% of time – compass used, but only to orientate map in poor visibility.
>
> - 7% of time – compass used to confirm direction of travel with rough bearing.
>
> - 3% of time – accurate compass bearing to walk on in poor visibility (and this is usually winter!).
>
> Patrick Hickie

> **The art of coarse navigation**
>
> Coarse navigation is what we do when we're following a feature on the map that doesn't have a map marked footpath. It might be a ridge, it might be a gully to a llyn / tarn. It could be direct route from a lochan to a bealach. It typically is a natural line to take, but there is no footpath marked on the ground. When you get there, there is a path, but you can't be 100% sure it goes where you want it to go. So, you have a rough bearing, a rough distance and you follow the rough path. Bring all three strands together, following the path, which should give the easy route, but only as long as it fits in nicely with your rough bearing and rough timing. This is the art of coarse navigation.

Using the compass: part two, poor visibility

This is when the compass really comes in its own. Yes, you can use a GPS device, I've heard this called the 'lazy persons' compass, this is because the GPS will point to a specific location rather than in a specific direction. If you have never used one for poor-visibility navigation try it, it's really good. This is also something that is getting easier to do with the apps on your phone. If you can operate your phone in the dark, when it's raining, and you are wearing gloves then this will be the way to go. However, for now the compass

THE MOUNTAIN LEADER

Practicing walking on a bearing in good visibility. This is essential practice for doing the same in the dark or low cloud.

A group learning how to walk on a bearing in poor visibility.

Poor visibility navigation, a key skill for the Mountain Leader.

remains the number one tool for finding your way in poor visibility. Don't let this type of navigation work dominate your teaching, we rarely use it in anger. Clearly you do need to spend some time on it, but your customers need to go away understanding how rarely it is done for real.

> **Top tips from Mountain Leaders**
>
> Always have the brightest headtorch on the hill. Skimping on light to save weight is counterproductive and at night, don't try to read OS maps using red light – the brown contour lines are invisible!
>
> Mike Hammill

Poor visibility navigation gets even harder in the dark, especially on cloudy nights when your headtorch will bounce back off the cloud.

Mobile phone in a case, with a stylus and a waterproof phone two solutions to using a phone in inclement conditions.

Navigation

You can make a table with your knee on which to rest your map. This keeps it stable for reading the detail and taking bearings.

The surveyor's tape in action for measuring an accurate 50 metres.

You can use a surveyor's tape to measure a 50 metre course.

Walking on a bearing

If we know, or suspect, we'll be needing to walk on a bearing, it's a good idea to prep it in advance. This can be done either at home or in a sheltered location and you can even write crucial bearings on your map. If you are taking a bearing on the hill, from the map, it's quite good to drop down onto one knee and make yourself a little table to work on. Double and triple check you are properly lined up at both ends. I like to use the black line in the compass housing for this rather than the edge of the compass. Clamp the map with your fingers on one side and thumb on the other, allow no movement until that bearing is read. The more perfect this bearing the less chance of going wrong. When following the bearing, let the compass settle. I like to hold my arms, elbows tucked into my sides, then clasp the compass firmly in both hands keeping it level. Let it settle, yes again. Now walk, literally five or six paces, stop, let the compass settle. Walk again, a little further, maybe twelve or fourteen paces, stop, let the compass settle. You really do need to slow things down and seek accuracy. As a Mountain Leader you have to do this on your own, there's no sending somebody ahead. If there is any visibility then obviously pick a point and walk to it, but when there is nothing at all to see you need to be able to walk on a bearing. If you think this is hard, wait till you do it in the winter! On its own, a bearing can't be completely relied on as it's too easy to drift left, or drift right, to drift uphill or drift downhill. In the dark, small slopes can seem like big ones, bogs will be encountered, walls and fences too. Walking in a straight line, which you must do, is really quite a difficult thing to achieve. We must, therefore, keep track of how far we have travelled, and this is where pacing comes in.

Pacing

When teaching or learning pacing it's well worth measuring out a 100 metre course. You might be able to use a rope to do this, but a 50m tape measure is not that expensive and is lighter to carry than a climbing rope.

It doesn't matter which foot you start on as long as you are consistent, you just need to count every time you put your right, or your left, foot down.

> **Note for Trainers**
>
> When teaching pacing don't let people walk next to each other, they'll fall into pace with each other. Get them to put their hoods up, drop their shoulders, relax and get people to walk as individually and as naturally as possible. Watch out for the last person as they will have a tendency to speed up to catch up with the rest of the group, warn them of this as it will affect their pacing. Get people to measure their pacing over 50 metres on some different terrain, then double it to get their 100 metre number. Don't go too steep as pacing soon fails to work as your footsteps become so close to each other that there is very little forward movement to measure. If it's a steep slope, follow the bearing and wait for a break in the slope upon which you can relocate. Don't try pacing downhill, people really struggle for consistency downhill. Remember pacing will be one of three tools so it won't ever be perfect on its own.

If you have to walk for multiples of 100 metres it might be worth having a method of ticking off each 100 metre leg. In winter, when this pacing can be taking place over some quite long distances e.g. the Cairngorm plateau, having a method of counting each 100 metre leg is very important. Most people just use some toggles to slide up or down a cord. In summer you shouldn't really have to count much more than three or four 100 metre legs, more than that would be an exception. I just use my fingers. You could use some small stones or some pieces of soft rush and throw one away, or collect one, after each leg.

When setting off on a bearing, as well as needing to know how far you will be going, you need to know what the terrain under foot will be like. Will it be uphill, downhill, level or a combination? Pacing is a kind of 'stop feature', in that if you haven't arrived at the desired feature in the distance measured it stops you walking too far in the wrong direction. Knowing the shape of the terrain gives you instant feedback. If you start walking uphill when you should be walking downhill you could be 180 degrees out.

Will changes in slope angle give you check off points? Changes in angle of less than ten metres don't necessarily show up on a map with ten metre contour intervals and coming across steep, seemingly bottomless slopes, is one of the very worrying things about navigating across open country in the dark. If this happens to you, double check your map to make sure you haven't missed a contour closing (two or more contours being squeezed into one on the map), or that you haven't missed a cliff. If these sorts of features are not apparent on the map, then proceed down the slope, with caution.

Navigation

I'm quite sure you've already worked out that, where possible, i.e. without a massive detour, it's a lot easier to handrail to an attack point, then make the shortest journey on a bearing you can, typically looking for opportunities to aim off and always being mindful of good catching features (catching features are sometimes known as catch features, as collecting features or as overshoot features).

Night navigation, headtorches are needed to read the map.

I remember ... a night hike

Poor visibility navigation isn't just for emergencies and escape; it can be fun. I remember vividly going on night hikes as a Scout. It was actually one of our favourite activities. We might do it from the Scout hut, though fields and around the village. Or we'd drive out to the moors, maybe Ogden, maybe Ilkley and have an adventure. I can still see the orange glow of the big conurbations either side of the Pennines. I can also remember coming across a rocking, parked car with steamed up windows – take young people on night hikes and they might remember them forever!

Note for Trainers

Try the 'compass rose practical'. Pick a small hilltop in a rough, but undulating area. Mark the hilltop with a walking pole, rucksack, or yourself. The group work in pairs. Each pair stands back to back at the marked point and walks off in the opposite direction to each other. They should pace and walk on a bearing. After about 80 to 100 metres they hide their rucksack. They mustn't hide it too well, just make sure it is not visible from the start point. They return to the starting point, checking the direction they have been walking in and checking the distance they have walked. Back at the start, they tell their partner where their rucksack is, in terms of distance and direction (compass bearing), they then go and collect each other's rucksacks. No one ever walks exactly in the right direction and no one ever stops after exactly the right distance, this helps you to reinforce the need for cross referencing three bits of evidence (direction – distance – terrain). It also helps you too see how accurately people are following their bearings, and how accurately they can pace. While it's very tempting to grab a brew and leave the group to it, keeping an eye on at least the direction they walk in, will feed well into how you follow up this activity and further develop the teams' skill set. Remember ... plan – do – review.

The 5 D's and DDT

Acronyms have long been used as a teaching aid. For some people they work well, for others not so well. One of the problems I've found with them is that they can be too long. Anything over three or maybe four letters is less likely to work. Take the 5D's for example. D for Description, D for Direction, D for Distance, D for Duration and D for Destination (other 5 D's are available!). Distance and duration are really one and the same thing and destination should include catching features. We've already established that distance needs converting to time to be useful to people. Try using DDT instead where D means direction, D means duration and T means terrain. A link we often make for climbers is that they are always seeking to use a three point belay and they need a good reason not to, like a big oak tree. It's the same with navigation on the hill, you need three bits of information, unless you are following a big, clear path (this is your oak tree).

So when teaching navigation, D – how far is it (pace or time)? D – what direction is it (cardinal direction or bearing)? T – is it up or down (steep or gentle)? Then, talk about making a film of the route in your head; what will you pass (tick off) and how you will know if you've gone too far (catching features). I endeavour to keep it that simple, but practise constantly in different places at different times, in different weather, working with different pairs and trying it solo.

Toolbox of navigation tools

I have another way of looking at the navigating skills. I compare them to a toolbox, well, two toolboxes really. Most people have some handy tools in their kitchen, possibly in a drawer, possibly under the sink, but somewhere within easy reach. These are the everyday tools, the things you use most frequently. In the shed or garage, you may have another toolbox, a box of tools infrequently used. In this toolbox are some specialist items that you only need to bother with in unusual circumstances, circumstances that occur infrequently. Navigation tools are like this too. Handrailing is in your kitchen-drawer toolbox, pacing on a bearing is in the shed toolbox. It's a really helpful way of illustrating how important each tool is. The importance of the shed toolbox navigation tools is often overstated or thought too much of because these were the tools that may have dominated the teaching on your training course. They do need teaching and practising under supervision, and they will dominate a large chunk of time on a training course. It's really important to get the perspective correct on this one. Pacing and bearings will, once ingrained into your soul, be left in the shed toolbox. You shouldn't however neglect to practise them from time to time.

From the shed toolbox

Below are four examples of the kind of tools that belong in the shed toolbox.

Boxing

Boxing makes perfect sense on paper and can work well with a perfect corrie, but is hardly ever used. A crude dog-leg maybe more appropriate, but let's be honest, most of the time, we'd just handrail the edge. Even in winter it's unusual you need to properly box. Boxing will fall to the bottom of the shed toolbox.

Dog-legs

You rarely need to do a long dog-leg using bearings. Dog-legs are much more likely to be small scale around an object, a rock, or small cliff. Just look to the other side, pick a spot, walk around the object and re-join where you started from after estimating how many paces you may have missed out. This might be near to top of the shed toolbox, you know, those handy little trays just under the lid when you open it.

Aspect of slope

Aspect of slope was originally taught as a winter technique. In a smooth snow covered corrie it isn't usually too difficult to work out where the fall line is, the line straight down hill, bisecting the contours at 90°. But try it in the Moelwynion or indeed any unruly, upland terrain; exactly where down is, is not always easy to ascertain. If you've been shown this technique, pop it in the bottom of your shed toolbox!

Timing cards

Timing cards are smart, fancy looking cards, often plasticised and usually logoed up. They are one of those things that look ace, but actually are next to useless and create a false idea of what a mountain leader should be doing. I struggle to understand why any mountain leader would need to know their timings over 100 metres walking at different speeds. If you were faffing about reading off a timing card to navigate on assessment, I'd be concerned about your grasp of actually what was going on and what you were being assessed to do.

Now, having upset at least half of my readership, let's put a positive word in for timing cards. Timing cards can help people to build up their knowledge of how fast they are walking and how long things might take. So, as an experienced walker you will soon get to feel the difference between walking at 3, 4 or 5km an hour, but during the early stages of practice, tools like timing cards can be handy.

The thing is, if you are walking 100, 200 or 300 metres in poor visibility then your speed will be variable due to the terrain underfoot, so making your timings less accurate. Legs of this length should be paced. Only when your legs get up to 500 metres, and this is pretty unusual in the summer, should timing come into play. These are poor visibility navigation techniques. If it's not poor visibility you can see where you are going and how far you've gone. You'll be handrailing, using tick-off and catching features so timing and pacing are pretty irrelevant.

You need to be clear that it is not normal to walk on a bearing while pacing in broad daylight, especially when leading a group.

Note for Trainers

When training you will inevitably pay more attention to navigation than other aspects of the qualification. It is important that you give context to the qualification and explain that you really need to push the technical aspects of the qualification during this training week. This is not so much to emphasise their importance, but to ensure a high standard is demonstrated and expectations of standards are clear.

Try to be very clear about progressions. Make sure people have consolidated before moving on, get them working in pairs, then different pairs, then solo. You can even get people choosing their own legs, this really gets them looking at the map. Try to be very clear about what is good visibility navigation and what is preparation for poor visibility navigation.

Teaching navigation

Navigation often gets taught in a linear manner, there is often confusion about which are the most appropriate techniques to use in any given situation. I've met people on assessment who've been following a bearing and pacing in broad daylight because they've been told that navigation is the be all and end all of the Mountain Leader qualification. This is clearly wrong. You need to be able to walk and talk and navigate and talk. Your chosen method of navigation must be the simplest one available. Simple is often better anyway. To aid this process I spilt my navigation teaching into three:

1. Navigation in good visibility

2. Preparation for navigation in poor visibility

3. Navigation in poor visibility

Navigation

If you are teaching techniques for navigating in poor visibility then, by necessity, you want to work through this in good visibility. You must make it absolutely clear that you are now looking at, and teaching, techniques to be used in poor visibility, in preparation for practising them in poor visibility.

Navigation in good visibility

- Handrailing, including tick off features and catching features (visualise the route)

- Timing for legs typically longer than 500 metres

- Introducing contours

- Working map to ground and ground to map

- Use the compass for identifying targets such as separating one knoll from another knoll. Use it for measuring distances. Use it for ascertaining the general direction of travel such as when leaving summit. You might also use it to take a bearing along a liner feature such as a path or a fence.

Navigation in poor visibility

(All of which has to be taught in good visibility first.)

- Handrailing

- Pacing

- Taking and following a bearing, including aiming off

Throughout all aspects, you should be building up route visualisation which includes tick off features and catching features. It won't be learnt until it has been practised in different places, at different times, with different people in different conditions. Think carefully about progression and build slowly on firm foundations.

THE MOUNTAIN LEADER

Note for Assessors

This should not be a navigation qualification. Clearly it is important that your candidates can navigate. However, they need to be able to do this while looking after a group. Just bear in mind that we do, sometimes, go out of our way to find tricky, navigation challenges to push the limits on this qualification. Maybe if you're ascending a peak you could let them choose the legs and organise the leadership handover. At the end of the assessment, you need to ask yourself if the candidate can identify their position, use the map alone and walk safely in the dark, while looking after a group. Another way to think is to ask yourself if they will be ok doing the sort of walk most Mountain Leaders do? In this case, their leadership qualities will begin to outweigh any minor, micro-navigational issues they may have had. Think of the bigger picture.

If you don't have a full complement of four people you could lead some legs and get them to show your position on the map, or even draw a line on a map to show the route you took. You also need to flag up that feedback isn't always given instantly and sometimes it will be a simple, noncommittal, usually monotone: "thank you". This non-judgemental comment is used so as not to put pressure on the rest of the team and to allow candidates the opportunity to change their mind later, or at least on the next leg or two.

Map-reading practice necessarily takes you off the beaten track.

I remember ... a case of two borderline candidates

There were two candidates, on the same assessment, neither completely convincing with their micro-navigation. One passed and one was deferred. How did we come to the decision? Quite simple really, the assessment is holistic and the logbook of experience is a key part of that. One candidate was actually short of the required minimum of forty quality mountain days while the other had walked the Munros. In the context of looking after people in the British hills, it was actually quite an easy decision to make and an easy one to evidence.

Navigation

Walkers puzzling over whether or not handrailing the fence is the best choice for the way ahead.

Route planning

Many of you will have made a detailed route plan at some stage of your walking career. You may use these as teaching tools to develop route planning skills. There is no doubt that working through a detailed route plan is a useful exercise. I remember constantly jotting down grid references and adding compass bearings to a table of notes. This is brilliant practise for inexperienced walkers. Mountain leaders, however, need to be able to look at a map and think that'll make a route, that'll be a good day, but if it isn't I can shorten the route here or extend it there. A Mountain leader likes options, doesn't like a fixed plan, must be able to respond to the needs of the group and the prevailing weather. It's pretty unusual today to find a route that hasn't been described somewhere before, so make full use of guidebooks and online resources.

Map extract with three routes on. Plan A, plus a plan B if things are going well. Note plan C if the day is going slower than hoped for.

Walking guidebooks, websites and apps like walkingworld.com, outdooractive.com, AllTrails, walkhighlands.co.uk, mudandroutes.com and ukhillwalking.com are just some of the places where you can find plenty of ready-made route plans. Even when using these sources of information, you should run through the options available in terms of extending or shortening the route. Run through the timings and take a look at the terrain. These sites do help you know if there is a clear path on the route or one which might not appear on your map, they are also handy at helping you find the best place to park.

Different ways of measuring routes on maps.

How to measure routes on maps has changed over the years. I remember laying out some string along our intended route, then measuring the string. You can still buy map measuring wheels and these maybe useful when introducing new people to maps, scale and route planning. Nowadays, the many phone apps will do this job for you too.

A wonderful day of high pressure on the Carneddau.

What is the weather doing and how will it affect us?

Weather

"A good guide knew the mountain well, knew the paths in all conditions, knows the mountain weather ..."

Enos Mills 1920

Of all the skills required to be demonstrated by Mountain Leaders, this area has probably seen the biggest change since the inception of the qualification in the early sixties. When I went through the scheme in the early eighties I remember having to fill in a proforma sheet with information gleaned from the shipping forecast as it was read out on the radio. We would then take this information and draw our own synoptic chart. We'd then read the synoptic chart to predict the forthcoming weather. You can still see synoptic charts, daily in the TV weather bulletins and they are easy to find on the Met Office website, they're labelled as surface pressure charts and we'll look at these later. Even if we were just listening out for the weather on the radio, here in north Wales, we'd listen out for the Irish Sea forecast as that would be the weather soon to be approaching us. Interestingly, if you were in the Lake District, you'd be following the weather across the same shipping area. These days we just reach for our mobile phones to get the latest hour by hour update.

THE MOUNTAIN LEADER

The path in Cwm Idwal during a very heavy downpour.

The three 'levels' of weather knowledge

I think weather knowledge comes at us on three levels now:

1. Just do an internet search although you won't even need to do this, as with apps, it can be there on the screen of your mobile phone. Work out which are your favourite apps and check two or three of them.

2. At the next level, you might need or wish to interpret a sea level forecast and apply it to the uplands; for those of us with a mobile handheld internet accessible device on our person even this is diminishing in its requirement as a skill. I still think an understanding of this is a good thing for a Mountain Leader as we can explain to our groups why the weather may deteriorate as we ascend.

3. The coverage of depressions, fronts, isobars and cloud types is really now just an area of interest. You really don't need to know what an isobar is to be an effective Mountain Leader. It is nice to know though and I would suggest that some meteorological knowledge is a good bit of environmental knowledge to have and it might be something you develop over time. The weather does, after all, completely dominate what we do.

Sources of weather information

Mountain leaders are expected to be aware of a range of sources of information on the weather. Well, it comes up immediately on your phone home screen, a quick internet search will give you a mountain forecast for wherever you are heading. My top tip is to update your weather forecast frequently on your mobile phone and simply screen shot it whenever you get reception. There aren't many places where you'll have no reception all day. While the valleys may have no coverage, there could easily be a signal wafting in over the tops. The weather forecasts are constantly updated and constantly changing so do check whenever you can.

The best sources are those that are dedicated to the uplands. Telephone forecasts for the UK mountain areas were developed in the eighties, and a phone call to the 'weather-line' was a normal part of a day's preparations. Of course, we now have a range of these available on our phones. The top two, most used and most beloved, are probably those from MWIS and the Met Office.

MWIS

The Mountain Weather Information Service was set up by Geoff Monk in 2003. Geoff is passionate about the weather. After graduating with a degree in meteorology he has spent his entire career as a weather forecaster, including 25 years at the Met Office. Geoff has always had an interest in local weather. After moving to Scotland in 1999 to run a private weather forecasting service he developed a particular interest in mountain weather and this led to the formation of MWIS. After an initial, trial period Geoff worked out that mountain users wanted detailed (but not overwhelming) levels of information written in a language that was accessible to both professionals and inexperienced mountain users.

MWIS now has a loyal following from the mountaineering and hill-walking community. It has extended its coverage to Wales, the Lakes, and the Pennines. MWIS is a big supporter of the outdoor community and it's worth a look at their website and clicking on some of the links. MWIS is funded partly through Sport Scotland and partly through individual supporters.

The Met Office

The Met Office was established in 1854 by Vice Admiral Robert Fitzroy. It established weather forecasts based on observations taken in several locations, to predict how the weather might change in any given place as the observed weather moved over it. Some of the ruins on Ben Nevis's summit are of a former Met Office recording station. Today the predominantly, publicly funded Met Office boasts one of the world's most powerful supercomputers capable of 14,000 trillion arithmetic operations each second. The Met Office provides a wide range of specialist weather forecasts, including mountain ones.

THE MOUNTAIN LEADER

A misty day in the mountains.

I usually look at both. I also take a quick look at a simple one like yr.no as well, just to get a simple overview with timings which are surprisingly accurate. Another favourite is MeteoBlue and it's fun Where2go feature. Check WINDY and Windy (yep, two different ones with the same name) and Windfinder. The BBC will also give you a good, localised weather forecast. I'm sure by the time you read this, you'll have come across some other favourites too. The key thing missing from most of these other forecasts, which will send you back to a mountain specific forecast, is the level of the cloud cover, for that you'll need to go to one of the above, more specialist forecasts.

It can be surprising, but reassuring, how similar weather forecasts from different sources are. The BBC currently uses information from Meteo France, while yr.no is Norwegian and the Met Office is, of course, its own data collecting organisation. All these meteorological offices collate a range of data from satellite imagery, to ships, to weather balloons and weather stations. They put together an impression of what the weather is doing now, how those weather systems are moving, and from this they suggest what the weather might be doing later. Look for a confidence level in the prediction, the Met Office start their forecast with the level of confidence in the prediction.

Anyone with any walking experience, certainly anyone with enough walking experience to have considered undertaking the Mountain Leader qualification will have some interest in the weather. Actually, most British people have some interest in the weather, even if it's just to pass the time of day!

The key skill for the Mountain Leader is to be able to interpret the information given in respect of how it may impact on their day in the hills. Should you head east or west? north or south? Stay low or go high? Do you want to walk with the wind or into the wind? How windy will it be on the ridges and in the bealachs? Although, in the past, you might make the best judgement you could about where to go, you would probably still carry everything. By that, I mean you'll always have your full waterproofs, a spare layer, a woolly hat and some gloves. Even if you added to these with sun cream, sunglasses and a sun hat, you'd still be very nervous about ditching the waterproofs. I have, only recently, started to do this. I can now look at the synoptic chart and make my own weather forecast, but more importantly, I can look at several, different weather forecasts online, made by expert interpretation of those very same synoptic charts. If everything lines up then I may well leave my waterproofs at home, something that I would not have dreamt of in days gone by.

So, the first trick a Mountain Leader needs to be able to perform is to know where to get a weather forecast from. You should be able to work with two or three different sources, evaluate the predictions and make judgements on how those predictions might affect your day. Always be aware of changing forecasts, make sure you have absolutely the most up to date information it is possible to get hold of. Be aware that sometimes there is low confidence in the predications being made.

I think it's useful to have an understanding of how the weather can vary with height gain and local geomorphology in the hills. Why it can be colder, wetter and windier in some parts of the mountains than others? Even if this is not essential knowledge for understanding the weather forecast anymore, I think it is useful knowledge about the mountain environment. Beyond this, it's just quite fun to be able to read a synoptic chart and so this is the approach we will take here.

Why is it colder on the hill?

It is colder on the hill, because as you ascend it really does get colder. There is an established scientific formula for working this out. It varies with latitude, but here in the UK it is around 1°C cooler for every 150m of ascent. This is very much a simplification of a simplification. The real sums have lots of strange symbols and end up with decimal points galore. Even the typically quoted 'norms' for the UK are a bit fanciful. You'll see quoted that the air is 1°C cooler for every 100m of ascent in dry air and 1°C cooler for every 200m of ascent in moist air. Obviously, here in the UK the air is rarely moist or dry and is typically somewhere in between, hence the simplification of 1°C for every 150m of ascent.

What this means is, that if you are in Fort William at sea level and the temperature is 10°C, by the time you've ascended to the summit of Ben Nevis it will be 0°C; that is, freezing. Most weather forecast apps mentioned earlier will build in an estimated effect of lapse rate so you should be able to see what the difference is. However, should you only be able to obtain a sea level forecast, then you can make a stab at how much colder it'll be as you ascend your chosen mountain. It's also a fun thing to talk through with groups from time to time.

The snowline, above which temperatures are low enough for precipitation to fall as snow rather than rain often stands out clearly in our hills and mountains.

Why is it wetter on the hill?

It is usually wetter on the hill than it is lower down. This is due to something called relief rainfall, or orographic rainfall if you want its academic name. Air is forced up and cools, as it cools, it condenses and this condensation forms clouds, when the cloud gets too heavy it rains. Think of the steam from a kettle spout, rising, spreading and cooling; if it then hits a cold surface, like a window, it turns to water and runs down the glass. This is the same principal as with relief rainfall.

We have a lot of relatively warm, moist, air which travels to the UK across the Atlantic Ocean. This air is coming from the equator and the Caribbean, so it's warm and it picks up moisture from the ocean. It's known as the tropical maritime air mass. This air mass dominates our weather systems and keeps our climate, predominately warm and wet. Obviously when this air mass hits Ireland, Eryri or any of our other western hills, it's forced up, cools and condenses and falls as rain. This is why it's wetter in the mountains, particularly the western ones.

There is some good news though, on a smaller scale it's often dry in the lee of the mountains. So, here in Eryri, Llanrwst in the Conwy valley gets half the amount of rainfall that Capel Curig receives per annum and if you head up to the coast, Deganwy gets half as much again. This is the rain shadow effect, there will often be lower rainfall to the east of our mountains. This might influence your route choice for the day.

Top tips from Mountain Leaders

Waterproofs should be the most accessible items in your rucksack.

Derek Clarke

Walkers out in the rain.

Why is it windier on the hill?

I suppose, in the grand scheme of things, it isn't really windier in the mountains. There are many plains and seas around the world where the wind blows for many miles without interruption and in doing this it picks up a fair amount of speed. The Southern Ocean regularly sees steady winds of 100mph plus. (Oklahoma in the flat, US interior records some of the highest landborne wind speeds, though these are mostly due to tornadoes.)

The increase in wind speed in our small mountains is typically due to a sort of squeezing. The troposphere is the lowest part of the atmosphere, and over the UK, it's around 7 miles deep. It is in this layer of the atmosphere that our weather operates. Our mountains form a small obstruction in the base of this layer of the atmosphere. So, as air moves across it, it is interrupted and ripples of wind will form. The increase in wind force over and around obstacles is known as the Venturi effect, after Giovanni Battista Venturi who first described this phenomenon in the late 1700s. What this means to us is that the wind will speed up over ridges and speed up through cols. There is no magic formula, as there is for lapse rate, so to work out how much windier it'll be the higher we go, we often suggest it'll be two or three times stronger at around 900m which seems to work pretty well.

The wind is a real issue for us in the hills. There are days where travel across them is simply not possible, or so difficult as to be not worth persevering with. However, armed with the knowledge that it won't be consistent across a range of hills you can start to pick your routes. Steep sided ridges like Crib Goch, Aonach Eagach and Striding Edge are best avoided as the wind increases above a predicted 20 / 25 miles per hour and definitely avoided above 30mph. There will always be other places to walk. The wind direction will be important too. The north ridge of Tryfan is not too

A group being buffeted by strong winds in the mountains. This is the entrance to Cwm Idwal, so clearly not a day to be heading much higher.

bad in strong westerlies or south westerlies, you can hide on the eastern side of the hill, but a corresponding easterly, fortunately quite a rare thing, would be really hard work. Check the wind direction for the day, look out for changes then take a look at the map; there will be places in the lee, and of course you don't always need to summit.

The wind can surprise you. You know it'll typically be windier on the tops and you know it'll be windier on cols. I have, however, battled up to a summit just so I can get over it and find some lee-side shelter, only to be surprised by arriving at a quiet, virtually wind free summit. The summit was sheltered as the windward slope had forced the wind up and over the summit, leaving the summit area calm and a bit like being in the eye of the storm. Similarly, I've ruled out the tops for the day but been blown off my feet, with a group in Cwm Idwal. It seems to come over the col by Llyn y Cwn and race down into the cwm below. It's often really strong around the north-west, north and eastern shores of Llyn Idwal, but usually a bit more sheltered tucked in around Rhiwiau Caws (The Idwal Slabs). You should observe and take note of this sort of phenomena on your own local patch.

What does the synoptic chart indicate?

You probably had a quite a good session on synoptic charts on your Mountain Leader training course, so this might just act as a reminder or a refresher to those who did it some time ago. These days you are not asked to interpret a synoptic chart. You have such easy access to people who can do this so much better than we can, that it would be a bit daft really. It is, however, a bit of fun to be able to look at a synoptic chart, or surface pressure chart as they are labelled on the Met Office website, and begin to understand why the weather forecast is as it is. You can also look at the

Synoptic chart
Credit: Met Office

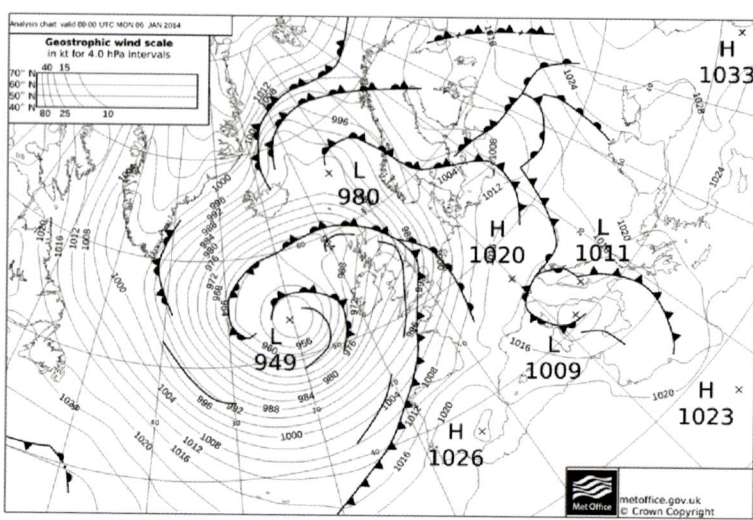

Weather

chart yourself, then check your thoughts against the professional forecasters. We can ask these four questions:

1. Is it a simple or a messy chart?
2. Is it dominated by low or high pressure?
3. Are there any fronts?
4. Are there many isobars?

Is it messy or simple?

This is the first quick way to get an idea of what is going on. A messy map will have lots of isobars, lots of fronts, lots of wiggly lines all over the place. This can't be good, a messy chart will mean messy weather. On the other hand, if it's a simple chart than that's good, it'll be simple weather, nice and settled with not much happening and easy to understand. Messy or simple, bad or good?

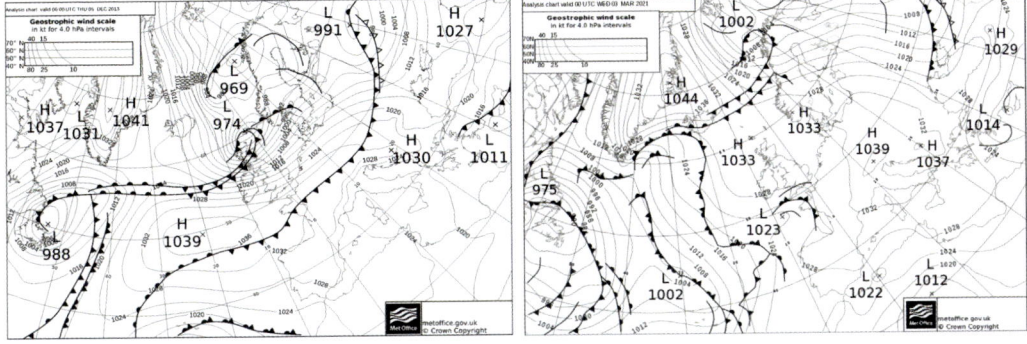

A low pressure synoptic chart
Credit: Met Office

A simple high pressure map
Credit: Met Office

Is it dominated by low or high pressure?

High pressure

High pressure is settled, sinking air and because it's sinking, it's stable. This is good, as it gives us fine weather. In summer, it can mean blue skies and hot sun. Gentle winds blow in a clockwise fashion around the high pressure system. In summer this can bring the sand from the Sahara to cloud our views and it can also lead to a heat haze which makes our views less clear. It is dry air and it's great – if you see an area of high pressure over the UK, get yourself out there. However, it might not cover the whole of the UK, so head for where it does. Sometimes you get a ridge of high pressure, a good day between poor ones, look out for these and use them. So confident are we in our weather forecasts today that these could be the times to leave your waterproofs at home, in the cooler months you might get some use out of your soft shell jacket too. Enjoy the highs, hi's are good, we like highs.

High pressure weather in the summer.

In winter it can go one of two ways. In the mountains, it could just be the best day you've ever had. Cool air will sink into the valley and condense, forming low-lying mist in the valleys, while warm air will rise around the summit, you'll be walking in a T-shirt looking down on a sea of cloud; these temperature inversion days are not common enough to rely on or to get completely used to. They are on the edge of the summer Mountain Leaders remit as they usually occur when we have good, winter conditions. As you descend back to the valley and into the cloud that has formed down there, it'll be cold and damp, quite a change. It's on days like this when you need to look out for Brocken spectres. If you see cloud below you, position yourself with the sun behind you and your shadow on the cloud below might have a rainbow halo around it – fabulous. In the valleys and in places like East Anglia, winter highs can be pretty miserable as the sinking cold air forms a layer of cloud or fog. This can be quite a thin layer, but it's at ground level and it's this layer most of us live in. I've seen it when Heathrow and Stansted airports have actually had to close, but up in the hills we've been having the time of our lives. Highs are great!

A Broken spectre in Eryri.
Photo: Rusty Bale

Weather

A moment above the clouds. This inversion gave great atmospheric conditions on this Mountain Leader assessment expedition.

I remember ... my first inversion

It was quite some time ago now. I was a kid, quite a small one. We were heading west from Yorkshire in the days before the M62, a family holiday of some sort I presume, but don't actually remember. What I do remember however, is leaving home in fog, that dark grey fog you used to get, full of smoke and fumes, not like a great, London smog but still pretty grim. Cold, wet and foggy, a grey world. We drove through Huddersfield and hit the A6024 (many years later this road would provide a spectacular stage on the Tour de France). We climbed steadily from Holmfirth and through Holmbridge and Holme, then, quite suddenly, we emerged from the cloud. Wow! We were now above a sea of low cloud, only masts and moors were tall enough to pierce it. The whole of Yorkshire was buried under a blanket of white, cotton wool, clouds. Above, the sun shone brightly and this was all that was needed to lift the mood – we smiled. I can still see that view in my mind's eye, today. It made a big impression on me and when I'm fortunate enough to experience a temperature inversion today, I think back to the first time I saw such a thing. Maybe, just maybe, you'll be lucky enough to be with a group when they experience their first temperature inversion. Our role as Mountain Leaders can be a privilege.

Low pressure

A map dominated by low pressure is all too familiar I'm afraid. The UK and Ireland are sat at a point on the globe where different air masses meet. From the north-east comes a dry, cold air mass called the polar continental; from the south-east comes an air mass called the tropical continental and from the north is a rare visitor, the arctic air mass. From the north-west comes the polar maritime air mass and from the south-west comes the tropical maritime air mass. If it's polar it's cold, if it's tropical it's warm, if it's continental it's dry and if it's maritime it's wet.

We are mostly under the influence of the warm, wet air heading up from the south-west. This is, for most of the time, a good thing. It means, along with the influence of a warm, ocean current, known as the Gulf Stream, our islands are good, fertile, non-extreme (weather-wise) places to live. Compared to other places at the same latitude as the UK and Ireland, this is a very comfortable spot to inhabit. However, it is wet and the air masses I've mentioned above really don't like mixing. One that is composed of colder air will push under, and lift up, one that is composed of warmer air. That warmer air is cooled as it rises, condensing with height and this leads to cloud formation and rain, not dissimilar to the physics involved with relief rainfall, it's just that it's an air mass forcing the warm air upwards, rather than mountains.

Are there any fronts?

A front is where two air masses meet. Typically over us, we will have the border between the cold and wet, polar maritime air mass and the warm and wet, tropical maritime air mass. The warm and cold air won't mix, it goes into a 3D spin, it's lifted up and spirals in an anticlockwise direction. You can see this in the charts. You end up with a segment of the warmer air mass surrounded by the colder air mass. Along the leading border is a warm front, cold air followed by warm air. The line is not vertical, it's sloping, it can sometimes be picked out by a descending line of clouds. Along the trailing border is the warm air, again being lifted, but this time from behind, by the undercutting cool air. This border, more precisely, a cold front which is steeper than the warm front and gives heavy, sharp downpours.

At some point the cold front catches up with the warm front and lifts the warm air mass completely off the ground. This gives us an occluded front with, you guessed it, loads of rain which is like having a warm front and a cold front over you at the same time.

There are lots of diagrams to illustrate this in other books and on the internet. All of these diagrams are simplifications of simplifications of simplifications. None of them can take into account the speed of the front passing over, any changes in direction of the air mass or local variations.

A sharp, heavy cold front downpour, this one had hail in it.

Are there many isobars?

Isobars join together areas of equal pressure in the same way that contour lines join together areas of equal height. When contour lines are close you know the slope will be steep, with isobars the closer the lines the windier it will be. The wind blows into the isobar at a slight angle, but the wind

Weather

direction is roughly along the isobar. The geostrophic wind scale helps us to calculate wind speed, you can see it in the top corner of the synoptic charts. It means that roughly for every isobar crossing the British Isles there will be about 5mph wind at sea level. So if there are four isobars expect a wind speed of 20mph at sea level, this wind speed could be two, or even three, times stronger at 900m. In a depression the wind spirals anticlockwise, in a high pressure, or anticyclone, the wind blows clockwise.

On the cusp of winter, wet snow on wet ground makes the going hard work.

These concepts are often taught as factual statements about the passage of a depression and what happens as one passes over. It's not really like that. Look out of your window, can you tell whether or not there is a depression passing over? Is the sky blue, has it got obvious clouds in it or is it just grey? It's often just grey. Always remember that the models we use to teach the weather are simplifications, the weather is a 3D concept which we try to reduce to 2D illustrations on paper. There are massive variations within air masses and fronts can move slowly, quickly or even stop. This movement is currently unpredictable. So, take all your weather teaching with a pinch of salt, it's interesting and the basic concepts are sound.

Enjoy the weather, think about microclimates, think about rain shadow areas, think about wind direction and strength, and when planning, think about how the prevailing conditions might change and how they might affect you. For the best information, use proper weather forecasting, as I've said before, lack of reception is no excuse so just screen shot it whenever you do have reception.

I remember ... more than once!

I know, I know, I'm all too aware that it gets colder the higher you go yet it still seems like a surprise. It's taken years of repeatedly not carrying the right kit to begin to nearly always have the right kit. There have been several occasions where just how cold it has been on top has surprised me. We talk about 'three-season' gear as being spring, summer and autumn. Let me tell you, that when it comes to the spare gloves in your rucksack the three seasons are autumn, winter and spring. It's those start of winter and end of winter days where a little summer complacency has slipped in. The rucksack has been lightened a little, the big gloves are back in the store and I really needed them! Think on, which three seasons are you carrying spare kit for?

THE MOUNTAIN LEADER

A group led by a Mountain Leader enjoying a sprinkling of snow.
Photo: Belal Younis, Peak Adventures UK

When is it summer?

Rather an odd question I know, but it is one we have to discuss with surprising frequency. The Mountain Leader qualification is called the Mountain Leader qualification. It isn't called the Summer Mountain Leader qualification or even the Mountain Leader (summer) qualification, it's just plain old Mountain Leader. The Winter Mountain Leader, on the other hand is called the Winter Mountain Leader, so when do we need to call up a Winter Mountain Leader?

There is not a clear border between summer and winter conditions, there can't be, and the leader will be expected to make wise judgments about where they should and shouldn't be going. It is winter, in Mountain Leader terms, when winter conditions of settled snow and ice prevail. This will be fairly clear-cut in the Scottish Highlands. There will be an altitudinal line for most of the winter period where it is clear that snow and ice are settled on the hill and an ice axe and crampons (and the skills to use them safely) should be carried. This will be less clear in the more coastal parts of Scotland, particularly in the west, where lower hills rise straight from the sea. In the Lake District and Wales winter conditions can come and go almost daily throughout the winter season. In other hill areas such as Dartmoor or the Pennines you can never rule out winter and people have died in avalanches in the Pennines, however, true winter conditions will be very much the exception rather than the rule.

A tongue in cheek suggestion as to when it's winter is that if you really need to take goggles and wear them due to wind-blown snow and ice biting your face, then it's properly winter. A more serious definition might be that if

A little more snow is pushing the limits, this group had to make some decisions as to where they should be and where they should not be. The tops were out of the question, but walking through the woods, as in the picture, presented little extra danger. The forecast was for thawing conditions.
Photo: Merfyn 'Smyrff' Jones

Weather

there is compact snow on slopes, to the degree that if you were to slip, you would continue to slide. In these conditions, crampons may prevent a slip and an ice axe may be of use to assist progress or even, in extreme cases, arrest such a slip.

All this means that a little bit of snow does not make a winter. It is perfectly safe be on the hill with a smattering of snow on the ground. Crampons would not normally be worn if there are some frozen puddles and a hint of snow in the air. Snow sitting on the heather is not a danger. Much more of an issue will be colder temperatures, shorter daylight hours and the physicality of walking through such a landscape. Paths may be hidden, your groups kit may not be adequate and cold, easterly winds can be wearing. It all, as ever, comes down to judgment. Are you matching the group, and its kit, to the prevailing conditions and the terrain to be encountered to achieve your goals for the day?

Fogbows and rainbows

Rainbows are well-known and wonderful to see anywhere, never mind in the hills. Fewer people will have come across a fogbow. It is similar to a rainbow, but without the colour, it can also be known as a white rainbow. Whereas in a rainbow, light is refracted by water droplets i.e. rain, a fogbow is refracted by water vapour, such as that found on a misty mountain top. If you have mist with sun behind then you might see a fogbow. As the water droplets in the mist are so small, the refraction of the light rays is broadened, this loses the colour associated with a rainbow.

A fogbow in Eryri.
Photo: Rusty Bale

Looking down on a rainbow on from the north ridge of Tryfan.

THE MOUNTAIN LEADER

Walking in the rain.

Note for Trainers

Let me refer back to the box of the three levels of weather knowledge. Is vitally important that everyone can do level one well. That they can interpret weather forecasts and understand what it might mean for the day's activities. They must understand the forecast in terms of how it will affect people and how that might influence route choice. This is much more important than understanding the passage of a depression, and therefore more time should be spent on understanding weather forecasts. You should do this every day on the training course.

Note for Assessors

While it would be nice to see that candidates can show some understanding of weather systems on a home paper it isn't necessary to question them about this on the hill. What is important, is that they are up to speed with the weather for the day and what that might mean for the group. You could ask them how the prevailing conditions might affect route choice with different groups, but it's hardly likely to change a result.

One farmer's response to roadside 'fly' camping by a popular llyn in Eryri.

What will we see on our journey and what issues are there in our uplands?

Access, Conservation and the Environment

"The guide finds treasures to right and left for followers in territory which to most people appears barren."

Enos Mills 1920

Mountain Leaders are expected to inspire, be enthusiastic about and expand the environmental knowledge of those they lead. This is really important and cuts both ways. Nature is good for people and we need to learn to embrace it, bathe in it and appreciate it more, but we also need to look after it, care for it and nurture it.

As leaders taking people into the countryside we have a duty to help people learn more about the places we go and how special they are. We need to raise awareness of the issues and challenges faced by the countryside and discuss some of the choices faced around future management of rural areas and, in particular for Mountain Leaders, our uplands.

THE MOUNTAIN LEADER

> **Top tips from Mountain Leaders**
>
> Make them fall in love with nature and our outdoor spaces, make them want to protect it and look after it. We need future generations to feel passionate about it.
>
> Mladenka Hooper

But being a Mountain Leader is all about safety ...

It is actually the case that there are not very many accidents in the hills and mountains of the UK. Even on Yr Wyddfa. The number of people ascending Yr Wyddfa on an annual basis is now well over half a million (590,984 in 2019), many are not experienced hillwalkers. All these people return down the mountain as well; meaning there are over a million ascents and descents or people movements on the mountain. In a typical year, the Llanberis Mountain Rescue Team, which has Yr Wyddfa on its patch, deals with around 200 incidents, but most of these are minor and easily dealt with. Serious incidents are very few and far between. This is still a significant number of incidents for a group of volunteers to deal with, but it just puts into perspective how safe hillwalking is.

I would like to think that one of the reasons that there are so few incidents is because Mountain Leaders are doing a good job. Even if they are volunteering, they are leading their groups well, making sure their group is prepared, appropriately equipped and that they travel with care.

It is also a fact that people tend not to fall off mountains. They might get ill, they might turn an ankle, they might slip or trip, but people are resilient and those who ascend and descend Yr Wyddfa, a hill which sees a lot of traffic from inexperienced hill-goers, have remarkably few incidents which require outside assistance.

You, the Mountain Leader, need to be knowledgeable and enthusiastic about the upland environment. This is an area of the syllabus that you will need to keep working at beyond your assessment. No one knows everything about the upland environment and you will meet many, sometimes overwhelming, specialists and the odd polymath. Your role, however, is to know just enough about everything to see how it all links together and what influences it all. It's really important to have some knowledge, some facts and some interesting stories to hook your group, but it's just as important to understand how it all fits together. I know many Mountain Leaders are intimidated about how much there is to know. One of the advantages of having denuded uplands is that, with a list of ten to twenty species you can soon have enough knowledge to be on the way to being an inspirational

Access, Conservation and the Environment

The summit of Yr Wyddfa can be a very busy place.

leader. I do think it's better to know a bit more about fewer species, than to be able to name lots of species but know nothing about them. Deciding what it is you really need to know is a voyage of discovery in itself.

Five flowers, five birds …

To develop your environmental knowledge, start simple, and build slowly. Look out for things that are easy to recognise and are abundant in the hills. Tormentil, bell heather, ling, common milkwort and heath bedstraw are pretty much omnipresent in our uplands. Find out about each one, what it looks like, when it flowers, where it grows, any uses it may have had, why it is abundant here and any quirky stories about it.

Flowers are one thing, but birds, because they refuse to sit still for long, are another. Look out for the meadow pipit, wheatear, raven and wren as these are frequently seen or heard. Your fifth bird could be a bird of prey, maybe a red kite in some areas, maybe a golden eagle in others, alternatively try cuckoo, everybody knows the call of the cuckoo and its range has shrunk to the uplands of the north and west. Find out what each bird looks like, what it sounds like, where it lives, how it migrates, what it eats and how it behaves in flight.

Tormentil is often confused with a buttercup. In fact it is the only four petalled member of the rose family and is not related to buttercups at all.

Wheatear, a summer migrant to our hills; look for the prominent white rump as it flies away.

THE MOUNTAIN LEADER

Why is nature good for us?

We know we feel better outside but these things need to be proven and, fortunately, it has been. There is a lot of research about this now and one study, in 2015, run by the University of Derby and The Wildlife Trust encouraged people to do something out of doors, something 'wild' for 30 days. They found: *"... that there was a scientifically, significant increase in people's health, happiness, connection to nature and active nature behaviours, such as feeding the birds and planting flowers for bees – not just throughout the challenge but sustained for months after the challenge had been completed."* They went on to say, *"children exposed to the natural world showed increases in self-esteem."* They also felt it taught them, *"how to take risks, unleash their creativity and gave them a chance to exercise, play, and discover."* Dr Richardson, University of Derby, also said: *"there is already research evidence that exposure to nature can reduce hypertension, respiratory tract and cardiovascular illnesses, improve vitality and mood, benefit issues of mental wellbeing such as anxiety and restore attention capacity and mental fatigue. But, more than that, feeling a part of nature has been shown to significantly correlate with life satisfaction, vitality, meaningfulness, happiness, mindfulness, and lower cognitive anxiety."* Richardson et al (2016)

Sometimes it is just great to be out in the hills, whatever the weather.

I remember ... walking up Yr Wyddfa

It was only a few years ago and if I'm honest I'd been avoiding Yr Wyddfa. It's become very busy and if there is low cloud it isn't the greatest summit to be on. But I had to head up there for work one day. I was meeting a group that had been camping out, in Cwm Tregalan, on a Mountain Skills course. There was low cloud and it wasn't a very encouraging day. I was, however, free from my usual leadership responsibilities, I had been working indoors for a few days and it was great to get out and walk and talk. Despite there being no view, despite it being cold and wet, I had a lovely time. The group were chatty and the simple physical exercise was just what I needed. At the end of the day, my legs were tired, but back home I had a smile on my face. The day out had just reminded me of the simple, physical pleasure of walking up and over a hill or a mountain, with good company.

Access, Conservation and the Environment

Mountain Leaders and the environment

Mountain Leaders have a special role to play in the upland environment. We are the people who introduce others to it and many of the people we lead will have little understanding of the countryside. We need to show them why it is special and why it needs looking after. We should raise awareness of the issues involved in managing the countryside, and use it to exemplify some of the large-scale impacts on our green spaces such as climate change. We need to be passionate about these places. We need to be advocates. We need to undertake our adventures with a high level of responsibility.

So we need to take time when leading groups to introduce the upland environment. They will appreciate that hillwalking oozes physical benefits but you may have to help them understand that it also feels good because it's outside in places we perceive as being wild. Try a 'take ten' exercise. Pick a quiet spot and get everyone to just sit down, face away from each other and look, listen, feel and smell (not taste at this point!). Do this in silence for ten minutes if you can. Get them to look at the view, look at what is growing around them, listen to the wind, listen to the birds, feel the rocks, feel the vegetation beneath them, smell the wind, smell the ground beneath them. You can maybe try taste when you chance upon some fresh pennywort, wood sorrel or, best of all, some bilberries.

Introducing people to the upland environment is also a great way to improve your day out. A little knowledge of some of the fascinating things to see will really help spur your group on. Just knowing what plants grow in boggy areas (so you can avoid them), why heather grows out of the reach of sheep (if it's too steep for sheep, it's too steep for us) and how different rock types produce different walking conditions (slippery or grippy) will all enhance the experience you can provide for your groups.

> **Note for Assessors**
>
> You just want some sort of enviro spark from the candidates, something that shows they care about the place they are in, that they have a sense of awe and wonder. You want them to show that they really love being outside and sharing the joys of hillwalking with people. You really don't want them to walk past too many interesting things. *"What is this little yellow flower? It's everywhere!"* Mountain Leaders also have a very important role in explaining to those they lead that this is not a pristine, natural wilderness, it is a landscape with issues.

THE MOUNTAIN LEADER

A selection of 'essential' reading for the Mountain Leader.

Look out for old and second-hand nature books, some of the old coffee table Readers Digest books were very good.

How do Mountain Leaders learn more about the environment?

To inspire and enthuse others, you need some knowledge yourself so how do we learn this stuff, top up this knowledge and keep up with the latest ideas?

Books

Books are brilliant. There are a few books written especially for you; books like my own *Nature of Snowdonia* (Raine 2020) which now has a sister companion for the Brecon Beacons. For Scotland, *Hostile Habitats* (SMT) is essential and alongside these you should be looking at Paul Gannon's Geology Series *Rock Trails* (Pesda Press).

You can learn a lot from these books. Depending on how you learn, you might need to head to a quiet spot in the hills and just sit down with your book and relate it to what you can see around you. On the other hand you might be someone who browses in the evening and soaks up the information.

I'd also recommend taking a look at the Collins series of *'Complete Guides to ...'* Their *British Wildflowers* is very good, as are their other titles in this series. I actually have the *Collins Bird Guide* on my phone as this version includes bird song, but more on apps later.

There is another group of books you might find useful and that is the old coffee table style of nature guides. They were often produced by groups like the Readers Digest or were publishing ventures following on from TV programmes. Look out for second-hand books on mountains and moorlands. Some of the information (be very careful on species numbers and distribution for example) will have changed. They may also have different attitudes to different land uses, reflecting the time of writing, but they do make good, easy background reading and can even be cut up and laminated to use in the field.

> **Top tips from Mountain Leaders**
>
> You can quickly find fascinating facts to impress your clients from the excellent RSPB books which are designed for youngsters. The information is accurate but simple and can help you educate adult clients with nuggets of nature knowledge that they're likely to remember.
>
> Rob Nicholson

The final group of books I'd like to recommend are the inspirational ones. It's incredibly hard to come up with a definitive list. I will leave more out than

I include here, and I'll upset some by leaving out their favourites. Plus, it's an ever-changing feast with new titles around all the time. This has been a growth area of publishing in recent years. Here are twelve of the best and my favourites, because they are well written, well researched, and have inspired me to some degree

Rewilding and nature-friendly farming

Feral: Rewilding the Land, Sea and Human Life, George Monbiot, Penguin 2013, 9780141975580

Wilding: The return of Nature to a British Farm, Isabella Tree, Pan Macmillan 2018, 9781509805105

Rebirding: Rewilding Britain and its Birds, Benedict Macdonald, Pelagic 2019, 9781784272197

English Pastoral: An Inheritance, James Rebanks, Penguin 2020, 9780241245729

Wild Fell: Fighting for nature of a Lake District hill farm, Lee Schofield, Doubleday 2022, 9780857527752

Farming

I Bought a Mountain, Thomas Firbank, (first published in 1940, currently out of print, but available second hand)

The Shepherd's Life: A Tale of the Lake District, James Rebanks, Penguin 2016, 9780141979366

Nature and the land

Curlew Moon, Mary Colwell, Harper Collins 2018, 978-0008241056

Wonderland: A Year of Britain's Wildlife, Day by Day, Stephen Moss and Brett Westwood, John Murray 2017, 978-1473609266

Meadowland: The Private Life of an English Field, John Lewis Stemple, Black Swan 2015, 9780552778992

Inglorious: Conflict in the Uplands, Mark Avery, Bloomsbury Wildlife 2015, 9781472973290

The Last Wilderness: A Journey into Silence, Neil Ansell, Hachette UK 2018, 9781472247124

THE MOUNTAIN LEADER

> **Note for Trainers**
>
> Do your best. This is such a big topic area and you won't have a lot of spare time. Nonetheless, don't miss opportunities when out on the hill. Foster an enquiring approach: What does this place look like? Why does it look like this? How might it change? Introduce some of the common species and, above all else role-model your passion for the environment in which you are earning your living. Further environmental knowledge and understanding will be an important part of everybody's post training action plan. Help them to find good sources and good ways of learning more.

Workshops and courses

Many of you will need practical, in the field help. The Mountain Training Association supports a series of workshops. Of course, workshops can be a bit hit and miss. I've been on some that were educationally poor with too much talking, and too much lecturing, but I've always picked up something and they are nice days out with nice people. Some workshops are free. These are often run by subject specialists, which is good, but you also need to look for someone who can communicate that information too.

Workshops for Mountain Leaders, aimed at you, delivered using a range of methods are a very valuable resource. I run some so please visit www.mikeraine.co.uk, but I can also recommend Jim Langley of Natureswork. It's about communicating and sharing the passion, but being able to do so in different ways.

Group on a workshop.

Group actively learning on a workshop.

> **Top tips from Mountain Leaders**
>
> Have a go at a volunteering day with a local conservation organisation such as Cymdeithas Eryri / Snowdonia Society or the Wildlife Trust. You can quickly build a bank of interesting titbits to talk about with your clients e.g. how path maintenance is carried out, why rhododendrons have been cleared and even how dry stone walls are built.
>
> Rob Nicolson

Apps and eLearning

Many of you will turn to apps these days. There is no doubt that there are some good apps available. There seem to be two kinds: one is the artificial intelligence app, the Google eye, the iNature, PictureThis or PlantNet style. You send a picture, and the app identifies it for you. You need internet access and the nous to know when the answer is wrong, which to be fair, isn't actually very often. The other type is simply a book on your phone such as *Mountain Flowers* by Alan R Walker or the *Collins Book of Birds*. You need to know what you are looking for, but they are incredible stores of further information to have at your fingertips. Both have their place, and both are, to some degree, game changers. It is however a fast-changing world, so keep a critical eye on the latest developments.

eLearning is an area which has been developing, particularly through the coronavirus pandemic. Much eLearning is lecturing; it's difficult to make eLearning sensibly interactive and some of the quiz type activities can seem more like trivial guess work than meaningful learning activities. The lack of a clear, on the spot, explanation from the tutor does detract. That said, putting out information in a format which can be easily digested is useful, and if it comes in a form by which you can pause and rewind the lesson then it can work. You do need to follow up and apply your learning in the field and that is down to you. You'll find good eLearning modules at www.mikeraine.co.uk, www.natureswork.co.uk and on the MTA website.

Nice to know – need to know

There is, it has to be said, an overwhelming amount of information out there and there is no upper limit to what you should know. While ultimately it is the interactions and interrelationships within the ecosystem that is of most importance, you aren't going to get far if you have no knowledge of what is in that ecosystem.

Here's a suggestion of minimum knowledge for you to aim for. You should be able to:

1. Explain why the geology of Eryri or the Lake District is complex in comparison to Dartmoor, the Brecon Beacons or the Pennines. In Scotland you might contrast the Cairngorms with Glencoe or Assynt, in Ireland contrast the Mourne with Donegal.

2. Describe and explain the processes of glacial erosion and transportation. Identify features of erosion and deposition.

3. Describe the lives of around 12 key mammals, bird or other living species in your area of operation.

THE MOUNTAIN LEADER

4. Recognise and describe, including some medicinal, historical and current uses, of around 12 plant species, including some upland specialists.

5. Explain how land use has, over time, contributed to how the uplands look the way they do and how this may continue to change, including some of the choices currently being discussed.

A small cliff on Crimpiau, just outside Capel Curig showing how complex the geology can be.

A sample of granite from the Cairngorms, an area with a more straightforward geological story.

An erratic boulder, above Nant Conwy with an accompanying striation.

A fine display of wild thyme in Cwm Idwal, Eryri. Can be added to salads, brewed to make a tea or used as an antiseptic.

Here a simple fence delineates different land uses. The near ground is used for sheep grazing while over the fence is forestry land.

A buzzard scanning for small rodents, but will be happy with a few worms in between more substantial meals.

Informing and inspiring others

How do we pass on our knowledge and inspire others to learn more and care about the environment?

This is the difficult bit. You can go on a workshop led by an environment expert and they know loads of stuff and have loads of tricks and resources. The thought of you having to put this knowledge across can be a bit overwhelming. Think about yourself, stood in front of a group. Think about plodding up Yr Wyddfa, it's bit cold, the team are a bit bored, there's not much to look at. This is what you need to prepare for. You need to ignite a spark in the eyes of those you lead. You need to tease out a reaction. You need to cultivate a sense of awe and wonder.

Laminated sheets, textbooks and games have their place, but you are the flexible, differentiated, inspirational, weatherproof resource. You need to learn your stuff, and think about how you will share it. Telling people things is a start, but will it inspire them? Will it trigger questions? Will it create a memory? By far and away the best way to tell people things is to tell them stories. We love stories. Myths and legends will be remembered by even the most cynical amongst us. So, if you need to talk about bigger issues, ecology, weather, archaeology or land use, try to find a story telling way of doing it.

Don't be shy about using books or other sources. I still use my copy of *Nature of Snowdonia* when I tell the Prince Idwal story or the King Arthur story, it just helps me to get the names right.

I've used laminated sheets and the Wildflower playing cards from Natureswork in different ways. One way is to give them out at the beginning of the day and get people to look out for their target, be it a flower or a tree. It's quite hard for them to do and I usually have to give them a nudge. People are often a little self-conscious about reading off their cards too, and if the whole group are doing it then each member will tend to only remember the bit they read out rather than anything anyone else has read out. This doesn't work with birds at all.

Top tips from Mountain Leaders

One of the most successful things I do is nature bingo. It works well when walking or stationary. Simply get people to tick a box on a pre-prepared, illustrated, nature bingo sheet (make sure it shows things that they will find). It's a great tool for collaborative learning.

Rob Goodsell

> **Top tips from Mountain Leaders**
>
> Do your research. It's not just about group management, it's about being a role model, inspiring, and educating your group on fauna, wildlife, geology, history, and folklore. A leader isn't expected to know everything, but doing a bit of research into the route that you're doing will make your life a bit easier when one of the group asks a question about a certain flower or rock formation – and believe me they will ask questions. Get on as many CPD workshops as possible. Not only is this a great way of networking with other Mountain Leaders (which can result in additional work), but it's a great way of keeping those ML tools sharp, learning new skills, and keeping abreast of up-to-date policies and procedures.
>
> Darren Parkinson

I have got people using apps themselves, using the identification books and using pre-prepared bingo style cards with the flowers we expect to see during the day. None of these work reliably well. They might be OK with one group, but flop completely with another.

Without doubt the best way is story telling.

The cuckoo and the meadow pipit

The cuckoo has one of the most recognisable calls of any bird. Everyone knows the sound of a cuckoo, but increasingly few people get to hear it.

The cuckoo is actually an African bird which spends a few weeks in the north and west of Britain in the early summer. It's attracted to a food source few others enjoy – hairy caterpillars.

When the cuckoo migrates to our shores it is, in a way, on holiday. When away from home the cuckoos begin to pair up and start to breed. The female cuckoo needs to lay its eggs, but would also prefer to fly back home, back to the forests of the Congo Basin. She can't make that journey carrying eggs, so she lays them in the nests of other species. The upland cuckoos of the north and west frequently choose the nest of the meadow pipit.

The meadow pipit is fairly abundant on our hills and any 'little brown job' you have seen is probably a meadow pipit. They nest in the rough grass, live on insects, sing a little tunelessly but are characterised by a wonderful parachuting, descending flight during their mating time. The meadow pipit is very discreet about where it nests, but the cuckoo is

Access, Conservation and the Environment

watching. When the meadow pipit leaves the nest a female cuckoo might pop in and lay one of its eggs. As the female cuckoo leaves the nest, she makes a chuckling call which has the same resonance as that of a bird of prey. The meadow pipit is distracted, she looks all around, she sees no threat and heads back to the nest unaware that there is now an extra egg taking centre place.

The pipit incubates its eggs, but one, fractionally larger egg is the first to hatch. On hatching this blind featherless chick pushes, with all its might, the other eggs out of the nest. The cuckoo has landed. This chick will be fed and cared for by the meadow pipits as though it were their own chick. The parent cuckoos are now far away on their way back to Africa. As the chick puts on weight it fills the nest, then one day it fledges. It hops, by short flights, from rock to rock in the vicinity of the nest, still being fed by its hard working, but now very small looking foster parents. Goodness knows how the next bit happens, but on a day in early August the chick takes off and starts to fly south. It crosses the UK, Europe and northern Africa to find its home in the forests of central Africa. It has never met is real parents but the foster pipits are proud of the big chick they managed to rear this season.

Cuckoo
Photo: Tony Pope

Meadow pipit

Butterwort

Sundew

Sundew in flower

Butterwort and sundew – insectivorous plants

The butterwort and the sundew live side by side in the bog. They like the bog as they have space and are not hassled by other plants straining to take their niche. They can survive where other plants can't. The bog is nitrogen deficient and too acidic for most plants. Oh yes, there is that vigorous upstart the sphagnum moss, but the sundew and the butterwort can stay one step ahead because they have evolved a very special trick.

They have sticky leaves. And upon those sticky leaves, passing insects, hopefully midges, might alight. They stick and they are doomed. The butterwort closes its bright green leaf around the unfortunate insect while the sundew, not caring for the insect's modesty, holds the insect, glued to globules on the 'rays' of it's bright red leaves. Either way, the insect's end is slow and exposed and the butterwort and the sundew slowly dissolve the insects they catch, they're after nitrogen. It's the nitrogen from these unlucky insects that feed the plant and enable it to thrive in a nitrogen deficient bog.

But, you may ask, how are they pollinated if the insects that land on them risk being eaten? Take a closer look when they are in flower. Both the butterwort and the sundew hold their flowers high, disproportionally high for such a small plant, this way pollinating insects can visit the flower and avoid the leaves. Hence the butterwort and the sundew have found their niche, in the bog.

Access, Conservation and the Environment

Pebble beach, Gairloch, Scotland

The pebble

I was a rock, a gnarly rock living in the mountains, I was tough, and I was chiselled, my angles were sharp and I stood out against the rain and the snow and the frost and the wind. I repelled the sheep, the goats and the boots of humans. Then one day it all changed. I was cut loose and I started to tumble. The storm had destroyed my hold on the mountain. I tumbled and fell. I knew it was the beginning of the end. Gravity would hold sway. I stopped, then it started again and I was caught in the mud as it slid down the hill. I came to rest in a stream, and that is when I realised that my journey had only just begun.

Many, many years later, I sit here on the beach. Occasionally someone crunches over me, occasionally the tide pushes me around a bit, keeping me smooth and polished, all my handsome angles gone now. I once was a rock, but now I'm a pebble, anonymous and the same shape as all those around me, my angles smashed off as I was transported down the river, rolled along the bottom and carried in storm surges. I sit here amongst many, some smaller, some larger. Some of those around me have been here even longer than I. They were pushed here by the ice a long, long, time ago and one day we'll all be nothing but grains on a sandy beach, or, worse, particles of mud below the tidal seas.

Top tips from Mountain Leaders

If you're refreshing your own knowledge and skills then periodically go on a themed, quality mountain day. You could try a 'flower' day in spring and simply concentrate on naming every flower you pass – try not to continue until you're reasonably confident that you know what it is.

Rob Nicholson

Where are we allowed to walk?

"Who owns these hills? The man who bought them or I who is possessed by them?" Norman MacCaig, A Man in Assynt 1977

We are actually pretty blessed with access to our uplands, and while at first glance things are different in Ireland, they do seem to work out quite well in practice. I think we are probably fortunate that the first climbers, walkers and mountaineers were from the Victorian upper classes. They either owned the land, their chums owned the land, or they didn't care who owned the land. They established de-facto rights of access which meant we've always been pretty much free to wander the hills, imbibed with the confidence of our Victorian forefathers. Of course, there are exceptions to this and the closure of land for hunting and shooting has long been something walkers and climbers have needed to watch out for. Contemporary laws however, especially if we are responsible, give us access to pretty much all the uplands. The law does vary across the home nations though and while Scotland has some of the most celebrated access laws in the world, the situation isn't quite as free in England, Wales and Ireland. The laws in England and Wales are currently the same, but could diverge as the Welsh Government continues to mull over the opportunities and threats that may be encountered by reviewing access to the countryside across the principality.

In many ways, Mountain Leaders have it easy, the places we want to go to, we can. The Hill and Moorland Leader is more likely to encounter shooting interests. Pity the Lowland Leader trying to follow rights of way across English or Welsh farmland or balance their rights with responsibilities as they cross farmland or golf courses in the Scottish lowlands.

England and Wales 2022

In England and Wales you are allowed to walk on public rights of way and on open access land.

Public rights of way

You are allowed to pass freely along any public right of way, you can stop to look at the view or stop to eat your lunch. You must keep your dog under control and follow the Countryside Code. Public rights of way can have different classifications: footpath, bridleway or byway. As walkers, we can use any of them, although we might share bridleways with horses and bikes, or byways with motor vehicles. There are some restricted byways along which motor vehicles are not allowed, but you can take a pony and trap. Our public rights of way are quite well protected under Highways Law and no one has the right to hinder your progress along them. It's worth noting that if you

Access, Conservation and the Environment

Waymarked right of way and access land signs. In the UK a yellow arrow is the official waymark for footpath which is right of way.

Unofficial waymarkers can be really helpful sometimes. It's generally in the interest of landowners to help us along the public right of way.

leave the path then you are trespassing, trespass however, is a civil matter not a criminal one, so you can be asked to leave, but you can't be arrested unless you cause damage.

Obstruction of a public right of way is a criminal offence and landowners have an obligation to keep them open and clear; there are even rules about how close to the path crops can be grown. Stiles and gates are the landowner's responsibility though councils and national parks will both help to replace or maintain them. Dairy bulls are not allowed to be kept in fields with a public right of way, while other breeds should be at least 10 months old and accompanied by cows. The landowner is liable if their animals attack people. (See Hazardous Animals, Cattle.)

Footpaths can be closed, but only after a long period of consultation and they can only be closed for up to six months, you'll mostly come across this associated with forestry work.

Open Access Land

The Open Access Land was dedicated under the Countryside Rights of Way Act of 2000 which enshrined in law a right to walk (or climb) in certain, mapped areas. Most of the uplands in England and Wales are designated as such. On the OS map they have a yellowish 'tea stain' shading. This is generally a law which has been welcomed, but you might be surprised about some of the things that are expressly forbidden by the CROW Act. Open access land can be closed for up to 28 days a year, but not including bank holiday and summer weekends. You are not allowed to bring an animal (other than a dog), camp, play organised games, hang-glide, paraglide, or use a metal detector. It is forbidden to engage in commercial activities on the land, such as: trading or selling and charging other visitors for things they do. It is also forbidden to film, photograph or make maps on a commercial basis without the owner's permission. You cannot light, cause or risk a fire, damage hedges, fences, walls, crops or anything else on the land. You must not leave gates open that are not propped or fastened open or leave litter, disturb livestock, wildlife or habitats with intent, post any notices, or commit any criminal offence e.g. move, damage, or destroy any plant, shrub, tree or root with intent. On the other hand the designation of open access land removes the landowner's liability for any injury caused by any natural features of the landscape including any tree, shrub, plant, river or stream, any ditch or pond, whether natural or not. It removes liability for people passing over, under or through a wall or fence, as long as they're making proper use of a gate or stile.

> **Top tips from Mountain Leaders**
>
> Most importantly make it fun regardless of the objective for the day. Even picking the litter can be fun if approached in the right way and kids love it.
>
> Mladenka Hooper

Cleary there is a lot of detail in laws like this and should you wish to know more visit www.gov.uk. There is also expert information available from the Open Spaces Society, the BMC and The Ramblers.

Scotland

Scotland has long had an informal 'right to roam'. This was formalised in the Land Reform Act of 2003. In Scotland, rather than delineating the areas of open access, the areas which aren't open access are delineated. These are, by and large, places you wouldn't want to go anyway. Such as mines, quarries, MOD land and gardens. Beyond these places you can pretty much go anywhere. Look out for the odd quirk, such as where you can cross a golf course, but not go on the green. You have to allow a reasonable 'curtilage' i.e. distance away from property and this gets bigger the bigger the property.

Entering a field through a gate. Walkers enjoying the Scottish rights of access responsibly.

Access, Conservation and the Environment

The law allows for walking and climbing but also cycling and boating as it applies to water as well as to the land. The Land Reform Act explicitly permits the activities of mountain leaders and guides whereas this is only clear in England and Wales if you are operating in an educational context.

You also have a right to camp but the law says this is meant to be lightweight camping and for no more than two or three nights in one place. Cleary this fantastic legal permission comes with some responsibilities, and they are centred around respecting the interests of other people, caring for the environment and taking responsibility for your actions. The Scottish Access Code has a lot more detail and can be found via www.nature.scot. If you have done most of your walking in England and Wales then it does feel very strange to have this free access, albeit with the responsibilities that we would tend to exercise anyway, and it does take a little getting used to. Once on the hill it's not very different, but accessing the hill, wandering around the coast, crossing fields and wild camping all feels a little daring until you get used to it (if you've come from any of the other Home Nations). It's well worth downloading the Scottish Access Code to your phone, then you can browse it at your leisure.

Ireland

Now it gets complicated! Most land in Ireland is privately owned, there are very few public rights of way and many landowners are fearful they will be sued should someone be injured on their land. That we are able to walk anywhere in Ireland seems like a bit of luck. However, in practice, there is reasonable access in all upland areas due to the goodwill and tolerance of landowners. Increased numbers engaging in outdoor recreation activities is placing greater strain on informal access arrangements. Maintaining the goodwill of landowners and thereby maintaining access is a shared responsibility across the hillwalking community. It is incumbent on mountain leaders and more experienced walkers to ensure that the situation is understood and accepted by all.

An injured walker would have to prove 'reckless disregard' on behalf of the landowner if they were to claim against them. Two high profile test cases, both of which went to appeal, have added strength to the Occupiers' Liability Act, 1995. Both judgments made clear that those who undertake outdoor recreation activities are expected to understand the risk that is inherent in their activities, to have regard to the nature of the terrain they are crossing, and to take measures to ensure their own safety.

There are many waymarked and agreed national trails in Ireland, all established with the agreement of landowners. Coillte, the Irish Forestry Service provide good access and waymarked paths too. Hillwalking has grown in popularity in recent times, and Mountaineering Ireland have produced a detailed and comprehensive good practice guide for walkers

THE MOUNTAIN LEADER

Sleive Bloom Way in Ireland

which can be found on their website. Again, as with Scotland, it is well worth familiarising yourself with these local ways of working before heading there. Irish farmers, like those in the UK, are most nervous about dogs not being kept under control and dogs are expressly forbidden in some hill areas.

It's a similar situation in Northern Ireland, where there is relatively little formally defined access and hillwalking is largely dependent on the goodwill of landowners. Access to their most famous walking area, the Mournes is by courtesy of Northern Ireland Water, the National Trust and private landowners. The Occupiers Liability legislation in Northern Ireland (1957 and 1987) makes clear that no duty of care is owed by a landowner to any person who willingly accepts risks – such as the risks involved in hillwalking.

Note for Trainers

Do remember that the qualification covers the UK and Ireland and that access law varies across this region. While no one knows all the ins and outs of access legislation, candidates should be aware that there are differences across the Home Nations and Ireland.

Up to date information about access

Mountain Leaders need to know how to find out about access designations. In England and Wales this is well marked on our OS maps, both the open access land and the public rights of way are clear. In Scotland we have access anywhere within the scope of the Land Reform Act. Over in Ireland it will be much more a case of searching online databases, guidebooks and using the support provided by the team at Mountaineering Ireland.

Access, Conservation and the Environment

The Countryside Code

The Countryside Code has been around for many years now. It's one of those things that has been devolved to the Home Nations Governments to produce so there have been some gaps in recent years as regards their promotion. In Scotland, the responsibilities which go with the rights enabled in the Land Reform Act are much more comprehensive that the simplified, Countryside Code.

The Countryside Code was relaunched in 2021:

Respect everyone

- Be considerate to those living in, working in and enjoying the countryside.
- Leave gates and property as you find them.
- Do not block access to gateways or driveways when parking.
- Be nice, say hello, share the space.
- Follow local signs and keep to marked paths unless wider access is available.

Protect the environment

- Take your litter home – leave no trace of your visit.
- Take care with BBQs and do not light fires.
- Always keep dogs under control and in sight.
- Dog poo – bag it and bin it – any public waste bin will do.
- Care for nature – do not cause damage or disturbance.

Enjoy the outdoors

- Check your route and local conditions.
- Plan your adventure – know what to expect and what you can do.
- Enjoy your visit, have fun, make a memory.

I suspect anybody reading this has by now internalised the key facets of the Countryside Code as common sense. This contemporary update comes with some quite detailed guidance and has been criticised for not being more direct. As the Countryside Code has been around since 1951 it remains to be seen

THE MOUNTAIN LEADER

if this latest version can be made to work. Our challenge is how to teach it, how to get our groups to follow it and to appreciate it. This is something that needs to pervade our day out on the hill. A fun demo I have seen is to take out a range of items, let's say a plastic bottle, a tin can, a polythene bag, a piece of chewed chewing gum, a paper bag, some orange peel and a banana skin. Get the group to place them in order of biodegradability. This is quite an eye-opener especially when you get to the fruit peel.

My biodegradable experiment

On 6th March 2015 I placed an apple core, a banana skin and some orange peel in a small cage at 195 metres above sea level in Eryri. The location was exposed, but the cage was tucked on to a shallow rock shelf at ground level. This would be no rigorous scientific experiment but would give us some idea of how long these items take to biodegrade if left on our hillsides. I took photographs on most days of the cage as it was very close to my place of work. I enjoyed the little morning detour and, on many days, saw an adder trying to warm up on a neighbouring rock. All went well for me until August when the bracken rose up and made access tricky through the dreadful stuff.

The apple core had been nibbled away by some small mammal, I could see its teeth marks in the first week, probably a field mouse. To most people's surprise the orange peel disappeared before the banana skin, it took a while and it dried out and sat stubbornly for a long time. It only started to be attacked by mould after it got particularly wet one week. The orange peel lasted five months. The banana skin hung on for another month and even then, the hard stalk remained in place. I suspected that an increase in altitude and latitude would slow this process down even further. In 2016 I placed the cage again but it was on the ground hidden in some heather at an altitude of 474 metres. This time, it was even between the orange peel and the banana skin and they both took nine months to biodegrade. So, quite unscientific but based on a real experience, so you can now be sure that any orange peel you may discard on the hill will sit there for at least five months (unless someone else clears it away for you). Your banana skin will sit there for a minimum of six months, so please take it away.

This is how the biodegradable experiment at 195 metres above sea level looked on day one.

This is how the biodegradable experiment at 195 metres above sea level looked after six months.

Access, Conservation and the Environment

Note for Assessors

It's really important that Mountain Leaders are ambassadors for the uplands. You must be convinced that they have demonstrated a knowledge and understanding of our hills and mountains. They must be able to inspire and inform. They should be aware of discussions around land use and conflicts. The syllabus is very clear on this.

They should have stopped, several times to show you things, such as flowers, rocks or glacial features. It might be that they have an interest in archaeology, birds or even hill-farming. They should have pointed out things of interest, explained them and told the rest of the group some sort of story about something to do with the upland environment. They should have led, or at the very least contributed to land use discussions. It's crucial that we keep an open mind on most topics, but remember that nature conservation is paramount. A good assessor will enhance a candidate's knowledge and inspire them to want to continue learning. They should also beat you to removing any litter chanced upon during your time on the hill.

Leave No Trace

The Leave No Trace movement started in the USA and has been widely adopted as a code of good practice for the outdoors. It's commonly used in Ireland and is growing in popularity in the UK

Leave No Trace determine seven principles:

- Plan ahead and prepare.

- Travel and camp on durable surfaces.

- Dispose of waste properly.

- Leave what you find.

- Minimise campfire impacts.

- Respect wildlife.

- Be considerate of others.

You can find out more at www.lnt.org

Caru Eryri

Caru Eryri was set up in response to poor behaviour by a significant number of visitors to Eryri during and following the Coronavirus lockdown periods. Eryri National Park, The National Trust, Cymdeithas Eryri / Snowdonia Society and The Outdoor Partnership teamed up to recruit and train volunteers to promote, support and manage the scheme on the ground. This scheme runs alongside the established volunteer service already operating on Yr Wyddfa. Similar schemes are now operating in other national parks as well.

Help make a difference in Eryri this year:

- Plan your campsite; book campsites in advance.

- Try to use public transport.

- Remember to reduce litter by bringing a bag and taking it home. Don't leave anything behind, take it all home.

- Don't use disposable barbecues and don't set fire to campgrounds.

- Protect wildlife and livestock from harm. Always keep your dog on a lead.

Traditionally known as the Snowdon Horseshoe, Yr Wyddfa shapes a classic view down Llynnau Mymbyr.

Access, Conservation and the Environment

Why our hills look the way they do

We live on a small island, a series of small islands, you might say. Every bit of them is owned, worked, managed, guarded over, watched over, manicured to some degree – even, nay especially, the uplands. Walkers are but one group of recreationalists, farmers are but one group of land users. Consider the following: grouse shooting, deerstalking, fishing, water extraction, forestry, military training, hill-farming, off roading, mountain biking, paragliding, caving, conserving, environmentalling (I made that word up!), birdwatching, botany, field studies, training, running, fell running, ultra-running, outdoor or wild swimming, foraging, bothying, kayaking, open boating, bog snorkelling, walking (or is that just part of mountaineering?), bouldering, painting, photography, hillwalking and hiking (they might be the same). I think you get the point, lots of people, doing lots of things. We have created national parks, and one of the key roles of national parks is to manage potential conflicts between these groups, a thankless, or a hopeless task? So, how does it all fit together, how does it all work? Do the hills have any chance at all?

Well, the first answer, is yes, the hills do have a chance and the nature upon them does too. They were there before us, and they'll be there when we're long gone too. We have, however, stripped them bare I'm afraid. It's a fallacy that the wildwood covered the British Isles from Land's End to John O'Groats. There have always been meadows, scrub, heathland, bushy areas, woodland areas and tundra areas, certainly since the end of the last ice-age, 10 or 12,000 years ago. Without agriculture, forestry and water collection our landscape would be one of clear fell tops, scrubby woodland up to about 2000ft (sounds so much better than 609.6 metres), or even 2500ft, with thickening forest, interspersed with clearings and meadows below this height and heathland around the edge of the woods.

Wood sorrel a classic woodland indicator species, look for it in shady spots under boulders or bracken in the uplands.

Woodland indicator species

We know how far up our hills and mountains that woodland should be growing by identifying woodland indicator species. Some of the more well known, amongst Mountain Leaders, might be tormentil, wood sorrel and wood anemone. Star moss, bilberry, cowberry and the heathers are all woodland understory plants too. I can take you to cow-wheat growing at 700 metres on Tryfan, you will have seen open meadows of bluebells on hillsides, where trees once stood. You might see the devil's-bit scabious growing just out of reach of grazing animals and you'll see the ubiquitous herb robert all over the place. These observations give us a woodland edge of somewhere approaching 800 metres, imagine that!

This forest had clearings, probably quite large ones that were grazed by the large herbivores that were present, such as mammoth, elk and auroch. The numbers of large herbivores were kept in check by large carnivores, as were medium ones, small ones and tiny ones. It is worth noting that, even without animal grazing, if left to its own devices, the continuous woodland cover would not return. There would be a great variety of partially wooded landscapes and that variety would depend on altitude, depth and fertility of soil, latitude and aspect.

It was us that cleared the so-called 'wildwood'. We cleared it for building, for ship building, for burning, and to remove hiding places. It probably was reduced by disease too. Anyway, the upshot is we have very little woodland left. In-fact we have about a quarter of the area of woodland typically found in other European countries. Into the upland space has poured agriculture, forestry and large shooting estates.

Shooting estates

I do find it interesting how shooting estates are much more open, obvious and, dare I say, brazen the further north you go. Their hold on Dartmoor, on the Brecon Beacons, on Eryri, the Lakes and big chunks of the Pennines is subtle. They begin to rear their heads in the Yorkshire Dales, particularly the beautiful, wild Nidderdale, interestingly not part of the National Park (surely, some power and influence steered that decision). Then the North Yorkshire Moors, a place of unease and on to Scotland of which more later.

I should at this point talk about moors. I know we are Mountain Leaders, but moorland, especially heather-clad moorland is a large part of our upland landscape. The British Isles contain around 90% of the world's moorland, a rare and endangered landscape according to those who own it, that is, the descendants of those who created it. The moorlands of Britain are a Victorian construct. Predominately managed very carefully for the rearing and shooting of grouse. Heather is, naturally, a woodland understory plant. You've seen it growing in the woods, in clearances, around edges and below open canopy. Moorland doesn't represent a climax vegetation, its vegetation is a marginal part of woodland ecology. An important part none the less, and the scrub and heaths in and around areas of woodland do provide an important habitat for many species. Large, open landscapes of heather moorland are as natural a part of the British landscape as a field of wheat or potatoes might be. It's no wonder that it's rare and endangered, it's doing its best to regenerate; to regenerate its woodland cover as it does not wish to remain as open moorland, in the same way a mountain erodes and doesn't want to be a mountain, it wants to be a plain. A good place to see mature, heather-dominated heathland is on Rhinog Fawr where there is a National Nature Reserve, which is also the only Biogenetic Reserve in Wales. This reserve celebrates an area of heath that has had

Access, Conservation and the Environment

The female grouse blends in well with the landscape, but if disturbed it's 'go-back, go-back' call gives it away.

only light grazing and very little human interference for hundreds of years. Here there are red grouse in their natural habitat, but also black grouse, merlin and hen harrier.

Grouse is an indigenous species, it belongs here and lives in the heather. It eats the shoots of young heather and grit to aid the digestion of this course, plant material. It's a tough place to live, it has lots of predators such as fox, stoat, weasel, peregrine and hen harrier, amongst others. Grouse have survived because they have found a niche, they survive as a species because, like blue tits, they produce a lot of young. Up to ten chicks will be reared, sometimes more but only a few will survive. As meadow pipits are the 'mars bars' of the grassy upland; grouse are the big 'chocolate bars' of the woodland edge, scrub and heather moors. The grouse is a large bird, it'll sit tight to avoid predators and only burst upwards at the last possible moment, cackling as it goes. This habit of cackling, "Go-back, go-back ..." and its flight path of steeply upwards makes it a great bird to shoot. A bit easy for some, but hey, it gets good results for others. Some even eat a handful of the birds they shoot! So, grouse attract men with guns (it is very typically men). Some other men who have decided they own the land (some long forgotten ancestor did a deal with some King or other) have organised the moors into 'shoots'. They pay local men to help a few more grouse survive than they might do naturally. Yes, it is a wild bird, it isn't reared in captivity (you might be thinking of pheasant, that's a whole other story) and it has adapted to the moors; not evolved, but adapted in the same way that garden birds have adapted to our gardens. It doesn't take a genius to work out that, to keep as many of those chicks alive as possible, in order to sell a day's shooting for a healthy profit, you need to 'manage' the species that prey on them. But what has this got to do with us, walking over the moors? Well, everything.

Our land is private. Our nature is depleted. This is where we play. But we get no say in how this landscape should be managed. Should it be the preserve of a few people toting guns, or should it be managed more effectively for nature?

BMC on grouse shooting

In September of 2020 the BMC decided to comment on the issues surrounding driven grouse shooting in light of greater awareness being raised on the issue. Below is an extract from their statement.

"Unregulated driven grouse moor shooting results in the illegal killing of birds of prey, the persecution of mountain hares, and the damage to upland peatland habitats is contributing to climate change. Now, the BMC wants to see driven grouse shooting regulated and for government to strengthen and enforce legislation to stop the illegal killing of raptors.

We are asking for:

- *An immediate end to the illegal killing and disturbance of birds of prey across the uplands.*

- *Protected sites managed to return to and / or maintain favourable ecological condition.*

- *A reduction in the intensity of managed vegetation burning and a cessation of burning on upland peat soils, particularly on SSSIs and in drinking water catchments.*

- *The restoration of degraded upland peatland and moorland, now dominated by heather, to a healthy environment with a more diverse range of flora and fauna.*

The BMC is not anti-shooting, but we are against the illegal killing of raptors, and support sustainable management practices in the uplands. We now want to see driven grouse shooting regulated and for government to strengthen and enforce legislation to stop the illegal killing of raptors."

We should be pleased that there are significant elements of the BMC's position which chime strongly with the position of those organisations that represent the ownership and management of grouse moors. In January of 2020, in response to a greater awareness of raptor persecution being carried out on moorland groomed for the driven grouse shoot the British Association for Shooting and Conservation (BASC), Countryside Alliance (CA), Moorland Association (MA) and National Gamekeepers' Organisation (NGO) along with the Country Land and Business Association (CLA) issued a strongly worded statement deploring wildlife crimes. They issued the following statement which condemns all forms of raptor persecution:

"There is no excuse for the illegal killing of any bird of prey, and we unreservedly condemn all such acts. The shooting community has been tarnished with a reputation for persecuting raptors, and while many reports of such persecution have proven to be false and confirmed cases

Shooting butts, old and new, all well maintained above Swaledale.

A trap set for predator control on Melbecks Moor just north of Gunnerside in Swaledale.

Access, Conservation and the Environment

Moorland in the Cairngorm and the Yorkshire Dales which has had strips of heather burned to create new growth shoots to encourage grouse. This patchwork of old and new heather growth with very little biodiversity, is typical of land manged for driven grouse shooting.

are decreasing year-on-year, the illegal killing of birds of prey continues to be carried out by a small minority of irresponsible individuals. We strongly condemn their actions and have a zero-tolerance policy towards any such incident. These people have no place in a sector that is otherwise overwhelmingly positive; one that is the economic driver for many of our more remote communities, and the largest contributor to conservation schemes in England and Wales."

Opponents of driven grouse shooting will also bring to your attention concerns about low pay, medicated grit left out on the moors, discarded lead shot, muir burn and the lack of woodland contributing to faster run off rates. The muir burn, the practice of rotational burning of heather to produce new shoots for grouse to eat, is particularly concerning as it stops natural succession, releases carbon dioxide and can damage underlying peat. The driven grouse shooting industry argues that the muir burn is essential to reduce fuel load (for so called 'wildfires' – which are always started by people) on the moors and also creates habitat for species other than grouse such as curlew, golden plover and lapwing.

In 2017 the Scottish Government commissioned an independent report into the management of Scottish land for driven grouse shooting. The report was led by Professor Alan Werritty of Dundee University. The remit was to: 'examine the environmental impact of grouse moor management practices such as muir burn, the use of medicated grit and mountain hare culls, and advise on the option of licensing grouse shooting businesses.' In November 2020, following the publication of the Werritty Report, the Scottish Government has decided it will move to licence the driven grouse shooting business in Scotland as soon as is practically possible. Interestingly, this has met with joy amongst organisations such as the RSPB and the Scottish Wildlife Trust. But has been condemned by the organisations which issued the statement immediately above.

Should you wish to develop an interest in an ongoing topical issue that is very visible to hillwalkers then, may I suggest, this one would be an excellent topic to consider.

Deer staking in the central highlands.

It's surprising how hard deer are to spot in the upland landscape. Here you can see how well two female, red deer blend in with their surroundings.

Deer stalking

If you are heading up to Scotland hillwalking between 1st July and 20th August, you might need to be mindful of deer stalking. It is unlikely to be a problem, the popular peaks and routes such as ridges are rarely affected. There is little, if any stalking on a Sunday. Given we do enjoy open access in Scotland it is not unreasonable for us to check before we go. The easiest place to check is www.outdooraccess-scotland.scot/practical-guide-all/heading-scottish-hills.

The whole business of deer stalking is another world to us, and by and large we can leave it be. That is until you find out that there are probably more deer than the land can sustain. It's an interesting issue which sees an odd conflict of opinion. The conservationists believe that deer numbers are so large they are denigrating the regeneration of the natural vegetation in the highlands, so deer numbers should be reduced. While the deer stalking fraternity are nervous about large-scale culls of deer as they fear this may bring numbers down on their estates or make it harder to 'stalk' the fewer deer that would remain. Anyone walking regularly in Scotland will tell you, it's not often you see deer, but it's not often you see trees either. Deer are herbivores and, like sheep they will nibble away at anything fresh and tasty, that includes the saplings of native trees. Deer would have been prey for carnivores, most typically the wolf, which would have kept the flocks on the move and kept their numbers under control. Without predation deer numbers have grown, this has been exacerbated by the need to provide stock for stalking. So, while deer management is and will continue to be done by people, you can see why there are people who argue for the reintroduction of wolves to Scotland to manage the deer. As you can imagine there are plenty of people opposed to such a notion. Deer have also been implicated in the rise of Lyme Disease, their ticks are one of the main carriers of the disease and if you are working in the outdoors this is a real threat to you and your health (see Hazardous Animals, ticks).

Access, Conservation and the Environment

Roads and bothys

A couple of interesting by-products of the management of large areas by estates in Scotland are the provision of roads and bothys. The rough roads can be great for cycling as they speed us on our way into the hills, some of the newer hill tracks unfortunately don't go anywhere except to remote shooting stations on the moors and are an eyesore. Bothys are often old estate buildings, some are still used but are made available to walkers and managed by the Mountain Bothy Association for the rest of the time. Old bothies can be wonderful buildings, however newer estate buildings are not always quite so attractive.

This is one of the better estate roads running along the shores of Loch Ossian near Rannoch Station.

This is a modern estate building on the shores of Loch Ericht. Built for security rather than aesthetic beauty.

The wonderful lochside bothy of Glendhu in the far north of Scotland. This bothy is left open for use by passers-by and is maintained by the Mountain Bothy Association.

Sheep farming

The major use of our uplands is sheep farming. There aren't many places in the UK where you can go walking and not be aware of the presence of, or the impact of, sheep. However, what do we as walkers, climbers and mountaineers know about the only other sizeable mammal to be found on our hills? In fact, sheep probably have a wider distribution than we do, they aren't fussy, they're as happy on a dull old moor as scaling the slopes of Yr Wyddfa or Scafell.

Heavily grazed sheep farming landscape in the Howgills. A lack of biodiversity and a dominance by poor quality grasses.

Most sheep are descended from the Mouflon, a wild grazer found in Mesopotamia (present day Iraq and Syria). Initially they were bred for milk, meat and skins. The woolly sheep with which we are so familiar today were developed for their fleeces as long ago as 6,000 BCE, they then spread into Europe, Africa and eventually the rest of world through trading. In each place they arrived they were selectively bred to bring out the best qualities for survival in that area. It's thought that sheep were brought to the British Isles by the Romans. By this time sheep were far removed from their wild cousins, there were many distinct breeds, and the British took to breeding sheep well. We developed lots of new breeds, their wool made life a lot more comfortable on our chilly, wet islands and the wool trade grew to become the most significant trade in medieval times. As in Spain, wool wealth was a primary driver of our colonisation and empire building through simply generating the funds required for travel and conquest. Wool money built our churches and filled the pockets of our nobility, and wool set the 'social dyes' that remain today. Through the medieval period, sheep rearing was a nation-wide activity. The uplands were worked by small-scale farmers, but it wasn't until the industrial revolution that sheep farming came to dominate. Through the medieval period upland farms were small, poor and family run subsistence units, there might have been some sheep, but cattle, goats, and geese were more important.

Sheep have supported families and developed a folklore and history of their own, they have shaped our landscape and now we are asking questions. Are sheep really the demons of our uplands? Are they really the thing that impact, with the greatest adverse effect, our beautiful hills the most? Well, they might be, but you might also be surprised to know it's not really the fault of our hill farmers.

Access, Conservation and the Environment

Some fine Swaledale sheep, commonly bred for lamb or mutton in the north, these were photographed on the Ardnamurchan peninsula.

If grazing animals, principally sheep, are excluded from an area it doesn't take terribly long for nature to regenerate. Here we can see healthy saplings which have been allowed to germinate and have grown up protected by gorse. Good for biodiversity but not so easy to walk through.

Yes, sheep are responsible for the state of our uplands. They over graze, they reduce biodiversity and this needs to change. But farmers are victims of the system. They have tried to make it work and many are conscious of the loss of nature, knowledge, and a decline in sustainable practices that have occurred over generations. They are aware that nature has suffered alongside the intensification of grazing. We should also note that it is the farming families that get involved in community institutions and run the shows and fetes. They volunteer to be councillors or school governors, they are the ones who'll tidy up around the war memorial, they'll clear the vegetation around the village sign, they'll loan their trailers and they'll help each other and anyone living in their village. The farming community and all its associations lay like a blanket over our uplands, a 'blanket' upon which we play out our games, a blanket upon which some of us make a living.

There is some unease about the sustainability of sheep in our uplands. They eat a lot, and they eat the best bits. Sheep are known as 'patch' grazers and they love the shoots of heather, bilberry, rowan, saxifrages and most of the other flowering plants too. They do, by their selective grazing habit denude the hill and reduce its biodiversity. They don't touch the mat-grass, except maybe when it's young, fresh and green, so this straw-coloured deciduous grass takes over the landscape, as it dies off in the autumn its fallen stems form mats along the ground, mats which stifle the growth of other species. Other unpopular grasses are the purple moor grass, this forms the dreaded tussocks, and the damp-loving soft rush, fine for a tale about rush wicks but not a great plant for birds, insects or for walking through. Sheep won't touch bracken, they'll nibble around it but, unlike cattle, they don't trample it and they are wise enough not to eat it.

It was wool which ushered in the industrial age. When John Kay invented the flying shuttle to make wider cloth more efficiently, he could not have dreamt of the new world his invention would lead to. The industrialisation of the woollen industry led to great changes. Instead of subsistence farming on the hills, flocks of sheep were turned out, people left the uplands to seek work in mills, factories, mines and quarries. Some didn't leave by choice but were ousted from many of the large estates in Scotland to make way for sheep in the infamous clearances.

Those people who inhabited our uplands before the industrial period, farmed them quite intensively. The tree cover was largely gone by this time, but they didn't farm on an industrial scale, farms were mixed and nature still had a part to play. This changed gradually as specialized sheep farming took over. Even so, for many years sheep farming wasn't the intensive business it has become today. There were many, many small farms, all making a living, all working for the 'wool cheque'. Change came post World War II when subsidies to farmers for food production intensified and modernised farming like never before, not even in the agricultural revolution of the 17th century. The subsidies implemented in post-war Britain to decrease our reliance on imported food led to a growth in flock sizes. This was exacerbated in the 1970s as we joined the European Economic Community and sheep numbers grew fast through the 1970s, '80s and into the '90s before starting to decline a little.

Sheep numbers on the hill increased as subsidies were paid per head of stock. Farmers were simply taken along on a government led journey and many did well. Lowland farmers with arable land or dairy farms did very well. The upland farmers always struggled. It was hand to mouth, or more correctly, hand to wool cheque. In some lower areas, or even just the hilly areas around the mountains, the land, while not good for crops, was good for sheep. In these areas larger, fatter, meatier sheep could be bred. The fells of Lakeland and the mountains of Scotland and Wales have very little of this 'good' land. The upland farmers in these areas always needed to take their sheep off the hills for fattening and send them out to lower, more fertile land on other farms, this hits the profits hard. There's no doubt today that the governmental, direct payments to farmers is all that keeps our upland farms going.

The spread of bracken

How big a problem is bracken?

You may have worked out that walking through bracken is a pretty unpleasant experience. It is a plant which spreads through underground rhizomes so a whole hillside can be colonised by one plant. Killing it in one place, doesn't stop the plant returning. Traditionally it was trampled by cattle on the hill and cut to use as animal bedding, but as sheep farming came to dominate the uplands (sheep don't eat bracken, it can actually poison them) the bracken spread.

Bracken is rich in cyanide; it causes cancer and strangles the growth of other species such as the varied grasses and tree saplings that should be here. It is of no use to farmers and it is of little benefit to wildlife. Bluebells will use its shade for a few years as a woodland surrogate to propagate, but this doesn't last for long. Few birds will rest on its stems, mammals shy

Access, Conservation and the Environment

Dense bracken, very unpleasant to walk through.

away and insect life is very sparse, though the disease carrying tick is not one of those and a rise in Lyme disease cannot be disassociated from the spread of bracken. Yet, this is a plant which now dominates large swathes of all our national parks and uplands.

Bracken is, by ecology, a woodland clearance plant, here it has stiff competition from other species, such as bilberry and the heathers which can grow on poorer soils. Bracken, will only grow on the better, deeper soils, typically found in ancient oak woodlands. There is an old country saying: 'Where there's bracken there's gold, where there's gorse there's silver and where there's heather there's poverty.' Which refers to the way bracken chooses to colonise the best soils and that heather can grow in the poorest of soils. Another way of looking at bracken is to recognise that it marks out the areas where woodland would thrive. So, if you do cross hillsides of bracken, this could be healthy woodland. Given that bracken is not useful for sheep grazing, then it's not impossible to imagine a scenario where the bracken covered areas of the uplands were fenced off to keep sheep out and could then be returned to woodland with little loss of grazing. Frost halts the uphill spread of bracken, limiting it to a height of around 1000' or 300 metres. Chemicals previously sprayed on bracken, called Asulam or Asulox, are now thought to be harmful to people, to other ferns and to insect life. It was never allowed to be sprayed near water courses, though this was clearly difficult to manage in our uplands. The implementation of the ban on this herbicide is of concern to those trying to limit the spread of bracken and other means of control are now being sought. Experiments are taking place involving the composting of bracken and creating a peat substitute with it. One particularly interesting development has been made by Dalefoot Composts in the Lake District. They mix harvested bracken with wool to create a peat free compost, a product worthy of further investigation.

Rewilding or nature friendly farming

There has been an interesting rise in rewilding initiatives in the uplands of the UK. In particular, several large estates, some private and some in community ownership are moving in this direction in Scotland. The movement is in response to the degraded nature of our uplands and the lack of biodiversity in many of them. Generations of single use, typically farming for sheep, has left the uplands in a poor state. It is an interesting movement for us as walkers and leaders. We still love the Lake District the way it is, we think the Carneddau are special and we take the management of the Scottish Uplands for granted. It's only when we think a little and look a little closer, we start to see the shortcomings. Haystacks has long been a favourite in the Lakes, most notably identified by Wainwright as a hill with a different feel to it. Compare Haystacks with its ragged heather, crowberry, bilberry and rowan top to the bland, 'white' grass dominated slopes of the nearby Green Gable or even Great Gable, which despite its wonderful rock architecture holds little in the way of biodiversity. And then, of course, the bracken appears; the Lake District is bracken from north to south and from east to west. The same can be observed over large parts of Wales and Scotland. We should welcome the groups of people who are starting to suggest that the nature of our uplands is just not good enough.

Cairngorms Connect

Cairngorms Connect is a partnership of neighbouring land managers and owners, including the RSPB, NatureScot and the Scottish Forestry service. The group is committed to a 200 year vision to enhance habitats, species and ecological processes across a large area within the Cairngorms National Park. This is a riverbank to mountain top project to reconnect nature throughout the area of the project. The area includes Glenmore and Glen Feshie to the east of Aviemore and stretches up on to the Cairngorm Plateau. Also in the Cairngorms is the National Trust for Scotland's Mar Lodge estate, which too is being managed in a more nature-friendly way, making Cairngorm a place of interest, and contrast, for the student of wilding initiatives.

This the understory in the Rothiemurchus forest, an area which is part of the Cairngorms Connect project. The woodland here is being allowed to regenerate naturally, it's a wonderful place to be.

Rewilding has become quite an emotive term, a bit of a clarion call to some, to others a thing to be dreaded, and opposed at every turn. We, as Mountain Leaders and mountaineering instructors, need to have some knowledge of the topic as we are at the forefront of taking people into many of the areas that could be considered ripe for rewilding.

The first problem is with the term rewilding; rewild to what? Rewild to when I was a kid? To when you were a kid? To a time before intensive agriculture? Before the Industrial Revolution, or

Access, Conservation and the Environment

Iron Age times, or Stone Age times, or even pre-people times? When? It is a question with no answer, just varying opinions.

I like the term wilding as adopted by Isabella Tree in her book *Wilding*. I like the move towards nature-friendly farming as described in *English Pastoral* by James Rebanks. I think we all need to be aware of the sheep-wrecked nature of our uplands, possibly deer-wrecked in parts of Scotland, as described by George Monbiot in *Feral*. We need to be aware that moorlands are not natural landscapes and that every inch of our countryside, including our uplands, looks the way it does because we've farmed it. In farming it we've created a culture, a people, who live on the land and provide us with raw materials and food to eat. They are a hardy group of people and care about our landscapes in much the same way as any hillwalker does.

Conversations around rewilding our uplands can easily become rather partisan and lead us into confrontation. The wilder landscape as described by Benedict MacDonald in his book *Rebirding* should be our goal. This is landscape with a patchwork quilt of native woodland, of scrub, of hedge and of meadows. It's a landscape within which we can produce food. Sheep, cattle and deer can live within it and we can maintain the lifestyles and cultures of our farming communities. There are large parts of our uplands where small shifts of the dial could move us in this direction. Where we see a hedge cut rotationally, where we see a hedge developing between a double fence and where we see native trees being left to take over areas of harvested conifers, we should celebrate. Our lands can never again be truly wild, but they can be wilder than they are; they can be a good home for more nature and we must recognise that people will be part of that story. It's going to take some time and it's encouraging to hear that future farm support payments may help to make these changes happen.

Look out for double fences. The idea is native species will colonise (some will be planted), between the fences and start to develop into a hedge. Hedges are great habitat and highways for wildlife.

Tree planting on Wild Boar Fell in the Yorkshire Dales.

We do need to develop some common language. For us, as Mountain Leaders, we need to read around the subject and open our eyes. Acres of mat-grass covered uplands do as little for us as walkers as they do for farming sheep. Either this land needs returning to good grazing land (including hedges, drystone walls and coppices as well as greener grasses) or leaving to go wilder, to achieve that, it'll need some cattle on it to break up the tough grasses and create openings for a more diverse biodiversity. I think we could have areas of both.

We are seeing Welsh black, belted Galloways and Highland cattle back on our hills, we are seeing tree planting and areas being left to go wilder. I'm not sure how we fit in plantation forestry. Some areas will probably need to be set aside for this particular crop as we need more card and more paper to help us cut down on plastic packaging. It's a complex set of problems with no easy answers, and people's livelihoods are involved, but a movement towards a wilder, more nature friendly landscape is in all our interests. Talk of returning bears and wolves may be premature, but there has been some success with beavers and white tailed eagles. Will lynx be next?

These things are the beginning of a story, a story not of rewilding, but a story of wilding and of nature-friendly farming. Working with farmers will be the pathway to restoring our insects, our birds and mammals to the landscape. A by-product will be some excellent quality, grass-fed, naturally produced meat as humans retain the place vacated by the large carnivores – for now.

Further pressures on the uplands

As Mountain Leaders we are in the vanguard of getting people outside and more active. It is an important role and one we all subscribe to and firmly believe in. Other people are keen on getting out in the countryside too, but they have different ways of doing it.

4x4 vehicles near Moel Siabod. One vehicle had broken down and blocked the track causing an unlikely traffic jam and making getting past very difficult.

One of the most difficult for us is the use of 4x4 vehicles and off-road motorbikes. There are places where these vehicles can go legally and there are many very responsible users. We may think that the use of an internal combustion engine in the quiet countryside, unless for bona fide farming use, is an intrusive and destructive thing (I do), but we do have to accept that they have their place. Their days are numbered though as we phase out such vehicles, they'll still be here in electric form, but at least that'll be less polluting and quieter. When they are a big problem, is when they are not where they are supposed to be. You will see evidence of their passage in some remote and wild places. If you do come across illegal use then try to jot down registration numbers and report them to the police.

Access, Conservation and the Environment

Motorbike tracks near Cnicht in the Moelwynion, sadly not an uncommon occurrence, far from where it is legal for them to be.

A thoughtless moment, scratching your name on the rock, will last a long time.

Typical litter found after a visit by people unaware of the Countryside Code.

A stark dividing line between commercial forestry and open country on White Mountain in the Blackstair Hills of Ireland.

General tourism causes many problems too. Fly camping, disposable barbecues, fire pits, dog poo bags and general litter are all problems left behind by ill-mannered visitors. We can educate the people we lead. We can, if sensible to do so, challenge poor behaviour. Often people are simply ignorant about what is expected and are simply doing what they would at home, sometimes they will undo the wrong they have done. Sadly, there are those who just don't care, and quite how we change that is a job for society at large. We can also clear up other people's mess. On the hills this is rarely a problem, there is very little litter and what there is can easily be removed. I actually carry some biodegradable dog poo bags for this purpose, it's easier to put the peel and skins I've collected straight into the food waste when I get home if I do this. Roadside litter is another matter

This is a modern farming landscape with very little room for nature. The fence has replaced a hedge or dry stone wall. The field has been enlarged by removing further fences and walls. The only trees to be seen are commercial non-native species. The grass has been artificially improved to sustain greater densities of sheep.

THE MOUNTAIN LEADER

This ground was burnt out at the end of the period of time when gorse burning is permitted. The fire got out of control and a large area was burned. The burn is superficial in that the tops of the heather and gorse were burnt. It would have damaged ground nesting birds, reptiles and insects, but the vegetation will recover in a couple of years.

This is in the same area of Crimpiau just one year later, you can see the bilberry coming through strongly.

and may require a return visit properly kitted out. You could join in with clear up events such as the Real Three Peaks. The Real Three Peaks is a brilliant annual event. Originally it was Mountain Leaders litter picking on Ben Nevis, Scafell and Yr Wyddfa all on the same day, but it's now spread to other peaks and destinations. Hats off to the organisers, led from the start, by Richard Pyne of Rich Mountain Experiences.

Other issues we might be able to influence could include people scratching their names on rocks or with spray-paint style graffiti. We must not contribute to superfluous waymarking, and we can work with events to keep their impacts as low and as fleeting as possible. We can also park sensibly.

I know it can be challenging, there will always be reservoirs, conifer plantations, left over wire bales and out of control fires on the hills. But let's do our best to not even leave footprints if we can.

Note for Trainers

You should lead conversations about land use and misuse. The training must make the responsibilities of the Mountain Leader clear and you must get trainees to challenge views and opinions. It is important to know both sides of an argument, but it is also important to develop beliefs, as this is the way to encourage, challenge, and action. The Mountain Leaders you train will be the 'front line' of environmental knowledge and understanding for generations of new walkers. Leave them in no doubt as to how important this role is.

Conservation

There really is very little truly wild or natural landscape in the UK or Ireland. Any conservation designation is flawed by this simple fact. We have designations that encompass modern land uses to maintain their existing characteristics which can, in many cases, conflict with a desire to return to a more natural landscape. Many of the more ambitious 'wilding' projects are

Access, Conservation and the Environment

Yellow rattle

taking place on private land. That is not to say, however, that our land managing bodies are opposed to a wilder landscape. Here and there, you'll see clues of where they are trying to assist with a bit of wilding when they can.

Yellow rattle meadow at Geirionydd

Yellow rattle (*Rhinanthus minor*) is known as the 'meadow-maker' it is a fantastic plant to use if you are trying to battle with stubborn grasses to create wildflower meadows. The yellow rattle is a parasite of grass and it extracts nutrients from the grass's roots. This minimises the spread of grasses and helps other plants, including wildflowers colonise the same space. A brilliant place to see this is on a meadow managed by Natural Resources Wales next to the car park at Llyn Geirionydd in Eryri.

Who's who of the conservation world

Conservation of our landscape has long been seen as a government responsibility. The response by governments around the world has varied. Here in the UK, as all land is privately owned, government organisations try to work with and influence land managers. The government responsibility, in the UK, has been devolved to the Home Nations. Government use various tools of designation to influence how land is used. There is also a group of charities who work hard to preserve and protect our landscapes. It's a complex, and at times confusing world, as charities can act like authorities and government organisations seek to fund raise in the same manner as charities. Get to know your own patch and use it to exemplify the complexities of the conservation systems that have evolved over the years.

Natural England

Natural England is the government's adviser for the natural environment in England. Its responsibilities include access, rights of way, land management, landscape, parks, trails and nature reserves, protected sites and species, recreation, wildlife and habitat conservation.

Natural Resources Wales / Cyfoeth Naturiol Cymru

Natural Resources Wales is an amalgamation of the Environment Agency Wales, the Countryside Council for Wales and the Forestry Commission Wales. Bringing together these organisations was thought, by Welsh Government, to be a sound way forward after devolution. As you can image in has taken a while to settle down, but NRW is now responsible for access and rights of way, protected areas, recreation, forestry, farming, and flooding, amongst other things. It's a wide-ranging organisation.

NatureScot / Buidheann Nadair na h-Alba

NatureScot is Scotland's nature agency and it has a role is to protect and promote Scotland's natural heritage. It is responsible for access, protected areas and the promotion of nature in Scotland.

Northern Ireland Department of Environment and Rural Affairs

In Northern Ireland public rights of way are the responsibility of local councils. They are not mapped as well as in England or Wales, neither are they signposted as well. Each council will have different priorities as far as public rights of way are concerned. Protected areas such as SSSIs come under the remit of the Department of Environment and Rural Affairs, who also are responsible for agriculture, fisheries, forestry and water, amongst lots of other things.

Environmental Protection Agency (Ireland)

In Ireland the EPA are responsible for mitigating climate change, air, water, waste and biodiversity. The national parks and other protected areas come under the aegis of the National Parks and Wildlife Service.

National Parks

The national parks of the UK and Ireland are slightly different to others around the world, no, very different! In other parts of the world, they are often government owned and managed. Yes, they are parks for people, but they are parks managed for nature and wildlife. Here, our national parks are not 'national' and they aren't parks in the urban sense of a place to play. All the land in our national parks is privately owned. It can be owned by farmers, large landowners, water boards, forestry enterprise or the National Trust. Each national park here has its own management committee, each one operates independently and each one has to balance the demands of the public with the demands of the people who own the land. Our national parks are government (under) funded organisations with a remit to manage the conflicting interests of recreation, industry and agriculture. They have a professional staff team covering such things as planning, education, wardens and special projects. Each national park has recognised its own special qualities and it's worth checking these out when you are operating in the national parks.

It's also worth mentioning at this point that each national park also has a group of 'friends. The Friends of the Lake District, Friends of the Dales, The Friends of Loch Lomond and the Trossachs, and Cymdeithas Eryri / Snowdonia Society are examples of this. Each body campaigns to safeguard the national park and hold the national park authority to account. This is really important as the national park is the planning authority for the area too.

Areas of Outstanding Natural Beauty were set up at the same time as the national parks and they are considered of equal importance for the purpose of conserving and enhancing their natural beauty. National parks, in addition to this though, have another purpose and that is to promote understanding and enjoyment of the area's special qualities by the public. Because of this extra layer of responsibility, they have their own independent national park authorities, staff and budgets, with full planning powers, running them. The national parks conservation and enhancement role specifically includes 'wildlife and cultural heritage' whereas cultural heritage isn't covered by AONB legislation.

Note for Trainers – 8' Slingland

An activity called 8' Slingland or, if you prefer, 240cm Slingland is a fun way of introducing conservation ideas. Pair up the group and give them a climber's sling or piece of string of about this length. They have to go away and choose a 'site' to conserve, which will be contained within the 8' sling. They have to explain why they chose this site, what its special features are, how it should be protected, how the land within should be managed and how visitors should be managed. It should stimulate some discussion and can always be related to contemporary issues affecting our protected sites and national parks. (If this is an evening session, in the dark or indoors, just use some laminated photographs of different views).

National Trust

The National Trust is a charity. It was established for the purpose of promoting the preservation of landscapes for their natural features, animal and plant life habitats and of buildings, of beauty or historic interest. While famous for

THE MOUNTAIN LEADER

The National Trust have been at the forefront of encouraging grazing of the uplands with old breeds of cattle. Here we see Welsh Blacks, which were common on the hill before the dominance of the woollen industry, happily grazing in Cwm Idwal.

stately homes, the National Trust has a wide ranging portfolio and it owns much of the Lake District and a good chunk of Eryri. You'll come across NT properties in our other upland areas as well. In Scotland it is the National Trust for Scotland and it owns some of our most special mountains including those in Torridon, Glencoe and Kintail. It owns Ben Macdui, Ben Lomond and Ben Lawers too. The National Trust has been criticised for its adherence to traditional farming practices, which is intensive sheep farming, on some of its properties but, on the other hand, it does protect and manage its land holdings in a sensitive manner, including footpath maintenance, waymarking, parking and information sources. You could always become a member and put your point of view across as such.

Local Councils

Our local councils across the UK do have quite a lot of responsibility for issues that affect walking. Not only do they manage country parks and tourism infrastructure, they're also responsible for public rights of way. Public rights of way come under the Highways Department and each authority should have a footpath team. I, personally, would love to see spending shift away from the dominance of the motor car to more spending on pedestrian and cycle ways.

RSPB

The Royal Society for the Protection of Birds is probably the biggest wildlife charity. It is now a significant landowner and is an influential voice in upland management. They have some excellent resources which can help us.

Wildlife Trusts

The Wildlife Trusts are probably less important for the uplands, but you will come across their reserves in much of our countryside. I certainly recommend you find out about your local trust and the reserves they manage. The Wildlife

Access, Conservation and the Environment

Trust produce some excellent resources and are always looking for volunteers to help out with the work they do maintaining their nature reserves.

John Muir Trust

The John Muir Trust believes that wild places should be respected and protected. They are sizable landowners in Scotland including parts of Knoydart, Skye and Ben Nevis. They also now manage the Glenridding estate on the eastern side of Helvellyn. They have set up the John Muir Award to encourage young people to foster their aims. The Trust is named after John Muir, a Scot living in north America who was the first person to recognise the need for national parks.

Open Spaces Society

The Open Spaces Society is Britain's oldest conservation charity and has been campaigning to conserve England's open spaces such as commons, village greens and parkland since 1865. They campaign to protect public rights of way and are strong advocates for our historical network of footpaths.

Campaign for the Protection of Rural England / Wales / Scotland

The CPRE is a conservation charity in England. It was formed in 1926 by Sir Patrick Abercrombie to limit urban sprawl and ribbon development. The CPRW was formed in 1928 to campaign in Wales while the Association for the Protection of Rural Scotland, with similar aims, was also set up in 1926. Well ahead of devolution were these guys!

BMC

The British Mountaineering Council campaigns on behalf of hillwalkers, climbers and mountaineers. It has a team of access and conservation officers. It owns some crags and has contributed to footpath work in the uplands. The BMC engages with landowners and managers on behalf, not only of its members, but all people enjoying the outdoors for recreation. They have a network of voluntary access officers who supplement and support the work of the professional team. One of their team is the dedicated Access and Conservation Officer for Wales. The BMC runs a Regional Access Database, more focussed on climbing but it's still well worth a look and can be downloaded to your phone as a user-friendly app.

Conservation Land Designations

To assist with the management of our countryside for nature it can have one of several designations. These designations dictate how the area is looked after and what can, and what cannot, be done in them.

Site of Special Scientific Interest (SSSI) Area (ASSI) in Northern Ireland

This is our highest form of protection for special places. They are designated and looked after by the government's environmental protection agency (NRW, NatureScot etc.) and any potentially damaging operations within these sites needs their approval. They can be designated for flora, fauna or geological interest. You can find maps of these sites and their reason for designation on each government's environmental organisation's web pages. Each one is of significant national, and often international importance.

Cwm Idwal

Many of you will be familiar with Cwm Idwal, those of you who aren't have a special treat awaiting you. It's a roadside mountainous area with geological and botanical features of special importance. Most of what grows on a British or Irish mountain can be seen, and seen relatively easily, here in Cwm Idwal. This is due, not only to its geology, which provides the right conditions to start with, but also to the way the place has been managed.

Cwm Idwal is an NNR, SSSI, SAC and a RAMSAR site. It's owned by the National Trust, it's in a national park and it's had a sympathetic tenant farmer.

In the 1960s and '70s small plots of land were fenced off to keep grazing animals at bay. In 1998, after much deliberation, sheep were removed from the Cwm and a shepherding routine which kept wandering sheep out, as far as possible, was instigated.

Today the cwm is managed in a partnership by Natural Resources Wales, the National Trust and Eryri National Park. It is a popular location for visitors of all kinds. It has a long history of interest to climbers and walkers. Botanists, glaciologists and geologists have wandered here and field visits are to be found almost daily throughout the year. There is a good path around the llyn which copes very well with the traffic. You won't see much litter, but if you do, presume it has been accidently dropped and bring it down with you. Even the 'tea shack' by the car park has a long history and it's well worth pausing here for a brew and chat.

While the geology is of the 'in your face' kind, it's the carpets of flowers that really stand out. Uncommon, infrequently seen, flowers such as purple saxifrage, mossy saxifrage, starry saxifrage and moss campion form splendid displays right alongside the footpath. Incredibly rare species such as tufted saxifrage, alpine saxifrage, mountain avens and the Snowdon lily / lili'r Wyddfa are all to be found within spitting distance of the path, a truly special place, please tread carefully.

Access, Conservation and the Environment

Cwm Idwal, with its magnificent back wall reflected in Llyn Idwal.

Local Nature Reserves

Local Nature Reserves are designated under the 1949 National Parks and Access to the Countryside Act. They are areas of local importance for flora, fauna, geology or habitat. They are designated and managed by the local authority often in conjunction with a local Wildlife Trust

National Nature Reserves

National Nature Reserves are habitats important on a national scale. They were established to protect some of our most important habitats, species and geology, and to provide 'outdoor laboratories' for research. NNRs are of a larger scale than SSSIs and could be high, mountain tops such as the summit areas of Yr Wyddfa (discuss!), Cwm Idwal, or areas of woodland, bogs or limestone pavements.

Other designations

You will come across many other designations. Some of these maybe of more relevance to Lowland Leaders than Mountain Leaders, they include green belts, country parks, village greens and common land. There are also a series of coastal and marine designations too. We have inherited some protection systems from the European Union such as Special Area of Conservation (SAC) and Special Protection Areas (SPA), these were part of a network of protected areas across Europe called the 'Natura 2000'. In Scotland commitment has already been made to maintain these sites, I'm sure the other Home Nations will follow suit in due course. Most of the SAC and SPA sites are already SSSI sites.

THE MOUNTAIN LEADER

International designations found in the UK

RAMSAR sites are sites of wetland with international importance.

World Heritage Sites

World Heritage Sites are designated by the United Nations Educational, Scientific and Cultural Organization better known as UNESCO. While many of them do have a high nature conservation value they are actually cultural landscapes, typically castles such as Caernarfon or cathedrals such as Durham are designated. In the UK, Stonehenge, Avebury and the Giant's Causeway are such sites. For us, however, the game changed a bit when the Lake District was designated as a World Heritage Site. This is interesting because it internationally recognises the traditional, hill farming landscape as a key part of the Lake District's appeal. To most of us, most of the time this is fine, but on looking at the detail of this, we see that large parts of the Lake District are dominated by bracken, or poor quality grasses, and the questions remain over how the Lake District can be farmed in a more nature-friendly way while retaining the characteristics of upland sheep farms.

In 2021 the Slate Landscape of North West Wales became a UNESCO World Heritage Site. It was designated as such for the way that it illustrates the transformation that industrial slate quarrying and mining brought about in the traditional, rural environment of the mountains and valleys of the Yr Wyddfa massif. There are six archaeological sites in the designation, all are related to slate industrial processing, historical settlements, both living and relict, historic gardens and grand country houses, ports, harbours and quays, and railway and road systems. We will also be aware that these derelict sites offer a refuge for nature. They are home to rare choughs and ring ouzels. Peregrines and ravens live here and we see the pioneer birch species spearheading the ecological succession processes.

A slate fence in the Croesor valley.

The Vivian Quarry above Llanberis showing how nature, and climbers, are thriving in this former industrial landscape.

Opposite page
A gold D of E group on Yr Wyddfa.
Photo: Matt Giblin

SECTION B
BEING A MOUNTAIN LEADER

Looking towards Ogwen from Crimpiau.

How do we look after people in the hills?

Leadership

Are you the right person to lead others in the wonderful uplands of Britain and Ireland? Can you look after them if things don't go to plan? Are you able to open their eyes to the nature that surrounds them? Do you inspire your group to care about our uplands? You have covered so much on the journey to becoming a Mountain Leader and this book will hopefully help you to remember some of the ideas, skills and topics you have covered. It might help you to think about some new concepts, and even to challenge some of your established ideas.

Above all else, do you like people and do you love our mountains?

Successful Mountain Leaders are not just passionate about our hills and mountains and the nature within them, they must also have an intrinsic interest in people, a desire to connect. To inspire and lead people in the mountains is an enormous privilege and incredibly rewarding. The vast majority of the time it goes well, but are you the right person to be there when the proverbial hits the fan?

Mountain Leader trainees ascend Y Gribin from Ogwen.

THE MOUNTAIN LEADER

A well-dressed Mountain Leader, looking ready to lead.

Leadership behaviours 'on the hill'

Look the part, turn up on time and look as though you are here to lead, smart and equipped with a tidy rucksack and map in hand. Smile, say hello and introduce yourself.

What are the characteristics of a Mountain Leader?

The Mountain Leader qualification is not a degree in leadership, but it does put leadership first and more recently has begun to identify the characteristics of good leaders and the behaviours required of such. A quick internet search will produce many wise words on leadership. Even if you narrow your search to 'outdoor leadership' you will still come up with plenty of material. A typical training course exercise would be to brainstorm some of the characteristics a good leader might have. You could well have come up with some of the following. A Mountain Leader should be: confident, well-mannered, diligent, enthusiastic, empathetic, sociable, inspiring, patient, knowledgeable, tolerant, well organised, non-judgemental, proficient, respectable, likable, approachable, engaging, positive, adaptive, flexible, proactive, equable and able to communicate with people including listening to them.

This is clearly a long list and, at the same time, can never be completely exhaustive. The challenge is to pick out between three and seven of the words and weave them, consciously, into the way you lead on any given day.

Leadership

A group being led by a Mountain Leader into Cwm Idwal.

A group being led by a Mountain Leader down the Miner's Path on Yr Wyddfa.

You should then come back to this list at the end of a day, evaluate yourself against it and then see how you can further develop your leadership and work on other characteristics; good leaders are reflective practitioners.

Note for Trainers

Try brainstorming your group for words they'd associate with characteristics of good leadership. Then in small groups they should choose three of the words and discuss how those characteristics might be exemplified when leading on the hill. The challenge is then to get the group to model these characteristics on subsequent days.

LEADERSHIP – BEFORE THE DAY

Good leadership begins before we go on the hill. There is a lot of preparation to do. It's all about our group on that particular day and our role is quite simply to care for them. This means we need to do some prior planning and preparation, spend some time working out what is the right plan for the group on the day and ensuring that everyone is prepared for what may lie ahead.

Responsibilities

A key theme in the Mountain Leader qualification, leadership section is responsibility. The responsibilities of the Mountain Leader are many and varied and they start, with you, yourself. If you don't look after yourself, then how can you look after the rest of your group? Make sure you are well equipped, well fed, fit for the day and in a position to be able to monitor the condition of your group. Do not underestimate the power of role modelling. We all copy, we should be the best Mountain Leader we can be as people will copy us and model their behaviours on ours. We should lead by example and demonstrate desired behaviours.

Looking the part

I know, I know ... it might sound shallow, but it really is important to 'look the part'. People form an impression of you very quicky on first sight. What do they expect when they see a Mountain Leader? Well, we don't have go into too much detail on that, as what is smart and what is not smart will vary enormously. Obviously you dress in your outdoor gear, but that gear needs to be as clean and neat as possible. I don't hold with the argument that scruffy and worn looks experienced; we're talking about presenting a professional appearance here. Tidy hair, tidy beards, cleaned boots and rucksacks packed well. You should wear your association badge proudly too.

Be careful with how you wear sunglasses, slip them up onto your head when talking directly to people so they can see your eyes. Smoking is a thing of the past now and would not be expected of a Mountain Leader, likewise, chewing gum is unbecoming of you. These comments may sound a little prejudicial – I'm sorry, but people will make snap judgments and if you present anything they don't like it'll take you a long time to win back their trust. Introduce yourself every time, it's polite and professional. Are you prepared to deal with 'normal' problems? Can you do some first aid? Can you keep warm? Can you deal with an emergency? Can you fix a boot? We'll return to the theme of looking after yourself later in this chapter.

Top tips from Mountain Leaders

Model the behaviour you expect of others.

David Tainton

Does everybody know what they should have?

Looking after your group means being responsible for them and making sure they have appropriate kit for the venture, that they have had the right nutrition, they have spare kit, they know why they are doing what they are doing and how long they will be doing it for.

When you meet with youngsters it seems OK to ask to see their waterproofs, extra layers, lunch and drink etc. Of course, you'll need a plan of what to do should their kit not meet your expectations. If you can't provide the missing kit then it may be the case that you will need to change your plan for the day. With adults it's a little trickier. You can ask if people have the kit, but they won't always be honest. If you ask a man if he has some long trousers with him, he may argue that he always wears shorts. Other arguments that you will hear are: 'I don't like wearing waterproof trousers', 'I prefer walking in these shoes', 'I think my soft-shell is waterproof'. You'll soon collect your own list of these tales. Some people might lie about having the right kit to save face in front of the group and not to look silly. This has a nasty habit of catching up with them, and you, later. Some of these problems can be lessened with good prior information.

Jeans and inadequate footwear have been two problems with which I've had to deal and it can't really be ignored, unless the weather is perfect. It is really tricky to manage the situation if you have given out information and it's been ignored. You may need to refuse to take someone or at the very least you may need to modify your route. Before being too judgemental however, go back to source and check that you have given them the information about what you want them to wear, clearly and prominently. Make sure there is a little warning in your advance notes about the right to refuse to take anyone inadequately clothed or shod. Most people will have a fleece, many sports shirts are made to wick and any waterproof will probably do. Gloves and hats don't need to be expensive ones, but they will need them. They might not believe you when you are at the bottom of the hill, but they'll be glad they had them up the top.

You must make sure that you have given out useful and accessible information in advance. This should include a proper description of the day's expedition. It should explain why extra clothing might be needed, it should explain how the weather can change as you ascend, it should explain why some extra food and plenty to drink should be carried.

It is entirely possible to head off up the hill less equipped than you might prefer, but you need to be weatherwise. You might need to change your route and you might need to shorten the day. Make sure you have the kit required to keep your group warm in the event of any mishaps.

> **Top tips from Mountain Leaders**
>
> A piece of advice I'd give to anyone working with groups whether you know them or not is to ask if anyone has new glasses or contact lenses.
>
> I was walking in the Cuillin with someone I knew well and he seemed to be stumbling and tripping over every tiny nubbin. I almost abandoned the walk up to Sgurr Nan Giilean when he remarked that he had new varifocal glasses and was struggling to see his feet!
>
> Knowing this, I confidence-roped him up and down until we were back on more sure terrain.
>
> Always makes me ask questions about new glasses now, and medications too.
>
> Mark Hardy

Food and drink

People in your group need to turn up with a drink and some lunch, ideally after having eaten breakfast too. We all have our own personal tastes when it comes to eating. On days when we aren't leading a group we might just take a malt loaf, or some flapjack and keep moving. When we are with a group, things change, and you really need your team to arrive with food and drink to fuel them up and down the mountain.

What to drink

Water is the best thing to drink on the hill. It's healthy and keeps people hydrated better than anything else. Sipping frequently, especially during and after walking up hill will help to keep the group hydrated and in good health. You shouldn't need to overdo it, however. Individuals, typically, don't need more than 750ml to a litre on a typical hill day. The thing is water is heavy, one litre is one kilogram so we want to carry as little as we can get away with. Remember, the recommended two litres per day is to be consumed over the whole day and it includes the water in food, in the milk that may be drunk and even in the tea and coffee most of us consume. A typical adult will need more than two litres over the whole day if hillwalking, but they won't need to carry this much on the hill. It might be worth thinking about

Leadership

Reusable water bottles and flasks

taking more when it's particularly hot, but then it might be possible that you can cut down on some of your extra clothing, it's all a balance. Encourage your group to bring water, at least 750ml in a reusable water bottle.

Leadership behaviours 'on the hill'

If you use a drinking bladder, as a leader, you can sip away all day and keep yourself re-hydrated satisfactorily. Do you though, check your group are drinking? When I'm leading, I find it best not use a bladder. I take a water bottle, same as the group. Whenever we stop, and we'll be stopping for all sorts of things, I get the group to sip along with me. We might stop to take a photo. We might stop to look at the route. We might stop to put on, or take off hats and gloves, to put on sun cream, to adjust layers. Every time we stop I slip off my rucksack and take a sip. I demonstrate this to the group so that when one of them has to stop for some reason, they all use that time, together, as one, to drink.

A hot drink on the hill can be a real boost. If you need a hot drink, you probably aren't in conditions that you want to sit around brewing up in and this means you need to carry a flask. Metal flasks are readily available these days and will be a sound and robust choice for any day on the hills. As to what to put in it, you can take what you like. Traditionally coffee and tea have been considered poor choices, but their diuretic affects are so minimal as to be irrelevant and the morale boost of your favoured tea or coffee certainly outweighs any such concerns. Of course, milk and flasks aren't a great mix. Some people will take hot fruit squash, some will take fruit teas or maybe a mint tea. It could be worth, depending on your group and the prevailing conditions, taking two flasks. The boost of a swig of soup or hot chocolate shared with your group mid-afternoon might just help them off the hill with a smile and give a little moment to remember.

I remember ... on Ilkley Moor

I must have been about 12 years old. Brought up on tea, bread and dripping, or jam. Ilkley Moor was one of the most accessible places for us to go walking. I was being led by Scout Leaders, fantastic volunteers who did a great deal to shape my life. It was cold, low cloud and blowing a hoolie. One of the leaders offered me something hot from a flask, I took it; "tea" he said. Oh, my goodness it was revolting, tea with SUGAR in, yuk! I politely refused any more. He thought this was hilarious and conjured up an image of poor little Michael Raine passing away on the hill, hypothermia getting the better of him, not because he was ba'tat (without a hat), but because he didn't like sugar in his tea! These days, if I carry a 'group' drink I take hot chocolate.

What food to take

You should ask your group to bring a packed lunch, but it's also worth mentioning how important it is to eat something before they meet you and actually get on the hill. I would also recommend asking them to have a 'good' breakfast before coming on the hill for the day. What constitutes a good breakfast could well be the subject of its own book, so here we are just pointing out that the day will be more achievable if people start with fuel inside them. Not having breakfast is less than ideal, but we do need to recognise that people will have different breakfasts. If they ask you, then the classics of porridge, or the trendy oat pancakes, work well, but to be honest, a traditional cooked breakfast isn't a bad option either!

It's worth getting people to think about taking some snacks to eat on the hill. Fruit-filled, chocolate topped flapjack is hard to beat for quick release and slow release energy. It may well be eaten before you leave the valley though! There's nothing wrong with sandwiches and most people can be trusted to bring something they find palatable. What you might need to do however, is flag up the fact that you may not be stopping for a 'lunch hour'. Idling on the summit for an hour is rarely a practical option so just inform them that lunch may be split into two stops and that these will potentially be before the summit and after the summit. It's always good to have something for mid-afternoon too, but this is where you, as the leader, might need to pull some sweeties 'out of the hat'!

You should also think about packaging for lunch. Encourage the use of reusable sandwich boxes rather than plastic film wraps. Encourage the use of reusable water bottles rather than disposable ones and try not to choose sweets that are individually wrapped. It's getting rarer to come across people who smoke, but if you do ask them to bring their 'tab ends' down to be disposed of properly.

> **Top tips from Mountain Leaders**
>
> Think about asking the group to put some food in their pockets to snack on rather than having one big lunch stop, ideal when the weather is poor, on the other hand, if the weather is beautiful nothing beats a picnic on a summit!
>
> Kath James

Leadership

Responsibilities to parents, guardians and next of kin

Your responsibilities extend beyond the individuals involved, you must be mindful of their parents, guardians and next of kin. Has everyone been adequately informed about what the venture really entails? We talk about informed consent. You may have heard the phrase that consent forms are not worth the paper they are written on. This is not strictly true. The consent form needs to step up a level and be more informative. Think about it; a 'walk in Wales' can mean many different things to different people. People unfamiliar with hillwalking might not quite see a 'walk in Wales' as a walk up a mountain. It doesn't help when we flip between the terms, walking, hillwalking and mountaineering. It doesn't help when we say we're going climbing, scrambling or mountaineering 'on the hill'. Conversely, the term mountaineering doesn't always conjure up a similar image in different people's heads. While we use the term mountaineering as a catch all for climbing, scrambling, walking, even bouldering, the general public, those we lead, may well have images of Everest, of the Matterhorn, of the north face of the Eiger in their heads, or even just the picture on a Toblerone bar! Informed consent requires an explanation of where you will be going, how long you will be walking for and an accessible description of the terrain over which you will pass. It might include some of the reasonable precautions you have undertaken beforehand to ensure the best possible care for those you are leading. This would include having gained the Mountain Leader qualification and potentially made a prior visit to the destination.

What the public might imagine when you say mountain. Photo: www.alexanderkay.co.uk

What we might mean when we say mountain.

Informed consent

Informed consent requires that the participant, or whoever is responsible for them, has a clear appreciation and understanding of what the proposed expedition entails. You may need to describe what hillwalking is. You may need to describe the terrain you will be walking on, the time away from roads, that there are no toilets on the hill and that lunch will be taken, potentially, sitting on a rock on top of a mountain (oh dear, what is a mountain!). Pictures may help.

If you have described the expedition clearly then it is not unreasonable for signatures on it to be taken as consent. As a further step some people use is the BMC participation statement. It lays it on a bit thick and feels a bit too climbing focused, but it is the industry norm and it at least provides you with a starting point. You could go on to say that accidents are rare, and you have an exemplary record. Remember, members of the public will have heard of mountain rescue and they presume that they are the experts. They could be completely unaware of the Mountain Leader qualification.

BMC participation statement

"The BMC recognises that climbing and mountaineering are activities with a danger of personal injury or death. Participants in these activities should be aware of and accept these risks and be responsible for their own actions."

Make sure people realise that hillwalking is considered one aspect of mountaineering.

You will also need to make participants aware that they are part of a group, a group with a leader, and the leader may ask them to comply with certain instructions regarding safety.

You will need some personalised statements along the lines of:

- I consider myself fit and able to take part in this expedition.

- I recognise that hillwalking is an activity with some risk of personal injury.

- I have read the description of what we are doing, I have understood it and I recognise my role in minimising the inherent risks.

- I undertake to not be under the influence of alcohol or other drugs that may impair my ability to safely take part in this activity.

You should also include a note about photographs:

- I understand that photographs and video may be taken by the leader over the course of the event and I permit / don't permit these items to be used in social media and any potential future advertising with my image in them.

You then need to ask the usual questions about medications, illnesses, allergies and pre-existing injuries.

Don't forget to have next of kin contacts and consider that you may need to carry these with you.

The Rhyd Ddu path on Yr Wyddfa.

Responsibility to organising organisations

You shoulder a responsibility towards any organisation that you might be working for or on behalf of. You would not want to represent organisations like your school, Scouting or the Duke of Edinburgh's Award Scheme in a bad light. In the case of any organisation, you must consider yourself the representative of that particular organisation. If you are running your own business, then you will behave in a manner which might encourage potential customers to engage your services again. Likewise, if representing an organisation, you must always do your best to reflect them in a good light. This responsibility covers everything from your appearance and manner, your kit, to the group's kit, the group's behaviour, and the way you impact on other people and the environment around you. These organisations will expect a pre-trip risk assessment to be completed.

> **Top tips from Mountain Leaders**
>
> Be professional. Consider how you portray yourself to your clients and your employer (and remember that you're also representing your employer). The outdoor industry is more professional than it's ever been and all of us, as instructors, should be looking to maintain and further the professional reputation we've worked hard to gain in recent years.
>
> Dan Lane

> **Top tips from Mountain Leaders**
>
> Stand out from the crowd. Anyone with an ML ticket can take a group up Yr Wyddfa, so make yourself attractive to prospective employers by finding a niche and standing out from the other ML holders. For example, knowing your night sky makes you more attractive for night walks, having a Mental Health First Aid certificate makes you more attractive for welfare walks.
>
> Darren Parkinson

Pre trip risk assessment

Written risk assessments are difficult for us to complete and always seem a bit arbitrary. Of course, there is a risk of a trip or a slip. There is also a risk of a trip or a slip walking down the pavement or up the stairs at home. What the reader of the risk assessment might not know or understand, is that you know that everyone in the group, including yourself, will trip or slip at some point in the day and that your job as a Mountain Leader, who is qualified to make dynamic risk assessments on the hill, is to make sure they don't slip or trip in the wrong place.

A risk assessment should identify potential risks. Think about how likely that risk is to cause an accident, how serious that accident could potentially be and then how to mitigate that risk. The higher the likelihood of an accident the more coercive the mitigation should be. Quite quickly you begin to see that we need a different risk assessment for different walks, and we need a different risk assessment for different weather conditions and we need a different risk assessment for different groups.

However, a typical pre-walk generic, written, risk assessment might cover: trips and slips, stream crossings, cliff edges, changing weather, stumbling into bogs and external factors such as other people. You might want to think about drinking water, tick borne diseases and if you are camping, you'll need to think about stoves and cooking very seriously.

Whatever you do, you need to make your own risk assessment. Printing out somebody else's to 'tick the box' does not cut the mustard. Handwritten, scribbled on and slightly grubby risk assessments indicate revision and modification in light of new risks being highlighted. I would add in something about making dynamic risk assessments on the hill too.

Dynamic risk assessment

It is hard to cover all possible scenarios in a pre-trip written risk assessment, you should include a line about your ability to make on-going, dynamic risk assessments. The ability to recognise and adapt to changing circumstances while on the hill is a keystone skill for the Mountain Leader and we'll come back to this later.

Responsibilities to the wider, upland community

This is everybody else. You have a responsibility to operate in a manner which does not negatively impact on other users of the hill, be they recreational walkers and climbers or professionals instructing, farming or conducting other work such as footpath maintenance. You must at all times remember you are a representative of other Mountain Leaders, of the association of which you are a member, of Mountain Training and the integrity of its qualifications. Do not undertake these responsibilities lightly. While we have a right to walk in most of our hills we should behave like good guests and leave no impact of our passing. Only this way can our voice be seen as one of reason and be offered with credibility.

There are many groups of people we can offend, not least other hillwalkers, so let's be quiet and respectful but do say 'hello' to other people out enjoying the peace and quiet of our hills and mountains. Farmers are trying to work the land, and whatever our personal view, we don't have the right to hinder their activities. That might be harder to say as regards hunting, motor sport, drone flying or even some of the massive events that take place in the hills these days but challenging these types of events while leading a group may not be the best plan. I do suggest you open up a discussion with your group about other land use activities as discussed in the environmental chapter.

Environmental responsibilities

This brings me on the next big area of responsibility. The environment. We take people into places that many people don't go to, don't know about and can even be a little intimidated by. We must be very mindful about introducing people to our hills and mountains. We should have an understanding of why the hills look the way they do, who looks after them, what is special about them and what challenges they may face in the future. All land in the UK and Ireland is privately owned and it is managed for many different things. Our pastime is just one of many that takes place in the uplands. We

THE MOUNTAIN LEADER

Path spreading along the heavily used Llanberis path on Yr Wyddfa.

considered some of these issues in the Environmental chapter. Some prior research of the area you are going into should be seen as very important. Look out for its special features, any quirks of land ownership, any recent changes and of course the legality of the access along your chosen route.

The old maxim of 'take only photographs, leave only footprints', is a pretty good starting point, though we do need to minimise the imprint of our footprints these days too. If there is a path, use it, if there isn't a path consider spreading out a little so that you don't create one. Most leaders actively pick up litter when on the hill. I've found bio-degradable dog waste bags very handy. They can be used for banana skins and orange peel which can then got straight in the food waste bin when you're off the hill. These bags can be useful for other waste such as sanitary products and tissues. I do carry a litter picker on occasions, but this isn't always appropriate as looking after your group is your main aim.

As a Mountain Leader act in a manner you would wish others to, and begin by communicating this 'code of conduct' in advance of the day to your group.

Operational responsibilities

A good way to start thinking about your responsibility to your group and to the places we walk is to really think about the aims and objectives of your walk. Your aim should be a broad, overarching theme for the day. It could be as simple as having an adventure, teaching navigation or introducing the upland environment. The objectives need to be more specific. Objectives could include achieving a particular goal such as a summit, teaching certain skills or developing teamwork. You should be providing an appropriately challenging experience which has been agreed with the group beforehand.

Whatever your aims and objectives, you need to really keep them in the forefront of your mind. You need to know what you are doing, why you are doing it and you need be able to communicate this to your group and to any organisation you maybe representing. It's brilliant when these goals can be agreed with the group and you can calibrate the level of challenge directly to their needs. Supporting the group, and individuals within it, to enable them to be part of the decision making process, wherever possible, will only benefit the development of their own problem solving skills and future competencies. The more of this that can be done before the day, the more effective it will be.

> **I remember ... helping out on a walking festival**
>
> I was a bit reluctant but didn't really have an excuse. I was tasked as being the first aider on a walk with a storyteller. The storyteller was no walk leader. Fortunately I had the kit and I knew the way. What I didn't know is where she wanted to stop. I asked, I received a clear answer. I checked. The route involved quite a steep hill, "no stops" she said, "we need to get to our goal so I can tell the stories". Off we set, slowly, the group were lovely, we chatted. The storyteller brought up the rear, dropping back some, and then dropping back some more. We walked slowly, feeling under pressure not to stop as the destination had seemed all important for the storyteller. Finally, we did arrive at our lovely, special, peaceful destination. We sat through the stories, patiently, but not over enthusiastically. At least it was a nice walk, we were polite to her, in that very British way where everything is fine, or lovely. The return was downhill. Again, I checked, is there anywhere you'd like to stop on the way? "No, no, let's just go" she replied. We did. We finished the walk. A couple of days later the event organiser said the storyteller had complained. Complained we walked too fast and didn't stop. I didn't complain about the stories, maybe I should have!

It will be with the aims and objectives of your journey in mind that as you move closer to the commencement of your expedition you will start to make evaluations of your team and their ability to achieve, or not achieve, the challenge in hand. A good Mountain Leader will be able to adjust the goals of a hill day to keep some challenge in the expedition, and it may be worth communicating that you retain the option to do this in advance of the trip. Having said that, there is nothing wrong with an early finish if the aims of the trip are satisfied. The leader should, however, feed this into the planning process for the next expedition, which may as a result be a little more rewarding if the challenge, in line with the weather and underfoot conditions, is increased somewhat. **It is this ability to constantly evaluate and re-evaluate both your group and your plan for the day that really sets out good Mountain Leaders from other walkers.**

> **Leadership behaviours 'on the hill'**
>
> Make clear what the objectives for the day are and how they may change.

THE MOUNTAIN LEADER

LEADERSHIP – ON THE DAY

You have made your plans and you've done your best to inform your group about what to expect and what to bring. Other people know where you are going and why. Any plan will need constant monitoring, and then changing accordingly in response to the needs of the group, the impacts of the weather you are experiencing and the demands of the terrain you are traversing. This may mean you need to adapt your behaviours and decisions throughout the day to meet the ongoing safety needs of the group. You will start by checking that they have brought the kit, the food and the drink that you asked them to bring. On greeting a group, a Mountain Leader will instantly cast a glance at the group's footwear. The leader will be making judgements about the group from the off.

You will form impressions of people within the group upon meeting them. It is perfectly normal to judge people on first impressions and develop theories about how the day may pan out for them. You will think about what the day holds for the individual as part of a team. It is however absolutely vital that you constantly revise your first impressions of group members. Some people will turn out stronger mentally and / or physically than you first assumed, others may need a little more support than had been thought on first impression. Treat them as individuals. This is no place for prejudice and fixed mindsets.

> **Top tips from Mountain Leaders**
>
> Young people would rather look cool in their dress than put their coat on when it rains or tie their shoelaces! At this point they will need some clear direction.
>
> Paul Sanderson

A mixed group out walking.

If you can get the group working as a team, chatting with each other, getting to know each other better, and starting to work together effectively this will greatly enhance the likelihood of you achieving the goals that have been set for that day.

> **Leadership behaviours 'on the hill'**
>
> Constantly revisit your preconceptions of everyone in the group.

The briefing

The first briefing should be positive and welcoming. You need to appear approachable as you will want your group to feel that they can confide in you if they need to. At the same time however, you need to be absolutely clear about what the day holds, how the weather might change and how strenuous the journey may be. You can sometimes pre-empt difficult conversations by doing this and people can make up a story with which they can save face as they pull out. Things like *"oops I've forgotten my waterproofs / lunch / flask"* etc. Don't argue with these people this could well be a cover story for them realising, before it's too late, that they should not be going on the hill today.

> **Top tips from Mountain Leaders**
>
> Briefing – If it's windy, stand with your face into the wind so your clients have their backs to the wind, look them in the eyes. Don't wear sunglasses as it's important that they can see your eyes to help create trust.
>
> Darren Parkinson

> **Top tips from Mountain Leaders**
>
> With a group of teenagers, you have approximately 30 seconds to get across what you want to do with them and how you will do it. Be succinct and build the detail along the way through pupil self-discovery.
>
> Paul Sanderson

I often do a rough and ready Naismith's rule for the anticipated journey with the team at the start of the day. They all want to know how far it is. Convert the miles to hours, it's much more useful. They can then 'know how much further it is' by looking at their own timepiece.

THE MOUNTAIN LEADER

Leadership behaviours 'on the hill'

Brief the group about where you are going and how long it will take, when we will have lunch, and why we are carrying extra gear. Make sure everyone has had the opportunity to use the toilet before leaving the valley, and they are aware that 'on the hill' there are no toilets (explain the alternatives).

Top tips from Mountain Leaders

Go before you go.

Adrian Sancroft

The summit shelter on Rhinog Fawr.

The importance of learning names and getting to know your group

If there is one quality of a Mountain Leader that should probably be above all others it is the ability to interact with your group effectively. You need to get to know your group really quickly. It isn't just a matter of 'follow me'. This is an important difference between being a Mountain Leader, behaving in a professional manner and someone just showing people where to go. You will be armed with knowledge galore about the places you are in, about how to deal with emergencies and how to navigate. It is really important to get to know your group as quickly as possible for the day to proceed in a manner which is beneficial, and creates minimal stress for everyone involved. You will have 'interviewed' your group, done some research on them and you will have shared goals and aspirations. It may be that the group has signed up for a particular walk, it may be that you have a group that you are teaching things to. The people you are with could already be known to you, or you may have a group that you have never met before. It is really important to observe them on the hill and develop your knowledge of them quickly so that you can learn all about their habits, and mannerisms. You will need to develop the experience required to be able to see through the words they give you and develop empathy for their feelings. All too often you'll be told 'I'm fine' when they are not.

Top tips from Mountain Leaders

I've taken almost 14,000 people out in the hills and mountains, and it's all about the group. That's the No.1 thing. People and their emotions. Their relationships and interactions with each other, with you, their environment, terrain and weather. How they are feeling is paramount. It's a given that a Mountain Leader can navigate in all conditions, that is the foundational skill that should be second nature. The most important thing by far is how people are feeling. At the end of a day in the mountains, if your customers say that they feel invigorated, empowered, they've learnt something and they want to do more, then you've succeeded.

Mark Reid

Start by learning names. Learn names in clusters, maybe three at a time. Asking people another question to go with their names really helps. Who are you and where are you from, we can usually make some sort of comment, maybe a joke or ask a question about a place people are from?

Remembering names

Questions about places to help you remember the name of the person who comes from there. Yes, I am trying to be humorous, I am trying not to be offensive, maybe just a little tongue in cheek. I'm sure you can add your own ...

- London – Do you know Dave, he lives there?

- Chesterfield – Where the steeple is bent.

- Hull – KR or FC?

- Cardiff – Why is the Welsh capital as far away from the rest of Wales as it can get?

- Birmingham – Mind the canal.

- Manchester – I'm sorry.

- Liverpool – red or blue?

- Leeds – Can you explain the road system to me please (could apply elsewhere too!).

- Swindon – ah, the magic roundabout.

- Bath or Cheltenham – oo posh!

- Newcastle or Sunderland – can you explain a clothing system that might work on a night out compared to those used on the hill?

- Essex – Actually that's where the posh jam comes from isn't it?

- Swansea – just say bye 'ere.

- Scotland or Ireland – Can I come and stay with you please?

- Yorkshire in general – oops sorry. My Dad said never ask a man where he's from. If he's from Yorkshire he'll tell you. If not, you shouldn't embarrass him.

Serious note – learn names, find a way to make them stick.

Not knowing people's names is simply not good enough. Knowing names provides clarity so the group know who you are talking too. It can help with safety so you can direct instructions if required, it helps the group feel like you know them and you care for them. Being 'no good at names' does not work for a Mountain Leader.

> **Top tips from Mountain Leaders**
>
> It's important to learn names early on and pick up on their individualities. We are all different, and we need to recognise and celebrate that when we try and work with them as a group.
>
> Mladenka Hooper

Engage with individuals

Speak to each member of the group on their own as soon as you possibly can. Use their name, seek connections and common ground. It pays to check on people more than once. A little time invested early on will be repaid handsomely later in the day. Check that people are not too warm, not too cold. We

Leadership

A well-equipped and logo'd up pair, ready for their charity hike, with Thirlmere behind.

often start off wearing more than we need, this is inevitable when going from a standing around start. Stop soon to readjust clothing. 'Be bold, start cold' is a good maxim, but it's actually quite hard to do as people can start to chill quickly while they wait for the whole group to get ready and for the journey to commence. I always take time to look at people's footwear. I'm checking the footwear is appropriate for the journey but I'm also looking to see if it looks comfortable. I ask specific questions about rubbing. I'm on the hunt for 'hot spots' that if covered up with tape now won't go on to become blisters.

Tops tips from Mountain Leaders

Get to know the group, find out their names, partners' name if they have one, what they do for a living, where they live; show an interest, the more you do this the more the trust builds. Emotional Intelligence goes a long way in this business so, use it to suss out your group and suddenly your job isn't about the hills and mountains but people. We coach people and yes, they are in the mountains but understanding the people / individuals allows us to coach them and interact with them so we can then get the message across about the hills and mountains. Plus it's really interesting.

Adam Harmer

Leadership behaviours 'on the hill'

Early on in the walk check everyone's feet are comfortable and that there are no 'hot spots' developing. If there are, deal with them before they become a problem.

There will always be a need to recognise and respect the different, individual strengths and abilities of each person within the group. It's not always possible, but if you can, get everyone involved – perhaps by taking turns to lead or bringing up the rear. Try to include them in decisions to be made on when to eat, when to rest, when to push on, even which route to take. You should strive to create a positive and supportive environment for the group to gel and work better as a unit. This is always going to depend on the group and the reason for the walk. On some days we're just out for a nice walk, on these occasions it may be that people do just want to be shown the way, or be informed about aspects of nature. On other days, the team building and personal development will be a key part of the day's journey. A Mountain Leader needs to be able to operate with a range of groups, with a range of reason's for going hillwalking.

Leadership behaviours 'on the hill'

Learn something about each individual. Does each individual 'buy in' to the plan for the day? Use gender-neutral language and remember that everyone is an individual. Hold no prejudice.

The importance of small talk

This author is very passionate about Mountain Leaders informing the people they lead about the places in which they are being led. Raising awareness of rural issues and the choices we face around upland management should be considered a key duty of the Mountain Leader. However, that is not your only role, you are here to look after people and help them enjoy their day. You will be a more successful Mountain Leader if you can engage with your groups.

Top tips from Mountain Leaders

Soon after I qualified, while working on a Yr Wyddfa sunrise walk, I asked my employer that day what he felt made a good ML. Looking back, it was the best piece of early advice that I got.

"Be interested, not interesting"

Top tips from Mountain Leaders

Knowing when to enhance the moment with some local knowledge and when to just ask questions and listen (and when to say nothing) is a key skill for Mountain Leaders which certainly wasn't covered on my training / assessment.

Paul Justin

Leadership

Top tips from Mountain Leaders

The bread and butter days are the charity hikes, the sunset and sunrise moments with large groups of people. Shadowing established and respected MLs gave me an insight into the group dynamics that you encounter, the different range of abilities you might work with and the patience, empathy, motivation and strength you have to develop very quickly. You can't just plan a route and march off, you need to find ways to connect with the people you are working with, engage them in conversation and ensure they have a fantastic day on the hill regardless of the conditions. This is something that I think is worth so much in this business and is maybe something that cannot be taught, it is something you must develop through experience.

Kerry Bason

Walkers on the traditionally named Snowdon Ranger path on Yr Wyddfa.

The real art of being a Mountain Leader is the ability to walk and talk. That is, to know where you are and where you are going while holding a conversation with someone in your group. While having a weather eye out, checking on the team's progress and caring for the environment, you should be listening to someone else's story. Facing forward, not looking at each other, exercising gently is a brilliant way to get people chatting in a non-confrontational, an open and honest, way. Be sure to listen just as much, if not more, than you talk and look out for the 'awe and wonder' as people discover new places.

Top tips from Mountain Leaders

Spiritual elements – one of my best experiences as a Mountain Leader was sat with a group of Explorer Scouts looking at the view from Stickle Tarn when one lad said *"why is this all here"*. I started to go down the geology route and glaciation route but he stopped me and said *"no, why is this wonderful view here"* and asked about God. What followed was a great discussion about various religions (Buddhism, Islam, Christianity etc.) as well as atheism, all prompted by the 'awe and wonder' of the environment we call our workplace. Never underestimate the effect the mountains can have on people and our responsibility to nurture that.

Albert Hinton

THE MOUNTAIN LEADER

> **Top tips from Mountain Leaders**
>
> Children experience the outdoors more intensely than adults, as it is a new learning experience for them and by just being in the hills they are out of their comfort zone. Don't underestimate the experience of others to what you find ordinary.
>
> Paul Sanderson

Walking skills

It comes as a bit of a surprise that you need to teach the people you are leading how to walk. While on paths, most people will be able to walk perfectly well, but should you head off the beaten track at all, you may notice people struggling with how to walk across slopes, up them or down them.

When ascending, experienced hillwalkers tend to place the whole foot firmly, in a location we have already spotted i.e. we look where we are putting our feet. This almost 'flat-footed' foot placement allows us to use the thigh muscles to push up rather than a typical 'urban' bounce on the calf muscle, toe / heel – toe / heel style of walking. When traversing, it is the location of the knees, slightly rolled towards the slope, and braced to maintain a level foot that will enable us to use the edge of our boots (this is when a boot with lateral stiffness, really comes in to play – see equipment).

Or, as Geoffrey Winthrop Young put it in Mountain Craft in 1920:

"In walking uphill, the foot should always be placed so that the heel rests on the ground. It is a beginner mistake to rush a hill and spring from the toes alone. If the flex of the ankle is stiff – men vary much in this respect – and the gradient is too steep to allow the heel to drop, look out for any little stone or excrescence, however small to set it upon. If the path is very steep, and without stones, it is more comfortable to set the foot slightly sideways, so that the heel gets some support."

I presume the flex of the ankle varies much in females too!

On descents, it can be a case of digging our heels in, particularly if it is grassy, but maintain body weight over the feet and don't lean back too much. When traversing or descending less steeply, a side-on, flat-footed, approach is good, particularly on wet grass, where we can 'edge' the boot into the slope. Occasionally, we can head straight down bare rock with a flat foot, gaining maximum friction too. As in ascent, zigzagging will greatly reduce the toil. Do not underestimate the need to teach these walking skills.

Feet planted firmly, using the whole sole and pushing up with the thigh, rather than the calf, when ascending steeper ground, take short steps, make lots of zig-zags.

Leadership

Descending on scree can be pretty hard work. The walker here is demonstrating excellent balance by having his chest over his knees, and looking forward to his next foot placement. His heels are well planted in the scree and leaning back, away from the drop below, would deposit him on his backside. Descending into Coire Lagan on the Isle of Skye.

Top tips from Mountain Leaders

Never stop on a tiny stone that's on top of a large flat rock. It can act like a ball bearing and then you may fall.

Derek Clarke

The menstrual cycle (for men)

Menstruation is a normal bodily function that affects half of the world's population. It seems odd that we find it so difficult to talk about it, but we do. To most men, the whole topic is poorly understood and readily ignored. It is unseen and rarely presents the leader with any issue. However, through being informed, we might manage to be more empathetic to women in our groups.

Menstrual bleeding (the shedding of the uterus lining with an unfertilised egg) can last between three to eight days. The menstrual period affects different women in different ways. The first few days are usually the worst, with heavier bleeding and for some women, stomach cramps. It should come as no surprise then, that women experiencing their period can appear in poor mood because they are having to cope with so much more than the inclement weather. Hormonal changes in the body can also negate a positive mindset. Mood can also be affected if a woman needs to manage her period and she is stuck halfway up a mountain with a group of men who cannot relate to her predicament.

If you are leading a group that has female members it is highly likely one, or more, could be having their period. You will not know who this is, you do not need to know who this is. Very occasionally I have been leading a group with young females who are in the early days of experience with the management of their periods. It can be hard to ascertain why they are feeling uncomfortable. You need to give them space, not an inquisition. Ask how you can help, if privacy is required, and if they can manage the situation themselves or with help from a friend. You need to be empathetic, think about the topography of the area, is there any privacy, do they need the group shelter? If your expedition is longer than 8 hours then any woman experiencing her period will need to find some privacy at some point and you will need to give her time and space.

Given the discomfort and regularity of the menstrual cycle in women, we should appreciate how seamlessly our female counterparts cope when out on hikes or longer expeditions. By being aware and empathetic, we can make their experiences just a little bit easier.

Physical literacy

I know a few of you have had some surprising experiences around physical literacy. One of my most exciting came after I hadn't been working regularly with youngsters for some time. I was with a group from a school in England and we were actually hoping to go gorge walking. As ever, we did a little warm up on the way in and ... well, if I hadn't seen it with my own eyes, I wouldn't have believed it! There was one boy who simply couldn't stand on stones. Honestly, he couldn't stand on stones. His whole life had been spent on manmade, urban surfaces and the challenge of using some stepping stones was beyond him. I'd started easy and had nowhere easier to go. Another boy was doing fine until he got his foot wet. When he screamed, I thought he must have broken something. No, it was the shock of the cold water on his foot. He screamed, leapt up and tried to head straight up the side of the gorge, I literally had to grab him before he gained any height at all. It was an eye-opening day for me.

On another occasion I met somebody who didn't understand how to walk across a slope, he could go up or down, but not across! At least he was good humoured and enjoyed the discoveries he made that day.

Expect the unexpected. We aim high, but sometimes don't realise just how low the bar has been lowered by the upbringing of some youngsters today.

Leadership behaviours 'on the hill'

If the prevailing conditions and the nature of the journey mitigate against a traditional lunch break, make sure you have informed the group that you will take a few nibble stops rather than one, long lunch break. Some instructors talk about 'first' lunch and 'second' lunch, this works well.

Leadership

Walkers enjoying some rough ground in the Moelwynion.

Pace

When you are leading a group one of the most important roles you have is that of setting and managing the pace of the group. We all have a tendency to walk quicker than we should when in front of the group, I can't explain quite why this is, but it just is. Quashing this tendency is something that many of you will have had to work hard at. Once you feel you have the pace right, the next problem is imposing that on the group. This can be done in several ways. You can hope they fall in with you and most will. You can insist they stay to your rear; you'll feel the pressure of them on your shoulder if you do this. Or you can explain the day in terms of how far we are going, how hard it will be, how much energy will be needed and how we have to ration its use so that we can last all day.

Top tips from Mountain Leaders

Pace is one of the most important things to manage as a Mountain Leader – if you go too fast your group spreads out and then you end up stopping and starting all day, with the slower people feeling rubbish because they always get a shorter rest. Find a way to manage your pace and you'll have a better day, and so will your clients. I pause between each footstep to help slow myself down, I also sometimes start a conversation with slower group members just before setting off, by chatting to them I am able to keep a pace that they are comfortable with.

Kath James

It doesn't stop there though because you will have people in the group who can walk quickly all day, and you will have people who'll struggle to keep a pace in line with the objectives for the day. Ideally, you'd split a group of this nature. Those ready first will typically be the quicker walkers, let them set off with one leader while the other leader collects the stragglers and walks at a different pace. This leader will have to decide whether to alter the finish time of the day or the route.

Quicker members of the group may need to be given some responsibility, they might be the back marker, they may give extra help to someone in the group, they could be the timekeeper for the expedition. One of the things I find difficult to manage is my desire to inform, so if waiting with the quicker group for the slower group to catch up, I often like to tell them some tale about where we are. The trouble is the slower members of the group keep missing out. With some groups it works well if you get those you've told a tale to, to tell that tale to the slower ones at the group's next stop.

There is no magic formula for keeping your group together. You must be aware of where everybody is and how they are feeling. It does get easier with experience, but this is a challenge that never quite goes away. Try putting the quick one at the back and giving them the responsibility of looking after those who are slower. Try putting the one at the back into the front after a stop, sometimes they discover a new turn of pace and you actually need to slow them down! Sometimes they gradually work their way to the back of the group.

> **Top tips from Mountain Leaders**
>
> Fifty percent of the view is behind you (take time to stop and soak up the view).
>
> David Tainton

One of the easy ways to gel the pace of the group is to manage stops efficiently. If one person needs to stop to drink or to adjust something, make sure everybody else thinks about doing the same thing at the same time. If you have a group of ten people who all stop at different times for five minutes the difference could be total stops of 50 minutes, versus one stop of five minutes! By managing stops efficiently, keeping them to a minimum and keeping a steady, though possibly slower pace, you'll find yourself buying time that can be yours to waste later, should you wish to do so.

Managing a group containing people who wish to walk at different speeds can be one of your trickiest challenges. You may need to use some direct language about appropriate pace for the whole group should the weather deteriorate, or some members of the group be consistently too far away for normal communication to work.

Leadership

Group adjusting kit and having a drink all at the same time.

On routes you do frequently you'll learn, and make a note of, how long sections take. You soon get the feel for the rhythm of the group and you'll soon be speeding up and slowing down to order, almost subconsciously.

> **Top tips from Mountain Leaders**
>
> Keep the group together and work as a team; drink stops, food stops, layer change stops, do it all at the same time as this is more efficient and means you can keep an eye on how everyone is doing.
>
> Kath James

Should I split the group?

It's a horrible moment. One of the group decides they don't want to carry on, they are insistent that you and the rest of the group should continue without them. They insist they will be alright and they don't want to spoil the day for the others, the others might agree, but do you? Should you go on, should you split the group? Should you let the odd person make their own way down? Should you ask them to wait at a specified location? What should you do?

Well, you've heard the answer before … it depends. It is not possible to make a blanket statement that you must never spilt the group. You should definitely err on the side of caution when considering splitting the group and it should be a very rare occurrence. It can only happen if you're completely happy that the person you are leaving will be safe, that they will be warm, that they understand your instruction, that they will either wait at the allocated place or that they will be OK wandering back down the path back from where you came. You cannot have a yes / no answer as each circumstance will be different. People are not fools, if you leave someone to follow the path down then, presuming it's an obvious path with nowhere to go wrong, they should be OK. Is your decision making sound? Have you thought through what could go wrong? Are you doing a reasonable thing in letting an adult (hard to imagine this being OK with a minor) make their own way down the mountain on a good, obvious path. Probably, but it depends ...

Top tips from Mountain Leaders

There can be a Yr Wyddfa or 'challenge walk' weirdness, because there are so many other people on those hills usually, 'doing it on their own', sometimes people in a group may feel the need to go their own way. One particular couple I encountered were just really annoyed that they couldn't walk at their own pace having booked on an open, guided walk. It was an amazing weather day and a busy mountain. I'd given the situation enough strategies and it was impacting adversely on the rest of the group so, bearing 'volenti non fit injuria' in mind I let them go.

Kate Worthington

Timings on Yr Wyddfa

I asked Keith Hulse, a regular Mountain Leader on Yr Wyddfa how long it takes to do it. He answered, immediately with the following (he just knew this):

- "Llanberis Path 4.7 miles: Three hours up, two hours down.

- PYG Track 3.5 miles: Two and a half hours up, I don't usually come down the PYG because of the terrain but would probably be about an hour and a half.

- Miners Path 4 miles: Two and a half to three hours up, two hours down.

- Snowdon Ranger Path: just under 4 miles: Just over two and a half hours up about two hours down.

- Rhyd Ddu just under 4 miles: Just over two and a half hours up about two hours down.

- Watkin Path 4 miles: Three and half hours up and two and a half down."

"The average is about 6 or 7 hours for a trip but that varies a lot! An 8 hour trip is not uncommon and 10 hours is not unknown.

As a leader you have to switch on very quickly to your group's ability especially somewhere like the Llanberis Path with the first road section. I have seen many people take that too quickly and paid the price later in the walk, some giving up at halfway, same applies to the start of the PYG."

I also know that Keith knows the timings of particular sections of each route; he can ask his group for twenty minutes of effort to get up a particularly steep bit, such as that just after Clogwyn Station on the Llanberis Path. He also knows where he needs to be by midday or by 2 pm for a successful day out. You should learn this about your regular routes or try to estimate it beforehand on unfamiliar ones.

Gender

It is disappointing that females continue to be under-represented amongst the ranks of the Mountain Leader population compared to the population as a whole. There are many reasons why this is the case. Those reasons are varied and combine in unique ways for each individual. Our job is to encourage, nurture and support everyone to enjoy the outdoors. We have already seen that some of the characteristics of being a good leader are to be empathetic, to listen and to inspire confidence. By being consistently non-judgemental and treating people fairly you will be doing your bit to portray an image of being a Mountain Leader that other people, regardless of gender, can aspire to. This is something that anybody with a love of hillwalking and people can do and gender should be irrelevant. Treat people as individuals.

The menopause

In a group with more mature women, it is also important to recognise the impact that the menopause may have on individuals and therefore the group dynamic. The average age for the menopause is 51 although most women will experience symptoms long before they hit menopause. These symptoms need consideration (and empathy): hot flushes, 'brain fog' and low self-esteem can have a serious impact on the enjoyment and well-being of a woman in your group. Being outdoors is, as always, the best medicine, yet some women may feel less fit or mentally focused as they once would have been, and a few may struggle with 'mind over matter' stuff. It is not my place to advise how women should cope, but to advise how, as leaders, we can be patient and encourage women in our group.

Working with minority ethnic groups

The issue here is about people's identities, and how these are shaped by multiple factors. All people, regardless of their race and ethnicity, will have diverse needs, values, and capabilities. As Mountain Leaders we want to make outdoor activities inclusive and accessible to diverse individuals and groups of people. Yet, when working with new people, we have limited information about them and commonly make judgements based upon people's physical attributes such as age or body shape and size, the clothing they are wearing and the kit they are carrying or the amount of previous outdoor experience they have. This is common and sensible as it feeds into the factors affecting our plan for the day and the dynamic risk assessments we need to make.

Nevertheless, there should be constant reassessment of these judgements as we learn more about the people we are working with in order to avoid prejudice, and to ensure activities are inclusive, accessible and enjoyable for those participating. Try to avoid making judgements which are based on race or ethnicity as opposed to the those outlined above. Treat everyone with equal respect, and ask if you are unsure about people's needs, values or capabilities. Make enquiries and this will be well received with the understanding that you are trying to provide an inclusive and enriching outdoor experience for participants. Work to identify and overcome any perceived barriers, be they social, cultural, religious or even practical. Think about transport, kit, food, toileting, and enquire about any other activities participants want as part of their outdoor experience.

Striving to centre your days and activities around the needs, values and capabilities of all participants, including those who may be currently identified as BAME (Black, Asian and minority ethnic), is good practice. Make sure you practise well.

People represented by the acronym BAME are a minority in our hills. They are under-represented as a proportion of the outdoor population compared to their proportion within the whole population. Change is, however, gradually happening. We are starting to see people who may be classified as BAME beginning, and completing, the journey towards gaining Mountain Training qualifications. As a percentage of the nation's population, the number of people labelled as BAME is set to increase to somewhere around a quarter of the population by 2050. Therefore, we might expect that 1 in 4 hill goers could be black, of Asian descent, or from other minority ethnic groups.

It is important to understand that BAME is an administrative term used to classify people who are racially and / or ethnically non-white and / or non-British. This label is arguably too casual and dismissive of the extensive diversity in the needs, values, and capabilities of the people it attempts to represent. Such generalisations can reinforce racial and ethnic inequalities by conveying the idea that as 'minorities' they are vastly different to the racial

Leadership

Mountain Leader trainees scrambling in Cwm Idwal.

and ethnic 'majority'. In reality, there are similarities within and between different racial and ethnic groups. So, while it is important to be aware of this social and political context, it is even more important to not label and define the people you work with in such terms. A survey conducted by the charity Sporting Equals in October 2020 reaffirmed this stance, with respondents finding the term BAME to be inaccurate and marginalising.

There is no uniformity between people who are black, brown or from other minority and ethnic groups. The term BAME is considered by some as lazy short-hand. The diversity within the black, Asian and minority ethnic groupings is staggering in itself. Some could be new arrivals to the UK, some could be the daughters and sons of several generations. There is great diversity in accessibility to the outdoors and in awareness of the outdoors. There are different groups within groups based upon religion, upon wealth and upon geography. There are different hierarchies within groups.

Leadership behaviours 'on the hill'

Stops. It's all too easy to be stopping every few hundred yards for an individual to adjust something. This is where time is lost and keeping 'on pace' is probably more about managing stops efficiently than it is about walking quicker.

Mental health issues

Mental health is another area you, as a Mountain Leader, need to be aware of. If people have an obvious physical disability you can see it and ask about it, take advice about it and lead accordingly. Mental illness can be hidden, but it's probably more in the open now than at any time. Mental health isn't that different from physical health, it's something we all have and we all need to look after. In the same way that you might have small issues with your physical health that are temporary this can happen to you with mental health too. It is of course the case, that from time to time, we can suffer greater injury to our physical wellbeing or to our mental wellbeing.

Good mental health means being able to think, feel and react in the ways that you need to while living your life in the way you want to. A period of poor mental health can hamper this and people may well find that thinking, feeling or reacting becomes difficult to cope with. This can feel just as bad as a physical illness, or even worse.

As with physical illness and injury most people will experience poor mental health at some point in their life. Currently figures estimate that 1 in 4 of us will have a diagnosed mental health problem at some point. As I write this during the Coronavirus crises, I fear this figure will, in the ensuing years, be higher.

People may well want to tell you they are suffering, simply ask them how you can help and what they would like you to do. Usually, they just feel more comfortable that you know. When people are open about such issues it can be challenging to you if you have no experience of these kinds of things, roll with it. Talking to you, walking with you, being in a group in beautiful places typically is a great help to most sufferers of mental illness.

You will also meet people who have challenging mental issues which have not been diagnosed. This can make things difficult. One of the least diagnosed, but common today and something you are highly likely to encounter is anxiety. There are different kinds of anxiety and you need to respect the anxiousness anyone suffering exhibits and be supportive. People who are suffering from anxiety might exhibit some of the following traits, so before you dive in with both feet and attempt what you perceive to be a witty comment such as 'cheer up', 'I'm sure it'll pass' or 'pull yourself together', slow down and think about it. Then, listen without judging:

- Worry

- Agitation

- Restlessness

- Fatigue

- Poor concentration

- Irritability

- Trouble sleeping

- Panic attacks

- Avoiding social situations

- Irrational fear

It's well worth going on a mental health first aid course. You won't get all the answers, but you will have a heightened awareness of some of the issues people are having to deal with in this modern world. Always remember each person is an individual and be guided by them. Listen and hear them, work with them, be kind and encouraging. They will want to be independent; they will try, you just need to be there when they are wobbling.

There really are too many mental illnesses to go into here but do visit www.mind.org.uk to find out more. Amongst illnesses with information about them on that particular website are, anxiety and panic attacks, bipolar disorder, body dysmorphic disorder, borderline personality disorder (BPD), depression, eating problems, loneliness, obsessive-compulsive disorder (OCD), panic attacks, paranoia, personality disorders, phobias, postnatal depression and perinatal mental health, post-traumatic stress disorder (PTSD), psychosis, schizophrenia, seasonal affective disorder (SAD), self-esteem, self-harm, stress and suicidal feeling. This is just a sample, as with physical wellbeing there are a wide range of illnesses that people might be facing. Finally, remember, there is no such thing as a throwaway comment when it comes to any concerns people may have about the shape of their bodies, the way they look, their eating habits or your perception of their mood.

Working with vulnerable people

You will probably have done some training on how to manage yourself around vulnerable people. Sound advice is to be careful, be open, be considerate and respectful. Avoiding touching, but touching the elbow is deemed OK and can be very useful in the way we work. We need to develop relationships and trust and human contact can be an important part of that.

We often talk about child protection, but there are vulnerable adults too. It may well be that a member of your group tells you something you perhaps wished they hadn't. We get on well with our groups, walking is good for people and they feel free and it's easy to talk. If you find yourself in this situation, the most important thing to do is not to promise confidentiality, you must make it clear you will need to share anything you are told, particularly if it could be deemed abusive. If you haven't done any safeguarding training, I do recommend you avail yourself of some. The BMC runs courses and there are online units you can do too. Most of what is covered is common sense and the sort of things you would do anyway, but it's reassuring and reasonable to update yourself with the best of information and support around.

THE MOUNTAIN LEADER

Reflective practice

Reflective practice is simply reflecting on how things have gone and wondering if they could have gone better; this is learning from experience. In the outdoors it's not quite that simple though, as wise mountaineers will learn as much from other people's mistakes as they will from their own. Take the time to reflect, take time to talk, take time to share. It's hard being open about things when they haven't perhaps panned out as you would have wished. It's hard acknowledging that you could have made some better choices. However, it does happen, and it keeps happening, although with experience it should happen less often. On most days, you will come off the hill with a warm, glowing feeling. It's been a good day and you took the right people to the right place on the right day and they had a 'reet' good time. Now and then though, it doesn't work out quite right. You aren't sure about the venues, you don't know the group very well, the weather is unsettled. You would be well advised to be cautious if this is the case. It's much better to come back with the feeling you could have done more than end with the feeling that your adventure was very nearly a misadventure. Lives can be lost in an instant.

Top tips from Mountain Leaders

If you only ever do the same thing every day with no reflection, development or improvement – you could do a job for twenty years but only have one year of experience.

David Tainton

Early morning in the Carneddau.

LEADERSHIP – FURTHER CONSIDERATIONS

Beyond the immediacy of what to do step by step on the hill, and further to the pre-event administration that needs to take place, a Mountain Leader has other things to consider. It takes time to get on top of everything and there is much to think about.

People can be unpredictable and so it is important that we consider potential issues that they may bring with them. In many ways it's much easier for us to focus on natural hazards which tend to be obvious. With the members of your group however, come a whole load of issues you need to be aware of. In no particular order here's a few that I've come across and that you should bear in mind.

> **Top tips from Mountain Leaders**
>
> A teenager's job is to be the best teenager they can be, that means not standing out from their peers. This rule is not always compatible with being safe, so set clear boundaries and get the group to police those boundaries with each other.
>
> Paul Sanderson

Lack of breakfast

Assume nothing! I know it might seem daft to us that someone would go without breakfast, but I have seen someone struggling and it's taken me a while to work out what the problem was. Ask the question: *"What have you eaten today?"* This might take you down the line of discovering that it isn't something they've eaten, it's something that they haven't eaten. I've been told: *"I don't eat breakfast."* Personally, I look forward to my breakfast so much so that this is hard to understand, but it's out there. Check what people have eaten before they joined you to go hillwalking for the day.

The night before

In a similar vein, you may not know what people were up to the night before. Were they up late? Were they partying and drinking? Consider how ready for the day your group is and be prepared to modify your plan. This isn't just about drinking and drugs. It could be emotional issues, such as having been bullied, having argued with someone or maybe having received bad news from elsewhere. Be prepared for anything.

Undisclosed medical issues

There can be all sorts of reasons why someone might not disclose a medical issue. I've come across a couple of incidents where the sufferer, who's been battling with a recent diagnosis, simply hasn't been ready to talk about it yet. One such case I encountered was an epileptic who had a minor fit, but was in denial as she knew she could potentially lose her driving licence. Another was a recently diagnosed diabetic, not far off becoming hypoglycaemic, fortunately some sugar fixed him. But, should someone look unwell, do ask them if there is anything you should know, anything they might not have informed you of before the day.

Pre-existing injuries

Pre-existing injuries are similar to undisclosed medical conditions. People may have reasons why they don't want to tell you about this. They may think it will prohibit them from taking part, or they may think it'll adversely affect the day for others in the group. Either way, you need to make it clear when you meet a group that you need to know these things. I once had to help a very large gentleman off the hill, fortunately we weren't too far from Ogwen Cottage. The group half carried and half supported him back to our vehicle after he'd stepped down off a rock and suffered a shooting pain in his foot. We took him to hospital, a bit mystified as to how he'd hurt himself so badly on such a minor step down. Turned out he had an existing fracture to his foot. He'd done it the week before coming away on the trip so kept it quiet. To be fair we'd been up Y Garn and we were well on the way down before his injury got the better of him. Not a great experience for the group, but one we all learnt something from.

The need to know

Most groups you are leading will have had to fill in a booking form to be there with you. This form will have space for any medical information that should be disclosed. It's well worth, on meeting the group, reinforcing the need for this information. It can be done in a friendly supportive way, you can explain why it's needed, because of the responsibility the leader will have and the environment you are going in to. You can suggest that something may have changed since they filled in their booking form. Be positive, but also firm. You can ask again, when you start the walk, and you must give the members of the group an opportunity to speak to you quietly about things. They don't have to share their medical details in front of the group, but they do need to share them with you.

Fear of dogs or other animals

It can be the oddest things that catch you out. I once thought I'd lost someone after passing through a farmyard; it turned out she was still on the other side of the farmyard and had refused to enter it. This was due to barking dogs. Now, they can be enough to intimidate anyone and I've certainly spent a little time looking at their chains and seeing how long they are. Be aware of this and work together as a team. Cows, spiders and even birds have cropped up as things to be scared of.

Lack of cooperation

Most of the people you lead will look up to you. You have assumed respect but it is yours to lose. Most people will listen to your every word and will be impressed by your experience and knowledge; some won't. They'll argue with you, they'll ignore you and they'll think they know best. Fortunately, this is rare and if you are working with groups like this then you've probably got special skills to be doing this kind of leading in the first place.

The only time it might affect most of us is if things are perhaps not going to plan; if the weather changes abruptly and you didn't expect it, if you find yourself temporarily misplaced or you've forgotten something you really should have with you. Any issue of this nature can affect your standing within the group, it can lead to a loss of respect and far, far worse, an unwillingness to follow you. You need to remain calm, confident, you need to be honest and you need to be able to find ways to fix any such problems.

Lack of kit, food and water

Before heading up the hill do check your group have what you expect them to have and this includes food and water. With youngsters I will ask them to show me what they have with them to eat and drink. Time spent at base checking this will be well worth it in the long run. I'd much rather set off a bit late than set off unprepared. It's the same with kit, if you've asked them to bring waterproofs, spare hats and gloves ask to see them. This approach may not, however, be appropriate with adults. You can really only ask them if they have everything and take their answers on trust. It's not unusual to have a group member who is colder than they should be because they've 'forgotten' a piece of kit. This is why you, the Mountain Leader, need to carry spares.

Walking in Ireland

> **AdventureSmart**
>
> AdventureSmart grew from conversations in Eryri between the North Wales Police, North Wales Mountain Rescue, Eryri National Park the BMC and Plas y Brenin. It is designed to be a simple and accessible outdoor code that everyone can follow. It could be a helpful resource for any novice walkers you may interact with.
>
> **Be AdventureSmart**
>
> Ask yourself three questions before you set off:
>
> - Do I have the right **gear**?
>
> - Do I know what the **weather** will be like?
>
> - Am I confident I have the **knowledge and skills** for the day?
>
> www.adventuresmart.uk

Toileting

Give some consideration to this. We're probably happy to nip off to a hiding place to use the loo when on the hill, not everyone else is. Make sure people have had the chance to go to the toilet before going on to the hill. When you are in a place with some cover ask again if anybody needs to go. Most people can go on a day walk without needing a 'number 2' as long as they've been beforehand, you need to make sure they have the opportunity to do this. More than once, a poorly person has turned out to be someone who just needed to go to the loo, but didn't know where to or how to. The big caveat though is any cover near popular paths may well have already been used. Getting someone to go out in the open is not really on, a group shelter could be used in some circumstances, maybe linked to the menstrual cycle. You really need to get this covered as best you can before heading into the hills or at least before leaving the forest!

Other unforeseen circumstances

There will always be a possibility of unforeseen circumstances. While I haven't come across someone who is agoraphobic, yet, I have come across a few people whose fear of heights has inhibited their progress downhill late in the day. A colleague of mine once had a poorly candidate on the final day of a Mountain Leader assessment expedition. It took us a while to work out that he was actually dehydrated, he simply hadn't drunk enough to fuel the exercise he was committed to. As you can imagine, given the context, we weren't expecting to meet such a scenario. You cannot foresee everything. This is why we need to be constantly risk assessing, adapting, thinking and above all else, caring for our group.

Medical matters

There are excellent outdoor first aid courses available and I would strongly recommend you do such a course. Look for one with a high, practical content and one that is run by an outdoor practitioner who is not just a first aid tutor. Here are a few things to think about in your role as a leader.

Getting too cold

Hypothermia in particular is something to watch out for. When the Mountain Leader qualification was established this was a major worry as we didn't understand it fully and modern technical clothing had not been developed. It can still be seen in inexperienced walkers heading up high on some of our more popular mountains. A Mountain Leader should be able to prevent hypothermia ever becoming an issue in their own group by thorough briefings, kit checks and by looking after your group, keeping any eye on them and looking out for people getting cold. I know it sounds a bit daft, but getting cold is the first sign of hypothermia. Adults will typically resist help, and will say they are alright, you may need to ask them to do you a favour and get them to wear a hat, some gloves or slip another layer on. This is usually works, but a little firmness should not be considered inappropriate in such conversations.

It can be tricky if you come across someone not in your group and you suspect them of being hypothermic or close to being hypothermic. No one likes being told what to do, and this is when you may need to take control of a situation. If someone is shivering, ask them if they can stop shivering. If they can stop then it's mild hypothermia and some adjustment to clothing and carrying on should work. If I'm on popular routes, I have a small bag of 'disposable' spare hats and gloves. These are the cheap, fleece lined wool gloves from the garage and hats found on the trail (washed of course). I can actually give these away to strangers without too much stress, it's definitely a top tip if you are on Yr Wyddfa at the weekends.

If you come across someone who is so cold that they can't stop shivering, this is serious. This is moderate hypothermia and rewarming needs to take place. I'd strongly recommend the carrying of a Blizzard bag or blanket and a group shelter. A tent and sleeping bag would also work if you were carrying those – as you would be on an expedition. Call 999 and ask for a rescue. You can always stand the team down if the casualty improves enough to walk off. Getting someone in a Blizzard bag or blanket, out of the wind under a group shelter and insulated from the ground should be enough to

THE MOUNTAIN LEADER

improve things. It's unusual that you'd need to remove clothing, but if you find that they have damp cotton next to their skin then this may well be worth considering, fleece is much better next to the skin.

Treatment at base is not recommended for anything beyond mild hypothermia these days. Rewarming should be done under medical supervision, there is a great danger of 'afterdrop', which in the case of serious hypothermia can lead to heart failure.

Survival bags

Survival bags are not what they once were. While a large plastic bag was considered revolutionary at one time they have been superseded by the Blizzard bag. I make no apologies for mentioning the Blizzard bag despite it being a brand. The superior construction of these lifesaving bits of kit is such that they are a significant improvement on other plastic or foil survival bags. They contain enclosed cells which trap air, have an elasticated skeleton and a heat-reflecting coating. Together this works in a way that not only keeps a casualty warm, but actively, though gently, rewarms them. Casualties who go to hospital after being cared for in a Blizzard bag are treated for their injuries rather than hypothermia. Casualties that have not been in Blizzard bags are treated for hypothermia before their injuries can be looked after. A Blizzard blanket, still the 3 ply model, may be a better piece of kit for a Mountain Leader to carry. The bags are quite hard to cut and a blanket is a little more versatile. I'll often just carry a Blizzard smock in the summer too.

Blizzard bags being tested on a cold day.

Getting too hot

It's not often that hyperthermia is an issue in the UK, I have come across it, but first, the names; oh, how confusing! Hypo is cold, hyper is hot (I remember this by thinking big things are hyper, therefore big numbers, therefore big temperatures). So, hyperthermia is getting too hot. Like hypothermia it comes in degrees and no one in your group should suffer from it. Like hypothermia, hyperthermia is avoided by good preparation and constantly

Leadership

The author dressed for the sun with a proper sun hat, sunglasses and a collar.

caring for your group. Are they covered up to prevent sun burn? Have they got a proper sun hat on, one that covers the ears, are they drinking fluids regularly? Could you start earlier or start later to avoid the hottest part of the day, or have a long lunch break in the shade?

Prevention of hyperthermia is easier said than done. You can inform people of what you'd like them to wear before a trip, but it's a tricky one to enforce. Long sleeves and long trousers are a good start, but you could get into arguments about people wanting to wear shorts. I advise strongly that long trousers are preferred, and I do it in writing before the event.

Sun hats need to cover the ears, baseball caps aren't good enough. Shirts should have a collar, to cover the back of the neck. So, if people turn up without these, and it's highly likely, it's well worth having some triangles of light cotton material in your bag, like triangular bandages. If they do start to suffer you can make a head scarf or at least a neck scarf. I've used a Buff® for this purpose and I've dipped it in every bit of running water as I've walked past, and it's made a real difference.

Drinking is important. Make sure people have enough water with them. Typically, a litre is sufficient, but on very hot days two litres might be required by people who are working hard or are beyond their normal comfort zone. It's a big ask for you to carry extra litres of water so this is a burden you must share with the group.

The big red warning sign for hyperthermia is when someone is obviously hot and they stop sweating. This is serious, this is life threatening. Rig up some shade and call 999. If you have sufficient water, or a stream nearby, use water to wet their clothing. You need to cool them down, focus on their neck and wrists, this will cool their blood. Drinking water alone won't be enough for this person. I recommend having some rehydration powders in your first aid kit if you sense overheating might be a risk.

> **I remember ... the long hot summer of '76**
>
> Yes, I'm that old. I was at school and we were engaged on a D of E expedition in Swaledale. We had a fantastic time in a wonderful place, and I remain grateful to the teachers that took us there. I do remember though, that they had their work cut out with one student. It was hot, very hot, it was dry and we were drinking water like it was going out of fashion. One blond, pale skinned member of the team really started to struggle, stumbling, mumbling and really not very coordinated. We just got into camp where one of the teachers took over. I don't know how the teachers knew it was hyperthermia, but they did. We sat the student in the shade of an old, dry stone wall, got her sipping some weird fruit juice concoction with salt in, we put wet clothes on her neck and her wrists and slowly, but surely she started to cool down. I remember it well and have been slightly paranoid about sun hats, sunscreen and full body cover ever since.

Medical conditions

Commonly encountered medical conditions should be well covered on your first aid course. Make sure you have the information you require about your group members. This should have been requested in written form in advance, but there is no harm in checking on the day. Make sure people have an opportunity to tell you anything you need to know about them medically. You can suggest that things occasionally get lost in any administrative system, or that it maybe something that has occurred since they booked the day. Just make it clear that you need to know about any medical issues they may have. You need to check that they have any prescribed medications with them and that they know where they are. You are not allowed to administer these but you may be in a position to help the casualty should they require it. Things to look out for, in particular, are asthma, epilepsy, anaphylaxis, and diabetes.

Asthma

Asthma is caused by inflammation of your breathing tubes. These tubes are highly sensitive to agitation and can, in certain circumstances, temporarily narrow. If they do narrow, it makes the exhalation of air more difficult, and very uncomfortable. This is a highly stressful condition to have to cope with. It can also be life threatening so immediate action to improve the breathing is required.

Typical triggers for an asthma attack can be, allergies (pollen might be one to watch out for in the hills), smoke (moor and gorse burning), pollution (collecting in low cloud around roads; an awful example of this can be found when crossing the M62 on the Pennine Way in a high pressure period, you can smell the motorway, as well as hear it, long before you cross it), cold air, exercise, or infections like colds or flu.

Asthma is usually under control and the sufferer will know all about the condition and will manage it appropriately. You may need to help them with their medication or simply by giving them some space or privacy from the group.

Do not underestimate asthma. The annual death toll is between 1,000 and 1,550 people with nearly two thirds of them being female.

Asthma treatment

Most asthma sufferers will carry a reliever inhaler. This contains a drug which helps to relieve the symptoms of asthma and will help the sufferer over the attack. It has to be taken as the sufferer breathes in and this is where they may need help. They should be sat down, any pressure on the chest should be relieved, and everything should be kept calm. Some people may use a spacer, this is a plastic bottle like attachment which is filled with the drug vapour making it easier to breathe the drug in, rather than having to time the in breath with the pump on the inhaler. In an emergency, a spacer can be made from a plastic bottle. If a sufferer's inhaler is empty it is OK to try with someone else's but be sure not to leave that person in danger. There is absolutely no shame in calling 999 and asking for assistance and an evacuation. Asthma, can and does kill people every year, so take this seriously.

The relievers are blue. Some people have a different coloured inhaler and this may be a preventer that they use every morning. It's hard to remember what every different coloured inhaler does, so you will always be advised to try whatever inhaler the casualty has. The preventers won't, I'm afraid, act as a reliever. Calm the patient, try them with whatever inhaler they have, be guided by them, call 999 if they do not improve.

Epilepsy

Epilepsy is a condition which affects the nervous system and can scramble electrical signals to the brain causing seizures and fits. These fits can be large or small, non-serious or very serious. If a member of your group has a fit and they are not a known epileptic then it is an emergency and you must call 999. If you have a known epileptic in your group and they have a fit lasting five minutes or more then it is an emergency and you must call 999. If you are out on the hill and you have an epileptic in the group and they have any sort of fit I would still consider 999 and an emergency evacuation. Most epileptics have their condition under control through the use of medications, so for them to suffer while out on the hill would be a matter of concern.

THE MOUNTAIN LEADER

> **I remember ... epilepsy in school**
>
> Back in the seventies school was a cruel place. Not far removed from its portrayal in the film Kes or Bob, Sue and Rita too. Don't get me wrong I did OK. Scouting, the great outdoors and sport kept me out of trouble. But it was the sort of place where if you had an affliction it would be mercilessly exploited and one, poor boy in our year had epilepsy. The controlling drugs weren't quite as well developed as they are now so the naughty boys, would from time to time provoke the poor lad, they'd stress him to such a degree that he'd have a fit. It's what happened next that I really hated. The shout would go up around school, "fit, fit, fit" and everyone would to race to the location to watch the awful scene. Kids can be cruel, very cruel.

Epilepsy management

Epilepsy can be managed in a few ways including a special diet and electrical implants. We are most likely to come across control by drugs. If you have an epileptic in your group you just need to ask if they have their drugs, ask them if there is anything they need you to know and generally check that everything is in place. Should they have a fit, you need to let them fit. You may need to remove other people from the scene, you may need to remove objects upon which they may harm themselves. You may even need to 'field' them to keep them away from sharp objects such as boulders or, potentially worse, large drops. Epileptics will usually tell you what needs to happen next. It is most likely that you should evacuate them off the hill as the sufferer will need to know why their management of the condition has not worked and what has triggered the attack. They could well be quite fatigued by the episode. It is possible they have wet themselves and are exhausted and in some discomfort. It is perfectly OK to let them sleep and rest a little. Make sure they are warm and comfortable, make sure the rest of your group knows what is going on. Have no hesitation in calling 999 and requesting assistance as around a thousand people a year lose their lives due to epilepsy related incidents.

Anaphylaxis

Anaphylaxis is an over-reaction to an allergy, like a super-allergic reaction. It's caused by a defect in the immune system and it causes the body to release chemicals which can lead to severe swelling of the bronchial passages.

It can be triggered by many things, but ones to watch out for on the hill might be nuts, fish, eggs and some fruits, wasp or bee stings and latex. You should be aware that some drugs including aspirin can induce anaphylaxis too. There are other triggers, and a conversation with the sufferer is essential as you may be able to remove, or avoid, their known triggers.

Symptoms of an attack might include a flushing of the skin, a rash, swelling of throat and mouth, difficulty in swallowing or speaking, abdominal pain, nausea and vomiting. It will be accompanied by a sense of great distress in the casualty, it may appear asthma-like and it will lead very quickly, if not treated, to collapse and unconsciousness.

There are degrees of severity around anaphylactic attacks, but they are fatal in around twenty people a year, they can deteriorate quickly and do need further medical help

Anaphylaxis treatment

An anaphylactic attack can only be treated with adrenaline delivered through an adrenaline auto-injector such as an EpiPen. This is fairly straight forward but rather alarming. You'll have covered it on your first aid course but do refer to the instructions on the pen. The dose of adrenaline delivered by the pen can last for something like 20 to 35 minutes depending on the physiology of the casualty. Therefore, you must locate and have to hand their spare pens. There is no limit to how many EpiPen's you can administer. In hospital they will be put on an adrenaline drip. They will also be given antihistamine, so if you are remote, say more than one and half hours from help giving them antihistamine is unlikely to make things worse. It is the time factor that is crucial. You must get this person to hospital as soon as possible. Do not hesitate to call 999 and do not hold back in telling the controller exactly what the problem is. Your rescue will be prioritised.

Diabetes

Diabetes is a condition that affects how your body turns food into energy. Most of the food you eat is broken down into sugar and released into your bloodstream. When your blood sugar level goes up, it signals your pancreas to release insulin. Insulin then acts to let the sugar into your body's cells for use as energy. If you have diabetes, your body either doesn't make enough insulin or can't use the insulin it makes as well as it should. Typically, you have a blood sugar low and sugar is required. In a minority of cases you have a blood sugar high. We cannot spot the difference, so the first aid treatment is to give sugar regardless, if it's a blood sugar low they will improve, if it is a blood sugar high they won't get any worse.

Diabetes does come in different forms. These are not a matter of concern for us and no judgement should be made. Diabetics will usually have their condition well under control and you won't even be aware of it. Where it may come to your attention is if they are recently diagnosed and they haven't got the hang of controlling it yet, or when they let it go a little too far and can actually become resistant to help. As ever, a conversation about what you need to know and how you should help, if required, needs to take place as soon as possible.

You may have heard of a 'hypo'; this is short for hypoglycaemia and it's what can happen if the condition isn't controlled. Look out for the following signs and symptoms: disorientation, sweating, paleness, palpitations, tingly lips, blurred vison, unusual hunger, tearfulness, fatigue, and headaches. Any of these things could be the signs of a hypo coming on. Have a conversation, offer energy gel to the sufferer or at least strongly suggest they eat some of their own sweet stash, even if it's just to please you. You may well find them resistant to help, be firm, but respectful. Another thing to be aware of, is that diabetics often have a regular eating routine to help with their conditions and this can be interrupted when on the hill. The numbers of people who die early due to diabetic complications is staggering, diabetics being more prone to strokes and heart attacks. Diabetes UK suggest that there are up to 500 deaths per week that are related to diabetes.

Diabetes for all

If we take a mildly flippant approach to this serous subject, it would not be unreasonable to suggest that the majority of people suffer a bit of a blood sugar low mid-afternoon. Hence the great British tradition of afternoon tea or at least a brew and a biscuit. This is easy to replicate on the hill and this should be built into your day. Find time to stop at around 3.00pm, adjust clothing, refocus on foot placements, have a drink and something to eat. Prevention is always better then cure.

A good Mountain Leader will always have a pocket full of sweets of some sort. To treat diabetes on the hill you can buy special gels, but these are quite expensive and any ordinary energy gel will do the job. Look after them in your bag though as a split energy gel is a messy thing. They also go out of date, so be aware of this too. I've tried taking glucose tablets, but a couple of diabetics have informed me that they won't work as well as gels. Still, I like them!

Leadership behaviours 'on the hill'

Afternoon tea – At around 3.00 pm it is always a good idea to stop. The concept of afternoon tea is an important institution in our country and it can assume critical importance on the hill. We know that most accidents happen in the afternoons and we know that most accidents happen in descent. Stop for a cup of tea, a piece of cake, adjust clothing, take a breather, slow down and focus. This is really important as, at this time of day, people are keen to get down and off the hill. This refocussing can prevent trips and slips or worse. It's also an opportunity for another moment of just soaking up the ambiance of the place we are in. If you feel you can't be bothered stopping, that you're just on a mission to get down, be bothered, it's important.

Leadership

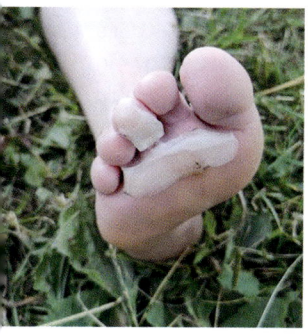

A nasty blister. I came across this on a charity hike. It just proves that prevention is better than cure, there's little we can do for a blister this size I'm afraid.

Blisters

Blisters are definitely less prevalent than they were. Modern boots are softer and generally much more comfortable than boots of old. Blister prevention is, however, the key. I ask people if their feet are comfortable very early on in the day, by early I mean after a hundred metres or so. I ask again after another couple of hundred metres. I then ask specific questions. What about your little toe? What about your big toe? What about your heel? What about the ball of your foot? I look them in the eye as I do it, searching for signs of hesitation. Most people will say they are fine, but if you spot a hesitation, dig a little deeper. If there is any rubbing at all, get the boot off, have look and get some tape on now. This will save a whole load of pain for the walker and earache for you later in the day.

If prevention didn't happen in time and a blister does form, there are various ways of treating them – popping isn't one of these. The fluids have gathered to heal the wound so popping blisters can lead to infection, the blister will pop or disintegrate itself as it heals. Cover them up, you might need to use a special blister plaster or some sort of artificial skin like Compeed.

Sprains

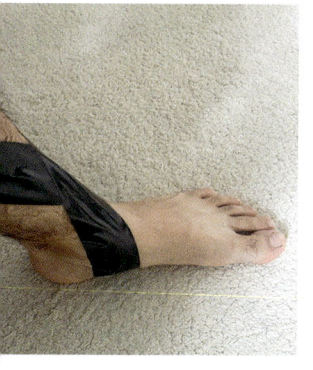

A sprained ankle supported with duct tape in a figure of 8.

Sprains are tricky and can actually be quite serious. They can involve torn or over-stretched ligaments and a whole phalanx of soft tissue injuries. If the sprained ankle, and it usually is an ankle, can load bear, can be rotated and the casualty can bear the pain when you try to squeeze the ankle, then they can probably walk off. Remove their boots, get some duct tape on their ankle, a sort of figure of eight around the ankle works well to support it and minimise it being turned again. If you a have walking poles they may find them helpful too.

If, when you take the boot off and the ankle swells to a degree that you can't put the boot back on, you may have more serious injury. Unless you are very close to the road and can self-evacuate, don't be shy about asking for help. You don't know how bad the injury is and walking on it may exacerbate it. Be cautious, call for a rescue.

Remote supervision

Remote supervision has been around for a long time, but it's really only come to prominence with the rise of the Duke of Edinburgh's Award and the expeditions contained within that award. When supervising remotely, you need to be fully up to speed on the groups abilities and you need to know the route. Many people will use the same route year after year for their expeditions. It's hard to argue against this as planning and learning a new route is not only challenging but time consuming as well. The route will never be quite the same due to changing weather conditions. If using the same route, again and again, you need to guard against complacency over any potential changes to the route. When you can sit on a hilltop with a pair of binoculars and watch your group going the right way it can be lovely. When you meet them at a rendezvous and they are in good spirits it can be lovely. When you manage to tail them and all is well it can be lovely. On the other hand …

I remember taking part in a Mountain Training workshop day once when we worked through a remote supervision exercise. We studied the map carefully, spotted every possible hazard, highlighted where tailing the group might work best, where we should meet the group or where we could take to the high ground to watch them. We veered their route away from a cliff line as the prevailing wind could blow them towards it. We thought of everything, we were good map readers, this was a doddle. To reward ourselves, we then went to walk the route. Not a word of a lie, we were no more than 200 metres from the start when the footpath was diverted! The variant we had chosen, away from the cliff edge was closed and the path was diverted along the cliff edge we'd cannily avoided. It just goes to show that there is absolutely no substitute for walking the route and for knowing the route. That you are aware of the confusing junctions, the misleading false paths, the places that might flood is absolutely priceless. Yes, there are more great days when out remotely supervising, fine food, fine company and great views, but never underestimate the potential for problems to occur. If it does go wrong it can be extremely stressful.

Some providers use electronic tracking, by GPS, by SPOT devices or other similar methods. The use of mobiles phones, sharing position on mapping software or even Google locate should be considered too. There can be rules on how to do this, for example the current Duke of Edinburgh's Award rule states that; 'It is unacceptable, at any DofE level, for Supervisors and staff to rely on text messaging or phone calls with participants for updates rather than seeing the team.' Check out the Mountain Training Remote Supervision booklet which is available as a download on their website. Check the guidelines of the organising

Allt Maenderyn on Yr Wyddfa

authority. If working alone, I would definitely experiment with whatever might be on mobile phones as everybody has one.

One other consideration to bear in mind, particularly when training or advising trainees, is that very few remote supervision days are going to count as a Quality Mountain Day. Yes, it's good experience for a logbook, but reread the criteria for a QMD and you'll find that a day such as this, which by definition is well known and cannot be varied, does not meet the QMD criteria.

Looking after yourself

While looking after yourself is not specifically mentioned in the Mountain Leader syllabus, Mountain Training is a key member of the Adventure Activities Industry Advisory Committee (AAIAC) and they have produced guidance which is worth your perusal.

Your physical wellbeing

Not surprisingly, safety features significantly in the AAIAC advice. Remember that the expedition you are leading should be to meet the ambition of the group rather than yourself. Trying to force less experienced walkers on a particular journey because it's the one that the leader wants to do can lead to problems. All too often a leader has been tempted by a route they love and want to share only to discover, sometimes too late, that it was, perhaps, not the best choice of route for those they were leading on the day.

While sharing out kit, if you have a rope get someone else to carry this, and any other bits of extra group kit you may have such as spare clothes or spare water. Right from the start you are involving the group in the running of day. You might feel a bit guilty about this, don't. You are spreading the load and looking after yourself.

Low cloud, wet rocks, ground upon which it is easy to stumble, don't neglect your own safety.

It is such a natural thing to do, but if someone is cold, tired or hungry you must be really careful about giving away your clothing and supplies. You'll be annoyed with yourself for getting into this situation, but really think through the consequences, particularly if there is a chance of the situation worsening. You are actually the most important person in the group, you are not solely a facilitator, you are a leader. If you were to encounter a casualty or the conditions worsened is it fair to the group to sacrifice your own safety?

Avoiding injury will always be a top priority for us. If we're injured we won't be able to get out there and lead walks. Think about warming up, in the case of walking this is just starting off gently, walking is, after all, a really good way of warming up for more vigorous exercise. We are all vulnerable to trips and slips. Make sure you are wearing the best footwear you can, for the walk you are undertaking, it should have good grippy soles and plenty of cushioning between you and the ground, particularly around the heels. Walking poles are something to think about, they do ease the strain a little when you are pushing up hill, they are supportive when going downhill and they will help you to arrest minor slips. Walking poles can be hazardous too. People have slipped and broken their wrist by having them caught up in the wrist loop, if the ground is slippery or uneven it's worth just slipping your wrist out of the loop. I've also experienced soreness in the wrist and elbows from using poles a lot and I know I'm not unique in this, so poles have their place, but be mindful of issues with them too.

Top tips from Mountain Leaders

Share the load – you are on the hill way more than your clients, I share out group kit amongst the group rather than shouldering it all myself, this lighter load means my body is not needing to work so hard and prolongs the time you can spend working as a leader.

Kath James

Harold 'Dickie' Bird was a cricketer and umpire for fifty years. Shortly after his retirement in 1998 he lost his eyesight; this was attributed to him being out in the sun for such long periods of time. Maybe we aren't out in the sun year round quite as much as 'Dickie' Bird was but we are out in the sun, and bright cloud quite a lot. Don't neglect to wear sunglasses. Please don't wear mirrored lenses though, they alienate you from your group. Photochromic ones are best and you still may need to push them up on to your forehead when talking to people. Sun cream (think about covering up) and a sun hat should go without saying too. There has been more than one case of outdoor people getting skin cancer, be sure to check out any skin blemishes that develop and hang around. Remember, you need to role model these practices.

A fine day for walking.

Take particular care to prevent against tick-borne infections. This is a real and present danger and the number of Mountain Leaders who have suffered debilitating illnesses contracted from ticks is now in the scores. Lyme disease, caught from ticks, is hard to pin down and hard to cure. Please make sure you are up to speed on the management and removal of ticks, there's more on this elsewhere in this book.

> **Top tips from Mountain Leaders**
>
> It's important to remember to take days off and actually rest on those days, you don't have to go out because the weather is nice, go and sit on the beach instead!
>
> Katie Cannell

Your mental wellbeing

There is a greater awareness of mental health issues now than there ever has been. We actually use the outdoors as treatment for mental health and know that walking in nature has a positive effect on our state of wellbeing, so how could Mountain Leaders be affected by mental health issues? It's more likely to be something like the weight of responsibility, the volatility of your income or the fear of turning down work, despite the fact that you need a break and you don't know when the next offer will come along. There is also the danger of being the first person at a serious accident. As the qualified Mountain Leader you may well need to take control. I'll talk more about this later in the book, but be aware that you will be expected to step up. Never, ever, underestimate the importance of talking your problems through. There is more than a grain of truth in the saying that a problem shared is a problem halved. Check out www.blackdogoutdoors.co.uk

www.mountainsforthemind.co.uk and the short Mountain Training video: The White Fox – Charlie Leeds. A lot of the training on offer is awareness of mental illnesses and can end up being a bit of a list. There is also Trauma Risk Management (TRiM) training which is risk assessment based before the event, but does have some follow up too.

> **Leadership behaviours 'on the hill'**
>
> Do take a moment or two at the end of your walk to reflect. Reflect on what you have seen, how everyone has performed, on what has gone well and what has perhaps not gone so well. How did your kit perform, was your timing up to scratch, did you have enough food, enough drink, do you need a new map? Do this with your group and do it on your own. Being a reflective leader is the only way you'll get better.

Enabling the group to look after you

You should always remember that, while not working alone, you are the person in charge, you are the experienced one and you are the person that knows what to do in the event of an emergency. Would your group know what to do if it were you that had a problem? We can all slip or trip and some of us may have medical conditions that the group should know about. Most leaders will carry a card with information about themselves and who to contact in the event of an emergency. So as not to alarm the group just build this into your briefing and sharing of kit. Make a point of getting someone else in the group to carry the group shelter, explain what it is and how unlikely we are to need it (though we may choose to use it at lunchtime). At some point just slip in the fact that your details and some top tips of what to do in an emergency are on a laminated card in 'this' pocket here, or this first aid kit which is 'here' (I know that if you are the one to fall off the cliff then this may not be helpful, but a quick risk assessment would suggest that this event has a low risk of happening. HSE law is about taking all 'reasonable precautions', you cannot foresee every eventuality and provide for it).

Working or volunteering for large-scale events

Working or volunteering on large-scale events has become a staple of the Mountain Leader's role. Many new walkers will be introduced to our pastime through these events and a good few more will be put off for ever! Events come in all shapes and sizes, take place on all sorts of terrain, vary in number, size and, it has to be said, in quality of organisation. Let's leave aside those events aimed at runners, like the ultra-trail marathons, the mountain marathons and the long distance races such as the excellently organised Dragon's Back Race and the Cape Wrath Trail. As walkers we'll be involved with sponsored walks of varying sizes.

Leadership

Working on a large sponsored walk on Yr Wyddfa. Yes, it's a lot of people, but they travelled by coach, they are using well-made paths, they are raising money for a good cause, they are outside being physically and mentally active. Yr Wyddfa was the draw for them so you need to chat to the group and raise awareness about the place you are in. You might also advise them of how to get into hillwalking.

Sponsored walks

Sponsored walks take place all over the place. One of the most bizarre I took part in was in the seventies. Before the M62 opened we had a 12 mile sponsored walk along the section near Cleckheaton, we all had sore feet after that! I've worked in schools that have annual sponsored walks, really well organised and part of their tradition. Sponsored walks are a good way of raising money, so it's no wonder people are looking for bigger and better challenges. Promotion of the Lyke Wake Walk over the North Yorkshire Moors actually stopped due to increasing pressures, though it seems to have had a revival recently. The Masters Hike has made a welcome return to the South Pennines around Huddersfield while the Ten Tors on Dartmoor is a very well established event. The Yorkshire Three Peaks is incredibly popular but, parking aside, now has a path surface that seems to be able to cope with the numbers. When organising these events, it's really important to engage with authorities, a national park if there is one, or the local council countryside service. There is rarely a problem in doing the events but you can imagine that it's well worth avoiding busy weekends in the Yorkshire Dales or the Lake District to undertake your challenge. The same might be said for Yr Wyddfa, which grows in popularity year on year. So coordination is important. Especially if you are thinking about the national three peaks.

When working on these large-scale events you can find yourself wandering along, trying to chat to people, who have formed their own groups as part of a long crocodile of people rather than the smaller groups formed by yourself that you may be used to. You might have a radio, but you might only see other team members occasionally. You need to be self-contained and with respect to the events guidelines, be prepared to make your own decisions. Wandering along at the back can bring a whole new set of challenges, for a start it can be hard to walk at the pace of the slowest!

> **Top tips from Mountain Leaders**
>
> Working at the back of a group, from my experience, can be the hardest both physically and mentally and a totally different experience to walking and leading at the front. Lots more encouragement / coaching / cajoling / patience / persistence is needed. Sometimes you are not looking to realistically get a customer to the summit, just higher up so they feel a sense of accomplishment and don't feel like a failure.
>
> David Tainton

> **Top tips from Mountain Leaders**
>
> You may find yourself working on a wide and varied range of events as a Mountain Leader, and not always in the mountains. You'll need to be adaptable, resourceful and reliable. You may be expected to undertake roles and responsibilities that weren't specifically covered on your ML assessment – applying good logic and common sense, and following the same decision-making principles as discussed on your ML courses will get you off to a good start.
>
> Dan Lane

The National Three Peaks Challenge

The National Three Peaks Challenge presents some problems. Each walk on its own is a great walk, and they have good paths and something approaching sufficient parking arrangements in the vicinity. It is the desire to do it all in 24 hours that is the problem. This means that more time is spent driving and that there is little time for positive input into local economies. The very fact that you are driving to just do Ben Nevis, even from Glasgow or Edinburgh never mind London or Birmingham, is a little rude given all the other wonderful hills that there are to walk up in Scotland. There is pressure to drive between the mountains, either fatigued or in a rush. The arrival at Wasdale in the dark to ascend and descend Scafell is such a shame for the participants, and a nuisance for locals.

On the other hand there are some very reputable organisers of this event. They play by the rules, are respectful and will look after you well. If people insist on doing this challenge then please encourage them to use one of these groups. It's such a well-known challenge now that it's hard to move people away from it. Being positive, it will, for some, be an introduction to a whole new world that they didn't know existed and they might just become hillwalkers. More than ever though, a Mountain Leader involved with these groups will need to work very hard to ensure no litter is left and that hill etiquette is sound. You will need to point out that charities and volunteers do the work of maintaining the footpaths and that mountain rescue, should it ever be needed, is run by volunteers and is a charity too. Now, spend a few moments thinking of other challenges with a better ratio of walking to driving ...

Do you really need to do the National Three Peaks Challenge?

You will need to aim to

- Inform authorities at Ben Nevis, Scafell Pike and Yr Wyddfa of your event – timing and numbers.

- If possible avoid weekends.

- Spread it over three separate days or even make it three separate events.

- Limit walkers to no more than 100 per event and group them into smaller groups, ideally of no more than 10 or 12. Each group should have their own Mountain Leader with them.

- Stagger start times and avoid congestion.

- Check equipment and experience levels.

- Plan to avoid arrival or departure between 12 Midnight and 5am at any location with settlement.

- To avoid congestion, completely avoid July and August.

- Brief all walkers, to go to the toilet when in the valley, not to leave any litter whatsoever, to keep the noise down and stick to the path.

- Have a plan for accidents, emergencies and poor weather.

- Try to encourage some 'visitor spending' in each destination.

- Use Glen Nevis visitor centre as the start point for Ben Nevis.

- Avoid starting at Wasdale, do not use Wasdale green as a car park. Water supplies are limited so bring your own.

- At Yr Wyddfa, parking is difficult at Pen-y-Pass. Disembark only.

- Do not speed between mountains; agree driving times before hand and observe legal speed limits. Only include the walking times in any 24 hour attempt, exclude the driving.

- Avoid bank holidays.

- Better still, do a different challenge, centred on one location.

Further specific guidance is available from the Institute of Fundraisers, Eryri National Park and the Lake District National Park. The BMC have produced a Green Guide to Challenge Events. Mountain Leaders should make themselves familiar with the contents of these guidance notes and if they do feel the need to get involved with national three peaks events they should try really hard to work within the guidance.

Working on charity events

Working on charity events can make up an important part of a Mountain Leader's calendar. These events are many and varied, the best ones are incredibly well organised and they give suitable status to the leaders employed. Your role is not so much about navigation on these events but you will need to heighten hazard awareness, be alert for medical issues, and, above all, have an interest in people.

You are unlikely to know the group and you will have to take their preparation for the day as it comes. The first time you meet these people will be on the day of the event, they will be strangers to you. While it is reasonable to presume that they have been well briefed and have a good kit list, you can expect to find people, within the group who didn't quite understand what they were letting themselves in for and didn't quite understand the kit list.

Hazards may well pop up where you least expect them. Many of the walkers will not be seasoned walkers and stiles, small rock steps and loose ground can all create problems for some walkers. Medical issues can be serious and you need to be alert, you will need to act in some cases. It might be a straightforward 999 call. In the traditional hill and mountainous areas this will be a Police and mountain rescue call, but you'll need to check the protocol if you find yourself working in lower areas.

People; these events are about people. People will be walking for good reasons, strong emotional reasons in some cases. They will be trying to give something back to a charity with which they have an affinity. It may be a charity that cares for, or has cared for, a close relative, you may need to be sensitive. You cannot doubt the motivation of the participants and far more often than not, you meet some of the loveliest people. As a Mountain Leader you do need to be able to talk to and listen to people, these events provide a celebration of your small talk skills. There may be occasion where you need to stop someone. They will not want to end the walk early. It might be that you become the decision maker and by taking the decision away from them, you will be doing them a favour. "They wouldn't let me continue" is actually easier for them to take home than "I couldn't do it". It's a fun role and more often than not you'll have a really nice time, in nice places meeting new people. You could end up dealing with some medical issues though, so be prepared. I challenge you to get one bit of environmental awareness into every participant with whom you hold a conversation.

Top tips from Mountain Leaders

One of my tips would be to learn to use a radio. This may seem simple enough, but learning how to use a radio and learning what information is relevant to support staff on the ground is very useful. Learn the local names of places on a map which often represent key points of reference on a walk, such as 'hole in the wall', 'crossroads, 'first junction' etc. Being able to relay quickly where your groups is, is vital, not only to support staff on the ground but other Mountain Leaders who are also on the event. I was quite awkward when I first used a radio, but knowing how to use one, what to say and give your location is essential, it's a skill and is relevant to your group, other Mountain Leaders and support staff on the event.

Clare Iley

Striding edge on Helvellyn, the tricky downclimb.

Working as freelancer

Working as a freelance Mountain Leader either full-time or part-time has become much more popular in recent years, and so it should. Some leaders set up their own business and advertise through a website and social media, others are happy to work for a range of providers. Realistically, even if you set up your own company, you will need to work for other companies while your business gets established.

Working as a freelancer has lots of advantages such as:

- Freedom to choose your working hours.

- More flexibility can give you a better work-life balance.

- Control over your career and the type of work you do.

- No office politics – you are your own boss.

On the other hand you need to be aware of:

- Not taking on too much work (there is a fear in the early days of saying no to work).

- You need to be proactive to find work.

- There is no employer pension or holiday pay.

- You're responsible for filing returns and paying your tax.

- You might need to chase up late payments from customers.

- Book keeping (list income and expenditure on a spreadsheet to start with).

- You'll need to buy all your own kit.

- You'll need insurance.

- You can end up working every weekend.

Typically you'll be a sole trader and responsible for making a tax return. It's well worth getting some advice on how to do this early on. There are apps to help nowadays but there's nothing like a using a real person, an accountant, to get you started. It's a bit strange working out what you can and can't put down against tax. Here are the rules www.gov.uk/expenses-if-youre-self-employed. It's a 'mind melt' working out which year you are in, which year you are paying tax for and which year you are doing the books for, I advise you to seek help.

You will need to manage your own PR though social media. This can be very time consuming and it will need attending to before, after and during every event you run. Some social media posts will sink without trace, others might see a healthy return on your time investment. Some might lead to further publicity as they get picked up by busier sites. Blogging is a key way to get your messages out. Some of the most successful users of social media are the vloggers and the podcasters. You will need to find what works for you as not every medium is right for every person. Have a think about the channels your prospective customers might be using. Have a look around the usual sites and see who pops up most frequently. Try to work out what they are doing and how you can raise your profile. The algorithms dictating what type of posts are more prominent are a moving feast and if you are struggling there are experts out there who can help you.

You will also need to monitor and check your kit, manage your diary, find new types of business and let people down from time to time, how you do this will lead into whether or not they ask you to work for them again. If you are working with young people you might need to have a DBS check, you might even need an ALAA licence, both these can easily be checked online. You will need insurance but the Mountain Training Association is a very good one-stop shop for this. You will be responsible for knowing when you need to renew your first aid certification.

DBS and ALAA

The Disclosure and Barring Service (DBS) helps employers make safer recruitment decisions each year by processing and issuing DBS checks for England, Wales, the Channel Islands and the Isle of Man. There are separate services in Scotland and Ireland that do the same thing. DBS also maintains the Adults' and Children's Barred Lists, and makes considered decisions as to whether an individual should be included on one or both of these lists and barred from engaging in regulated activity. Visit the gov.uk website to find out more.

An Adventure Activities Licence (ALAA) is required by anyone providing facilities for adventure activities to young people under the age of 18 in return for payment. Facilities for adventure activities means facilities that consist of some element of instruction or leadership, around caving, climbing, trekking and watersports. Visit the HSE website to find out more.

THE MOUNTAIN LEADER

Top tips from Mountain Leaders

Keep your paperwork in order. Keep your accounts up to date, as it can be a real pain at the end of the year trying to balance the books for that dreaded Tax self-assessment. Having an updated CV means that you are quick off the mark when a job advert that you like comes out. Having an up-to-date annual, safeguarding policy and DBS certificate, first aid certificate, mental health first aid certificate, clean driving licence with D1 (minibus) on your licence, shows that you're keeping ahead of the game, and definitely keep your DLOG (digital logbook) up to date.

Darren Parkinson

I also spend a lot of time on preparation and pre-visits to locations I want to use. I make sure I can park where I need to and at what time I need to be there to ensure that. I look to see if it is possible to get to work on the bus (it actually is sometimes). I always have a plan B. Communicating with your customers is easy with email, but it can be time consuming. Online booking systems which integrate with your website work really well, as do stand-alone ones, but they do cost.

One thing you must not do is canvass for your own customers when working for other people. What you'll actually find is other people doing the same as you will be really helpful. It's a strange world where people are technically in competition at times, but still remain best of friends and supportive of each other. This will come as a great relief, as being a sole trader can actually be quite lonely at times. You have to do everything yourself, on your own. You need to be open and honest with the people you live with, you need to lay down some personal ground rules about how often you check social media and your emails. Use holiday messaging when you know you won't be able to respond to emails. There is always stress that someone will write something bad about you on social media, hence your obsession with regular checks. If you've done your job well, you'll have more supporters than detractors. Every time you post, or email or speak in public, think about how this will be received by those people who you hope might employ your services. You need opinions, you need your own USP (unique selling point), you have to have confidence in assertions you make, but you need to be reasonable and open minded. I guess a hint of arrogance is required to be sure you are offering the right product at the right time in the right place to the right people. I was once told that if it is something you like and you enjoy then others will too, they are your customers. Good luck with it.

Top tips from Mountain Leaders

Do not feel isolated and alone, there is support at every point.

Andy Merrick

LEADERSHIP – STYLES AND MODELS

There is a great deal of theory about leadership. I've tried to condense an enormous amount of study into what might be relevant and useful for you to refer to when leading in the mountains. Think about things beforehand but, if nothing else, these notes on styles and models of leadership will give you a framework for reflection.

> **Leadership behaviours 'on the hill'**
>
> When you get to a stile always gather on the other side. When a section of the walk ends at a stile always get the group to go over the stile as they finish the leg. This means that when you start off again, you'll start off together and you won't be waiting for the group to climb the stile. This will avoid introducing a delay which, straight away, splits the group.

Leadership styles

In its simplest form the styles of leadership can vary from the 'laissez faire' approach at one end of a spectrum to autocrat at the other. No one should sit on either end of this spectrum, at least not all the time! You must let your group take part in all aspects of the expedition, you must fully brief them about where you are going, how long it will take and the subsequent decisions you have to make around achieving those goals. You'll only get 'buy in' for any changes in plans if you have your team onboard. Unlike in some fields, you need to be their friend and confidant, you need to know about their health, about their worries, things they might not share with everyone.

Leadership spectrum

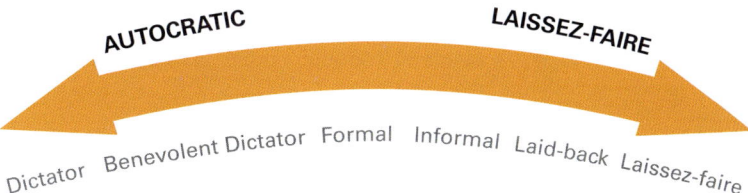

On the other hand there will be times when you will need to be autocratic. You will need to talk sternly to someone in your group, it may be along the lines of showing command in a deteriorating situation where you really need to get a move on. It may be in a safety situation, someone wandering near an edge, you'd rather they stayed away from. In these cases a firm command may well be what is required, but it'll only work if you know the person's name. "Oi you," has never been a great communication strategy.

Leadership models

Below are two useful models that illustrate a practical approach to leadership.

INSPIRE

Mountain Training has adapted the INSPIRE model for transformational leadership. There are some great resources on their website for working through this model.

- **I**nspire and motivate your followers with a unified vision
- **N**urture an environment of team-focused goals
- **S**et the example you want to see in your followers
- **P**raise, and give constructive feedback to help your followers develop
- **I**nsist on setting high standards, relative to each individual
- **R**ecognise and respond to each individual's needs
- **E**ncourage followers to create and implement their own solutions

Inspiration

Inspiration comes from optimism. Turn the negative into a positive. Always try to look on the bright side, be a glass-half full person rather than a glass-half empty one. On the other hand, optimism can be a bit wearing. Nobody likes to hear: "oh it's just round the corner now", when it really isn't. Flick back to your chat on timings and throw the ball back to them; if there is still an hour to go they might be looking at a false summit thinking it's the top, you do need to be realistic and honest sometimes. We've all been disappointed by another corner or indeed, another false summit.

Nurture

Nurture the team. Converse with them and share with them. Good briefings, asking for feedback, and knowing who they are will all help.

Set the example you want to see in your followers

Setting an example probably should go without saying but do think about your behaviours? It's not just about appearance, it's about the way you respect people, use language carefully and trust people.

Praise, and give constructive feedback to help your followers develop

Good feedback is often quite tricky to deliver, but a dialogue with your group should suffice on a day long walk. Do give praise where you can, but you must be honest too. You may need to tweak your plan later in the day and if you spent the morning telling someone how amazing they are, then it might not go down so well if you basically tell them they aren't strong enough to complete the desired route.

Insist on setting high standards, relative to each individual

High standards should be apparent in your role modelling, but never underestimate people and give each individual the opportunity to shine whenever the opportunity presents itself. Know their names (I may have said that before!).

> **Top tips from Mountain Leaders**
>
> Look the part. Apparently people make their mind up about a person within the first few seconds, so little things like having a shave, having clean boots, being dressed correctly may help the clients make their mind up about you and help create some subconscious confidence in you.
>
> Darren Parkinson

Recognise and respond to each individual's needs

Upon meeting a new group you will inevitably form an early opinion of the capabilities within the team based on first impressions. This is normal, but you need to constantly re-evaluate what you are thinking. Don't rely on those snapshot early judgements, engage a growth mindset and constantly evaluate the team, their aptitude, appetite for adventure, and their ability to succeed.

Encourage followers to create and implement their own solutions

Rather than giving answers to problems try to get anyone in the group with a problem to come up with the solution. Consider sharing the problem and see if the group can help with a solution, this is teamwork. Sometimes it will be down to you though, you are the expert. Just don't jump in too quickly like a proper 'know it all'. Give them a chance to work it out. Nudge them gently in the right direction if you can and never be condescending.

THE MOUNTAIN LEADER

> **Note for Assessors**
>
> Assessing leadership can be difficult. You may need to frame the assessment with some questions about leadership characteristics or leadership styles. A home paper task can flag this up well but do consider something of this nature after day one of the assessment. The candidates can then model the behaviours they have described to you. You are looking for someone who can lead in a manner which will inspire others to follow them. Do you see evidence of role modelling, engagement with the group and use of names? Can you work against a checklist of leadership behaviours that they have created? Look for evidence of the INSPIRE model having influenced their thinking, look for good leadership behaviours as highlighted in this chapter. If in doubt, reread the syllabus, if someone is not convincing as a leader then you must have the confidence, and evidence, to either defer or fail the candidate. You must, however, match this deferral with words from the syllabus e.g. *"The candidate has not, consistently, made suitable route choices or revised routes where necessary to manage risk."*

> **Leadership behaviours 'on the hill'**
>
> If you are feeling cold then you can be sure someone else in the group is too. Stop and adjust clothing. Make sure everyone is adjusting their clothing at the same stop if at all possible.

CLAP

The acronym CLAP is one that has come from paddle sports. It's very much about safety management, but it does encapsulate a lot of what we have been taking about in this chapter. It's also short and snappy.

Communication

Paddlers talk about having a visual signalling system. This is because of the noise of water and the fact that the leader could be bodily out of sight and might need to wave a paddle. How would this translate to a mountain situation? We mostly use quiet, but clear, verbal communication. A well timed shout might be applicable, but perhaps think of a signing system if you let some of the faster ones go on ahead. I have used mobile phones in some situations too.

Communication also refers to such things as the importance of briefings and having a conversation with / getting to know the members of your group.

Leadership

A kayak leader on the sea, using the CLAP leadership model.

Line of sight

Pretty much as it says on the tin. Do you know where everybody is? Who's in front of you? Who's behind you? How far away are they? Can you see them? Can you communicate with them? Watch out for people sneaking off, maybe for a sneaky smoke or perhaps just to go to the loo. Out of sight, is most definitely not out of mind. Where is everybody in my group?

Avoidance is better than cure (or even a rescue)

Back to the planning. Are you doing the right thing, in the right place with the right group at the right time with the right kit? A fun (if that's appropriate here) theory to use is the Lemons Theory (see below). Keep looking ahead, what could happen next, what will happen next?

Position of maximum usefulness

Most of the time it doesn't matter too much where you are within the group. Moving about within the group chatting to everybody is the ideal, as long as you know where everybody is. There are times however, when you need to be in the front, you need to be steering the group, micro-route finding and ready to spot. Make sure, particularly as it gets steeper or route finding gets trickier, that you are in the right place in the group.

The Lemons Theory

I have to admit to some confusion when I first heard the Lemons Theory. It comes from the lining up of fruit, in this case lemons, on a slot machine (sometimes known as a one-armed bandit). Not being familiar with these gambling machines, I didn't understand how lining up lemons would be bad. It turns out that lining up the lemons on a slot machine isn't a bad thing! So why lemons? I like lemons, but the word lemon has been used to describe something that isn't sweet, on the understanding that sweet is good and a lemon is a dud.

This convoluted background helps us to understand why, in 1993, a Kiwi, named Catherine Haddock framed the Lemons Theory. Each lemon represents something not good, if you get more than one thing that is not good, your lemons start to line up. For us, leading in the mountains, we can deal with the odd lemon. We can fix a boot, we can change our route, we can provide extra kit, a spare hat for example, but when these negatives start to collect, it leads to the lemons lining up. Only in this case the 'jackpot' is some sort of accident or misadventure. You'll see this happening in some of the stories recounted in this book. Watch out for the lemons. Accidents in the hills rarely have one causational factor.

Applying the Lemons Theory

Here are two real life case studies in which the lemons all lined up. Should the Mountain Leader have used the rope, or should they have counted the lemons lining up and made some different decisions?

1. The Llanberis Mountain Rescue Team was called to assist a teenager with a suspected back injury following a tumbling fall on Crib Goch. The group had been carrying expedition bags with the intention of crossing Crib Coch and Yr Wyddfa to then wild camp on the south side of the mountain. The group were inexperienced in the mountains and struggled with the terrain. They were climbing down a rock step between the pinnacles which was damp and had some loose rock. The group were close together on the rock step and one member fell and crashed into another member of the group, which resulted in both of them tumbling down a gully. The rescue team were called as there was a suspicion of spinal injuries. The rescue was a difficult one to manage as both casualties required medical assistance and the rest of the group were, understandably pretty shocked at what had happened.

2. A leader with a small group was working their way up the north ridge of Tryfan. It was early spring and cold. Looking up at the ridge, there were no signs of any winter conditions, however the higher peaks in the area did have a dusting of snow above 900m.

   "I was out with two adults on a mountain skills course and a Mountain Leader with their team was ahead of us for most of the duration. What was noticeable throughout the journey was the leader was struggling to manage the group effectively, with instructions often being ignored by the group. Higher up the scramble, the leader was getting increasingly flustered over which route to take. We were

taking a fairly adventurous line which was ideal for my clients and we soon lost sight of the other group. At around 800m we were finding snow and ice patches on ledges which had not been visible from below. It was manageable, but required more care and consideration.

I topped out on a short section to see the leader over to one side on top of a difficult rock step, frantically shouting instructions to the group who were following up the rock step. It was a serious situation and one that was difficult to watch. A fall from there would be very serious. I was unable to assist at that moment, but with my clients we made our way over to the leader. By the time we got there I asked the leader if they were ok and if they would appreciate some assistance. The group had all made it up the rock step by this point (thankfully). The leader was embarrassed and said they were finding the route much harder to follow than the previous time they'd been here, which, it turned out, was only once before. I suggested that they could follow me and my team to the summit, which they were very pleased to do. On the summit I went to over to check how the leader was feeling. The leader was much happier now and admitted that the group's behaviour had distracted his attention from the route finding. I asked about the rock step and whether he considered stopping and dropping a rope down to the team to safeguard them up. The response was 'on my ML I was told not to use the rope unless it's an emergency', 'I was scared to use it in case I got in trouble."

Bryn Williams of www.bwmountaineering.com

> **Note for Trainers**
>
> You might like to take some laminated cards (see next page) on the hill. Discuss how these factors could be applied when leading in the mountains and how they might help mitigate against the lemons lining up.

Llyn Idwal, Llyn Ogwen and Tryfan.

THE MOUNTAIN LEADER

Coach-speak

Much of what we do as Mountain Leaders can be described as coaching. Certainly, as we become more comfortable in the leadership role and start to make decisions about how people within our groups can progress to independence, we are moving beyond the realms of simple leadership. Coaching adventure sports has been an academic study for many years, now there are boatloads of papers and a fair few books on the subject.

To most of us they are hard work to read, but it's a good thing they are there. The authors are constantly explaining that we make decisions about the progress of those we influence, in an environment which is potentially hazardous. It wouldn't be a great navigation lesson if you walked off a cliff or someone in your group slipped and slid a long way down a steep, wet grassy slope. It is because of the requirement of 'situational awareness' that the relationship between the people we lead and the changing nature of the environment around us presents challenges which go beyond those of the everyday sports coach. Typically, we will be making decisions around the location we are operating in that respond to the prevailing environmental conditions, and the changing needs of our group and the individuals within it.

Leadership behaviours 'on the hill'

Mountain leadership is about caring for people and caring for places. Demonstrate that care throughout the day.

Key points to use as a discussion point. This can be laminated to take out on hill.

GOOD LEADERS	CLAP
The INSPIRE Model	**C**ommunication
Inspire and motivate your followers with a unified vision	**L**ine of sight
Nurture an environment of team-focused goals	**A**voidance of hazard
Set the example you want to see in your followers	**P**osition of maximum usefulness
Praise, and give constructive feedback to help your followers develop	**Leadership spectrum**
Insist on setting high standards, relative to each individual	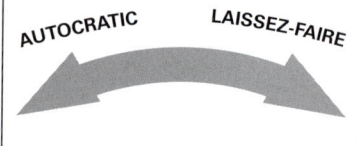 AUTOCRATIC — LAISSEZ-FAIRE
Recognise and respond to each individual's needs	
Encourage followers to create and implement their own solutions	

THE LEGAL BIT

Leadership changes you as a hillwalker. Once, you were walking without a care or a worry, but now you are someone who has responsibilities. You will always have these. In law, regardless of payment, by the very nature of your experience and qualification you will have a duty of care to your group and to other people. The key phrase in health and safety law is 'reasonable precautions'. Should you be unfortunate enough to be involved in a mishap on the hill then you may be asked to explain the reasonable precautions you took to attempt prevention of said mishap. A court of law will use expert witnesses to ascertain whether or not these reasonable precautions were just and sufficient. Failure to prove that you took all reasonable precautions is negligence and a failure in your duty of care. It is rarely a case of there being one person to blame. An adult is subject to the 'In volenti non fit injuria' principle. This literally means that someone who chooses to partake in an activity, knowing the risks, is, at least partly, responsible for their own safety, as long as they follow your guidance. Hence, the importance of properly informed consent. The leader has more responsibility with younger people and under 12 they have whole responsibility. Young people assume more responsibility every two years until aged 18, when they are deemed adults and can take full responsibility for their own actions.

The Cairngorm tragedy

During the November of 1971 six 15-year-olds from Edinburgh and their two leaders were crossing the Cairngorm Plateau when the weather deteriorated. They sought refuge from the storm by heading towards the (now removed) Curran Shelter near to Lochan Buidhe. They failed to find the shelter. Their failure to find the shelter was fatal for five of the teenagers and one of the leaders.

It is a very sad story. The inquest refused to put the blame on any individual, but big lessons were learnt. The parents of the deceased had not been fully informed about the nature of the trip. The party started out late. The experienced leader took another group separately; they found the Curran Shelter then descended first thing in the morning. The severity of the conditions was, although forecast, underestimated. The Cairngorm Plateau is no place to be in a storm. It was thought that the existence of high shelters made matters worse. Instead of descending, the group went in search of the shelter. Finding a small shelter in drifting snow, high winds and poor visibility would challenge anybody. It's a story that gave a higher profile to the mountain training qualifications, the shelters up high were removed and informed consent became a requirement. Interestingly, no laws were introduced. The efforts of those involved were recognised, the leaders tried hard to retrieve the situation and the mountain rescue teams pushed the limits to get to the parties. There was some poor luck involved for sure and before being too critical, we must ensure we learn the lessons from incidents such as these ourselves.

The Lyme Bay tragedy

In March of 1993, eight school children and their two teachers were led by two instructors on a kayaking expedition into Lyme Bay, on England's south coast. Four of the children drowned as the sea was too rough for the craft and kit they were using. Waves soon swamped the boats and the youngsters ended up in the water being blown further offshore. The instructors accompanying the group were not sufficiently experienced or qualified to cope with the situation. The manager of the centre organising the trip was found culpable. He was charged with and convicted of corporate manslaughter. There was a series of failings of which the young instructors found themselves caught up in and part of. The centre had sent out two inexperienced, essentially unqualified, instructors with a novice group, in unseaworthy craft, with no spray decks, inadequate buoyancy and no basic training. The sea state was relatively calm close-in but there was an offshore breeze and conditions were less benign further out. There were delays in calling for help as the young instructors had no radio and no flares. This terrible tragedy led to the licensing of commercially provided, adventurous activities for under 18-year-olds.

The Helvellyn Affair of 2020 – a press release from the Health and Safety Executive

On 5 March 2020, the group of 13, Year 10 pupils from The Gateshead Cheder school were on an organised trip to Helvellyn in the Lake District, led by one teacher and a teaching assistant. Weather conditions on the day were cold and icy. Despite reviewing the Lake District Weatherline report, which stressed the dangers to those ascending above the snow line, the school decided the trip should still go ahead as planned. Their route included ascending from Wythburn via Birk Side, and descending Helvellyn via Browncove Crags.

Despite the winter conditions many of the school children did not have suitable equipment, a number of them were wearing school shoes and school trousers; and others were wearing trainers. In winter conditions it is essential that hikers wear full winter clothing, including mountain boots, and that those venturing above the snowline carry appropriate equipment including ice axes and crampons.

Leadership

The adults leading the trip had no formal qualifications in mountain leadership or any experience of mountain environments in winter conditions. The party had a map but relied on a smartphone app as a compass.

During their ascent, at least two members of the public warned the Gateshead Cheder party to turn back, but the group continued their ascent and managed to reach the summit of Helvellyn without incident. However, as the party made their descent, they inadvertently ventured off the path and unknowingly began traversing the west face of Helvellyn towards a section of steep terrain featuring vertical rock faces of around 20 metres in height.

While descending, one of the pupils slid on the ice and fell several metres sustaining minor cuts. This caused another pupil to panic and run from the group down the mountain. The two adults remained with the injured pupil and the other school children. By this time, it had begun to get dark and the temperature was dropping.

The party were eventually located and rescued by Keswick Mountain Rescue Team, who cut steps into the snow to assist the party back to the path and down the mountain. The other pupil was lucky enough to make it back down the mountain and was found by members of the public.

An investigation by the Health and Safety Executive (HSE) found that neither of the adults with the party had the appropriate skills, knowledge and experience to lead the trip, and that the school had not taken advice from a suitably competent person to plan or organise the excursion. There was no effective system to check the suitability of the clothing and equipment the children had with them and no effective contingency plan in place if conditions became too difficult to proceed.

The Gateshead Cheder Limited of Bede House, Tynegate Precinct, Sunderland Road in Gateshead pleaded guilty to breaching sections 2(1) and 3(1) of The Health and Safety at Work (etc) act 1974. The school was fined £30,000 and ordered to pay a victim surcharge of £181 and costs of £4,574.90.

Speaking after the hearing, HSE inspector Stephen Garner said:
"On this occasion, none of the party came to serious harm, however, the school were aware of the weather and ground conditions, but decided to proceed without the appropriate planning, equipment, or suitably trained leaders. Those taking part in the trek that day were placed in serious danger and there was a clear failing by the school to adopt sensible precautions to ensure their safety.

THE MOUNTAIN LEADER

> *Excursions into mountains, particularly in winter, need to be led by people with the appropriate skills, knowledge and experience. If a school does not have access to the necessary expertise in house, then licensed adventure activities providers are available to manage the technical aspects of this type of trekking activity."*
>
> He added: *"This incident was entirely avoidable. HSE recognises the benefits of outdoor learning activities including those involving hiking or trekking in mountain environments, however schools need to take sensible and proportionate measures to control the risks involved. This trip should not have gone ahead without such measures in place."*

Care

It is hard to pin down leadership characteristics and behaviours for Mountain Leaders. It is hard to quantify them. It is an important conversation and a journey through some of the issues will enhance clarity about expectations and working as a team. For me, the bottom line is **care**. If in doubt, if you are confused or if you are feeling a bit overwhelmed (and this works for trainees, Mountain Leaders, Trainers and Assessors) think **care**. **Care** for yourself, look after number one. **Care** for your group as a team and as individuals, know their names, listen to them. **Care** for the places you visit, know about them, know how they got like this and the issues they face. **Care** for other people, keep your impact as minimal as you can, be quiet and respect other land users. **Care** about what we do, how we do it and where we do it.

Take care.

A CHECKLIST FOR LEADERS

Here's a checklist to help you to prepare for leadership on the hills.

- Are you cognisant with the appropriate safety and safeguarding policy?

- Are you operating within your guidelines?

- Are you operating within your competence?

- Are you operating in a manner appropriate to the participants' experience and ability?

- Do you have their informed consent?

- Have you ensured that any personal equipment used by participants is suitable for the task and is in an acceptable condition?

- Is your kit and your group kit suitable for the task and in good working order?

- Does everyone have fluids and food?

- Have you given due regard to care of the environment and other users? Can you share any relevant codes of conduct with your group?

- Is the route matched to the group's ambitions rather than yours?

- Do you have a flexible route plan?

- Are you the sole leader? If so, have you informed the group of your needs and what to do in an emergency?

- Conduct dynamic risk assessments throughout the journey. Monitor your group and respond to change in them or the environment.

- Learn names, invest in your group, enable them, care for them.

- Impart knowledge, skills and enthusiasm while paying heed to safety matters.

- Make time for reflection and feedback.

> **Tips for Trainers of leadership**
>
> Model the checklist for leaders throughout the training course. Ask candidates to build this list into their action plans as a way of thinking.

Exploring the sinkhole and entrance to Great Douk Cave on Ingleborough.

What sort of things could go wrong and how do we deal with things if they do go wrong?

Hazards and Emergencies

Our mountains can be hazardous places, of this there can be little doubt. It is, however, an unusual occurrence for those hazards to be unmanageable with good judgement; this is what a Mountain Leader does. Hazard management is a constant interaction between place, people, weather and the kit we use to manage that interaction. That the mountains are as safe as they are, that we travel through them aware of, but not overawed by hazards, is down to our experience based judgements. We juggle a constantly changing set of factors as people tire, as weather changes or as the land becomes rougher. We need to stay alert and be vigilant, but keep the fears under control, typically nothing goes wrong and we all have a good day, but the environment commands, and deserves, our respect.

Looking back along Striding Edge from near the top of Helvellyn.

THE MOUNTAIN LEADER

The hazard management pyramid of constantly changing factors. We choose the place depending on the weather and equipment available to suit the needs of the people.

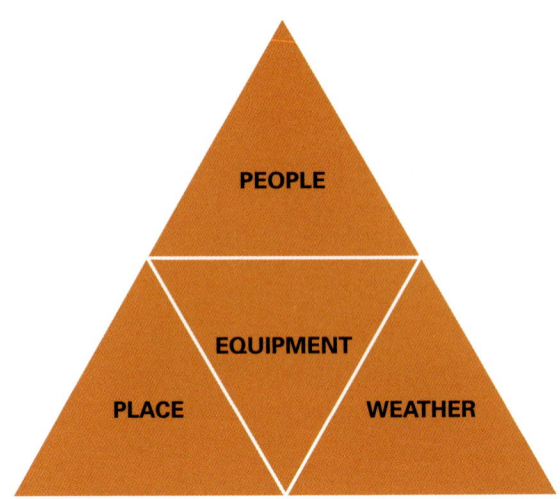

> **Top tips from Mountain Leaders**
>
> An experience of the outdoors that is challenging young people beyond their comfort zone is awesome and they will remember it for the rest of their lives. This experience may allow them to think they can achieve more than they ever thought possible and gain confidence from it, this is at the nub of any child's education.
>
> Paul Sanderson

What is a hazard?

Hazards are all relative in our mountains. As we've already seen our mountains are pretty safe places for people to be. You could easily argue that the hazards we discuss here are not really hazards. They only become a hazard when you add people to the equation. A cliff, for instance, is just a cliff sat on its own minding its own business. It is not a hazard. It only becomes a hazard if we wander near it, if we are disrespectful to it, or if we make poor decisions while in its vicinity. If you, and your group, stand close to the top of it in a position from which someone could slip, or if you stand at the bottom of it in a position whereby any falling object could land on you or one of your group, the situation will require some management from the Mountain Leader. So, avoid cliffs; easy? No not really, there are many paths that traverse above or below a cliff. Stay as clear as you can from the bottom, move carefully when above them.

Hazards and Emergencies

The Idwal Slabs (Rhiwiau Caws), a dangerous cliff to sit or stand below.

CASE STUDY – Idwal Slabs – don't sit here

There is a very busy path around Llyn Idwal in Cwm Idwal. Walkers use it to access the Glyderau, geographers use it to study the cwm and climbers use it to visit, amongst other crags, the cliffs of the Rhiwiau Caws, probably more widely known as the Idwal Slabs (the 'cheese slopes' is how the Welsh name translates). As you walk past (look out for the roche moutonnee on your right) you'll see climbers around the base of the slabs, mostly wearing helmets.

So, take the hint, don't, with your walking group, go to the base of the cliffs. Keep to the other side of the path away from the cliffs, it's easier to study the slabs and count the climbers from a little way back anyway. I've personally seen climbing kit, stones and sheep tumbling down this cliff, none of these are things you'd like to have land on your head. Avoid cliff bases if you can, if you can't, look up and check for people, check for sheep and check for goats. If it's windy be super careful and pass along as quickly as it is safe to do so. Look after your group, don't show off to them.

Hazard management

When qualified as a Mountain Leader, you should have the experience to avoid or manage hazards. Route finding and making choices appropriate to the group, your objectives and the prevailing conditions will always be more important than responding to hazardous situations as they may occur. Most hazards are predictable; indeed it may be part of your objectives to actually seek them out. Helping your group to understand the nature of upland hazards and how to avoid them is an important role of a Mountain Leader. Mountains do have steep ground on them though. A tongue in cheek definition of a mountain is that it's a hill that you can't afford to fall off because it might not end well – simplistic maybe, but better than arbitrary height delineations. In this section we'll look at hazards associated with the environment, the atmosphere, animals and those created by people. We'll look at ropework for Mountain Leaders and the management of incidents including first aid.

Dynamic risk assessment

In many ways this is the key element of a Mountain Leader's repertoire. The ability to make judgements on the hill in response to changing situations is absolutely key. Written pre-planned risk assessments are always a bit lame for walking in the mountains. Yes, you could turn your ankle on uneven ground, you could also turn it on a kerb stone, yes you could slip on wet rocks, you also can slip on a wet shop floor and so it goes on. People do not tend to fall of cliffs willy-nilly, what happens is people slip. The trick is to make sure you slip in the right place. So, you, as the leader, may well allow some slippage, as part of the learning experience in the right place. You cannot allow it in the wrong place, where there might be consequences. The thing is, where the right place is and where the wrong place is varies with the group and how fresh or tired they are. It varies with the prevailing weather conditions, as increasing wind or rain could increase the chance of a slip. You need to be expecting the unexpected at all times. Experienced Mountain Leaders are on the lookout for sloping bits of damp rock, especially if they might be a bit lichenous, in the wrong place these can trigger a bad fall.

Take the photos opposite. On the left, the bridge is safe (photo 1). It will be intimidating to some people, but it is dry, and the chances of a slip are minimal. A trip however is not out of the question, so speak to your group, get them to focus and all should be well. You do need to consider how bad things might be should someone fall off the bridge. There is potential for injury, but you'll be very unlucky for it to be serious. This looks, on this day, like an acceptable risk, probably less dangerous than crossing a road or climbing carpeted steps wearing socks (I bet you've done that and slipped!). Although the dangerous bit is actually none too obvious, the leader has spotted it. Can you see she's looking down at a sloping piece of rock which is damp? This is where a slip may occur. The persons following may be so relieved to be over the bridge that they cease to concentrate on their foot placements, and they stand on the sloping wet bit and slip. This is where the leader will station herself and she'll refocus attention and try to steer the group away from the sloping, wet rock.

Hazards and Emergencies

Photos 2 and 3 are a different proposition. Same bridge – different day. Clearly the bridge is wet, and a slip is possible. Clearly the consequences of a slip are potentially fatal as the speed and force of the water would carry a falling walker downstream and over a waterfall. I can also tell you it was extremely windy on this day which added to the seriousness of the situation. This is probably not the day to be taking a group over this bridge.

Clapper bridge over the Afon Llan on Yr Wyddfa. This area is often referred to as the 'Watkin path pools'.

Leadership behaviours 'on the hill'

Dynamic risk assessment is a constant process revolving around the group, the terrain and the weather.

Environmental hazards

Let's start by looking at identifying and dealing with, or avoiding, environmental hazards.

Route choice

Firstly, the big picture. When choosing the route up an area of rough ground, let's use the example of a ridge, you need to be able to 'read' the terrain. Look where the heather is growing. These areas are little grazed as even the sheep prefer to avoid them, this means they will be on the steep side for us and covered in straggly heather, which is also difficult to walk through. There may be some scree; look at the size of the scree. Large scree can be stable and easy to make progress on, though if it has not been trampled there could be unstable blocks awaiting the unwary. Small scree can be tough going, particularly with the less experienced, with much slipping, sliding and, potentially serious, dislodgment of rock onto people below or behind. Watch out for people putting their hands down, as fingers can be damaged by rolling stones. Rocky areas can be lovely, with a solid surface, which has good solid holds and great friction. On the other hand, it maybe loose, wet and have downward sloping strata.

A great clue as to what lies ahead is the colour of the rock. Wet rock is typically dark, light rock is typically dryer. Yes, this will vary with rock type and is harder to pick up on naturally dark rock, but try it out, look ahead. If the rock is dark it might be wet. If the rock is wet the grass to its side might be wet. If it's wet it might be slippery, but if it's light it might be dry, the grass could still be wet so the rock might give a better route.

One of the key skills a Mountain Leader needs to employ is looking ahead, constantly looking ahead. Gauge where you'll be in an hour, or in two hours. Observe the descent route and look for identifying features. But what are you looking for? Never have a fixed view. Think, *"I bet it goes that way,"* or *"I bet that bit is tricky,"* or *"I wonder if there is snow where I planned to go down?"* Look ahead, think ahead, what is going to happen? Theorise, keep an open mind.

Pick the best-looking line to match your group. It may not be about avoiding the rocky areas. Smooth, solid, well-weathered, rocky lines can often offer ease of travel with limited danger of a slip, what's more, height is gained quickly and progress is fun. If there are drops alongside, rather than trying to stay away from the drop, it can better to be closer to the edge where the going is good and upon which it is easier to make progress. Sometimes being further away from the edge on loose ground, or slippery, wet ground can actually be more hazardous. Wet grass can be deceptively dangerous and steep, wet grass (especially when it is short and sheep cropped) can be very slippery. You sometimes get a slippery, wet, top layer which is quite thin, on a harder, drier base; these conditions can be lethal as any slip will be accelerated when a victim slides down the grass.

Hazards and Emergencies

A – Looks steep and rocky here with dark vegetation in between. No obvious line. Might be able to weave through, but straggly heather, indicated by the dark vegetation, would make this uncomfortable.

B – Notice the darker vegetation on the steep ground. This is heather. It grows here, out of reach of sheep. If the ground is too difficult for sheep then it probably is not good terrain for walkers either.

C – Steep looking ridge with some rock protruding. Provides a nice ridge line. On checking the scrambling guide we find it's a grade two scramble. On checking local knowledge, however, we find this lower part of the ridge can be scrambled at grade one.

D – There's a stream in here and it doesn't look too steep. On closer inspection there is an old path up the side of the stream which might provide an interesting variation on the normal route.

E – From a distance this ridge line is grassier that the other potential routes meaning it's been sheep grazed, meaning it's probably of a more amenable angle. On looking at the map there is a path marked up this ridge. On the ground it is a made and maintained path.

F – It looks steep and rocky here. On checking the scrambling guide it's a grade two scramble. This is no place for walkers.

G – There looks to be some scope for a route here. There is a continuous line of scree up the back of the cwm. While face-on it looks quite steep, we know that slopes always look steeper face-on. While a route is probably possible here, one would have to wonder about how pleasant it would be, being on scree the whole way.

H – This is the line the path takes on the map so is an attractive proposition. There are clearly steep slopes either side of the ridge so some care and awareness of heights will be required.

THE MOUNTAIN LEADER

The leader looks back to check the group are following the chosen route.

Micro-route finding

Within any mountain journey you will constantly need to make micro-route finding decisions, left of this rock, right of that rock. It is when making these choices you have a lot of factors to weigh up quickly. You need to know your group, and will have tested them previously in safer locations where a slip would not present a serious threat. Perhaps you have done some movement skills on rocky terrain near a path, taught them how to smear with the sole of their boot or to edge their boot on smaller holds. At some stage you will have taught them to take small steps, making it easier to shift weight from one foot to the other. They will have learnt not to lean into the rock but to keep themselves upright, so their weight goes down the leg and through the boot to the rock. A weighted foot never slips ... All this will have been done, path-side, in a non-serious place. You will know the names of your group and you can coach, coax and cajole individuals as required.

On the north ridge of Tryfan a group has spread out to investigate micro-variations. Could you take any of these ways or would you steer your group to a particular one?

We are here, mostly, talking about terrain where you really want the group to follow your lead. So now the leader is, indisputably, leading from the front. The person immediately behind you will have a good view of where you are going, and number two and three should be able to follow. However, by the time it gets further down your group there can be a tendency for them to move away from your line. Is this a problem? Sometimes it isn't, but often it is. You need to be very wary of this and constantly be watching your group.

Hazards and Emergencies

After stepping through with the left foot the walker will be well balanced to place their right foot, rather than being in a rock 'hugging' position.

A zigzag approach to ascent will aid this process. It all too easy to say, 'watch out for this, don't slip here, mind that rock,' without being very specific about the hazard you are pointing out and how it should be tackled. It is instruction like this that can be lost as the message travels (or doesn't) to the back of the group. Think about who you want behind you, the fastest, the slowest, the weakest, the strongest? How do you arrange this in a sympathetic way, respecting people's modesty and apprehensions?

Starting off on the wrong foot

It's sometimes the case that to negotiate small steps it's best start with the 'wrong' foot. The right-hander will naturally lead with the right foot and the left-hander will naturally lead with the left foot. By pointing out which foot to start a rock step with the leader may well prevent their followers from tying themselves up in knots trying to place their next foot.

Take a look at the picture. As the walker has started on to the rock step with their left foot (not shown in the picture) they now have their right foot in the best position, on a good step, to swing the left leg through to the next obvious step. By stepping through here with the left foot they will be in a good balanced position, unhindered by the rock step to see where to put their right foot next. The alternative way round would see the walker in a position of hugging the rock, with less visibility to the next step.

Managing steep ground

Assuming you have chosen to lead your group into steep ground, be mindful that this is one of the areas that puts the mountain in the Mountain Leader qualification. While the Hill and Moorland leader should be able to see steep ground and walk around it without too much stress. The Mountain Leader needs to be able to not only travel through unavoidable steep ground themselves, but be able to lead groups safely, up, down and across it. This part of the qualification is very much about looking after people in ascent and descent on steep, sometimes loose, sometimes rocky terrain. You need to be able to pick the best route for your group and you need to spot them when appropriate.

Leadership on steep ground

On your Mountain Leader training, and assessment courses you would have been trained, and assessed, in how to lead people on steep ground, this will tend to be on ground beyond the path, rarely trodden ways (except by trainee and assessee Mountain Leaders!), it could involve scrambling of around grade one.

What does scrambling grade one mean?

The scrambling grading system was first codified by Steve Ashton for his 1980 volume *Scrambles in Snowdonia*. Steve defined three classes of scramble. His grade one scramble was a scramble from which it is easy to escape onto easier ground and would be a good route in descent. Unfortunately, his exemplar route was Bristly Ridge which is neither of the above and is often considered grade two nowadays! The BMC have suggested: *"A grade 1 scramble is essentially an exposed walking route. Most tend to be relatively straightforward with many difficulties avoidable."* In the preamble they do recognised hands will need to be used at some points and their exemplar routes are Crib Goch, Striding Edge and Jack's Rake.

The point is, scrambling grades were invented by one person and used by everyone else as a rule of thumb. They are not defined grades, into which hours of discussion by hundreds of scramblers have contributed, unlike rock climbing grades into which hours of disagreement has led to a consensus, mostly, on each grade.

Take scrambling grades with a pinch of salt. The cynic might suggest some ridges got a scrambling grade to make them eligible for the scrambling guidebook, others got grade one, based on tradition. I venture to suggest that the Deaer Ddu ridge on Moel Siabod is an awful lot easier than heading directly up the north ridge of Tryfan, both are grade one.

Scrambling on grade one terrain on Moel Siabod's Daear Ddu Ridge.

It is entirely up to you and your experience as to whether or not you choose to lead people on this terrain. For some people the north ridge of Tryfan and Crib Goch are bread and butter Mountain Leaders days, for others they are completely off limits. Remember, your Mountain Leader qualification is made up of an assessment process and your logbook; your logbook is who you are and what you have done. This is the crucial evidence to help decide whether or not you should be leading in such steep, and potentially consequential, places.

Leadership behaviours 'on the hill'

Match your route choice to the group, not too hard, not too easy. It's tempting to always take the easier way, but this isn't always the best for the group you are leading. Sometimes the perceived easy way has hidden dangers whereas the perceived hard way can actually be safer.

Hazards and Emergencies

Scrambling on grade one terrain on Helvellyn's Striding Edge.

Top tips from Mountain Leaders

With some groups, you can afford to give some leeway. It is their day so give them the tools and information that will help them to make informed choices and let them make the choices. Easier route, harder route, longer or shorter route, there are many different ways up so in a few different places give them options (want to go that way or this way?). I even let different members of the group go slightly different ways (within reason) so that everyone can get what they want and enjoy the day and freedom without feeling constantly restricted or herded.

Mladenka Hooper

When ascending steep ground, you will have all your attention either on your feet or on your group. You should be nervous, you should be alert, you should be working hard. So, don't forget to look at the view! Be mindful that exposure may have crept up on your group and stopping suddenly in an awkward position they could freeze. However, when you do get to a good stopping place, a nice commodious ledge, don't forsake the opportunity to take it all in and have a chat about the place you are in. Remember, you are here to inspire, we want people to love this place, care for this place, appreciate this place and think about returning for their own adventures. You are responsible for their future involvement in the uplands.

THE MOUNTAIN LEADER

Steps in spotting, showing height limits. In the first photograph we can see it is easy to spot someone. In the second picture, at this height different people of different builds may or may not be comfortable. In picture three the person ascending is too high for spotting.

Spotting

There are times where a slip could be dangerous. This is the time when spotting should be deployed. Spotting is not catching; it is merely preventing a slip becoming a fall. In the context of the Mountain Leader qualification it should only be done by the leader. If spotting is required then it is the leader's responsibility to get it right should it be needed; this can rarely be delegated. Spotting can be on a tricky step with a poor landing, or on an easy step but where a slip could have consequences, i.e. there is a big drop below.

When spotting, brace yourself, one foot in front of the other and push into the person you are spotting. Expect them to slip and you will be fine, any hesitancy will be cruelly punished.

One of the awkward areas surrounding spotting is the touching of people. Spotting usually takes place in public, in front of the group and this is a good thing. You must explain clearly what you are doing and why. It should make sense to the group. Try to touch, even a reassuring push, on their rucksack, before touching them directly. You can get a long way with the hips, maybe the thighs on smaller people, but avoiding the buttocks is preferable. I say preferable, but it may make more sense to push someone's

Hazards and Emergencies

buttocks than let them slide to a gruesome death. It will depend on your stature and the stature of those you are spotting as to what the height limits are. Generally, as someone's hips get out of your reach, they are really too high for safe spotting.

> **I remember ... spotting works**
>
> I was once heading up on to Mynydd Perfedd from the Nant Francon with an ML assessment group and we chose to go a slightly awkward way in order to do some ML ropework. I clearly remember being tied on at the bottom of a rock step and standing patiently to the side while my leader started up a slimy groove. Something inside me clicked. I untied the rope and stepped in below the groove in order to spot. My leader slipped, lost his footing and came down the groove, I stepped in, leaned in and pushed him back into the groove, I stopped the slip become a big slide; I had spotted him. As we drew breath I looked down at the long wet, smooth grassy slope below us and could only ponder what might have been. If I hadn't switched roles, from waiting patiently to actively spotting, then things could have turned out differently. Spotting works.

> **Leadership behaviours 'on the hill'**
>
> Spot in the right places. This is usually where a slip could become consequential because there is a drop, or steep grassy slope below the step.

Atmospheric hazards

While we deal with the weather, forecasting, and its influences on our chosen route for the day elsewhere, it's worth mentioning a couple of the dramatic atmospheric hazards here.

Be prepared to brace when you hear strong gusts of wind heading towards you.

Gusty wind

We'll obviously mention the wind in the weather chapter, but I just wanted to say here, listen out for gusty winds. Yes, listen out. You can hear them coming, sometimes you can watch them crossing the surface of water. It can be a ferocious noise, terrifying. If you hear it brace yourself, you know what's coming next and you need to be in a firm stance to resist being blown off your feet. Any wind over 30 or 40 mph has the strength to blow you over. Make sure you are not at the top of a cliff. I'm not the only one who's used a confidence rope on a member of my group in these conditions.

Lightning

Lightning is an unusual, but not unheard of, hazard in the British and Irish mountains. About two people a year are killed by lightning, that's a one in 33 million chance. In the event of lightning, standing on top of high things isn't wise.

If lightning threatens, act early and vacate any ridges you are traversing. If possible, head down into the valleys and get away from any high points that are more likely to attract a lightning strike.

People have been caught out when sheltering in a cave or below an overhang, as you are in the position of completing the electrical circuit from the lip to the floor. It's probably best to stay out in the open, but not be on the highest point on a ridge. If you are on a high point it is best to keep moving and head for a less exposed location. You may have a few scary moments.

Most fatalities have occurred when thunderstorms are forecast in the afternoon or the early evening. Should you suspect the risk increasing then decide early to go for shelter, as most people have been hit on their way to a sheltered location. If thunderstorms are forecast, reconsider your route plan.

Hazards under foot

These are hazards related to the ground on which we are walking.

Grass

It might seem strange to include grass as a hazard, but if you've ever found yourselves struggling through tussock grass you'll know why it makes this list. Tussock grass is typically purple moor grass of the Molinia family, and it's hated by farmers and walkers alike. It'll be in wet, boggy areas of acidic uplands. Do you balance on the tussocks, or do you try to step between them? Either way a turned ankle, a full-on fall or, at the very least, a wet foot are all possible consequences. Should you find yourself in a patch of tussock grass, reverse out and go around it.

Sheep cropped grass can be surprisingly slippery.

One of the most surprising and benign looking hazards is steeply sloping, short, sheep-cropped grass. This stuff can be lethal when it is wet, you get very little purchase, avoid if you can, especially when it's above cliffs.

Loose rock

I mentioned earlier about the dangers of sitting at the base of cliffs and we know that scree is characterised by loose rock, watch out for finger injuries here.

Hazards and Emergencies

If you find yourself on solid looking rock that doesn't mean there won't be any loose holds. You might need to teach your group how to check holds. Use a technique similar to that with which you check anchors for your Mountain Leader ropework; place a flat hand on the rock and tap next to it with the side of your clenched fist. Teach the group not to pull outwards on holds, but to try to press in and down on them. You may need to point out any holds to avoid. Be particularly mindful of this danger in the spring after a winter of freeze thaw.

Scree

Move well, move with care, look well to every step. A brilliant exercise for encouraging this in people new to walking in the mountains is to get them to walk silently. It's a trick stolen from teaching climbing when the instructors want the new climbers to focus on foot placement. For walkers on steep ground it works really well. The hardest place to do it is on scree, but this is potentially the place where a bit of stealthy movement will have the greatest application. It'll really get your group looking where they are putting their feet and transferring their weight more carefully.

Managing a group on scree is an area that has caused some confusion over the years. Clearly, we might like to avoid scree, but many of our popular mountain paths do cross scree. There is usually a pretty solid, well trafficked, way through, but not always. The key is to be aware of where falling stones might go. So, having people in line down the hill might not be a great idea. By walking one behind the other across a slope you ensure that no person is down slope of anyone else. On the ascent, keeping a group tucked in nice and close together will not allow any dislodged stones to gain momentum, but it may well be a stumbling person that lands on you rather than a rock. Still, if you are fairly close this shouldn't be too much of a problem.

A pair of walkers walking carefully, and silently, on scree.

A group being led safely across an area of scree.

THE MOUNTAIN LEADER

You may need to zigzag up or down a slope, particularly if it is in a gully. The group will need to cross the gully in a line, not one at a time as this is unnecessarily slow, then regroup on the other side as they progress up or down the slope. This ensures that no person is below another in the fall line.

Scree running, regarded as great fun years ago, is now frowned on, because of environmental damage, and you should really try to get your group over the scree with as little impact as possible.

Unseasonal snow patches

Sadly, not much of problem in Wales or England, but in Scotland you do need to be mindful of this. The ones that will catch you out are where a descent route has been banked out with snow at its top. This deep snow might well be quite hard and therefore slippery. You can often get round it, but proceeding onto it without an ice axe, and the skills to use one, might just be a rather stupid thing to do. Be prepared to have to change your route. It's not impossible to come across ice on paths, sometimes it's verglas, or black ice, you can usually walk around it, but be alert and careful.

This picture was taken in June in the Cairngorms. In some years there can be some quite challenging unseasonal snow patches. Typically, you can walk around them, but not always.

I remember ... a June snow patch

I remember going into the Cairngorms in June one year. My wife and I were keen to do a classic rock climb called Squareface. The guidebook suggested we locate the top of the route then 'walk down grass slopes to the base of the route'. Unfortunately, when we got there, and it was a long, long walk, the grass slopes were covered in hard snow, quite deep as well. We didn't have ices axes and probably should have changed our plans, but where's the adventure in that? We managed to get round, below the route, using our 'movement on steep ground skills'. We then had to scramble up some very unappealing terrain, loose, steep, gravelly and scary. That got us level with the start of the route, but with a snow patch to cross. We had the rope out by now and we improvised ice axes from stones to enable us to rope across the snow in some semblance of control. The climb was easy after that. We also got to use our 'navigating in poor visibility' skills to find the way off and back to the valley. A most excellent adventure, but well beyond the scope of ML!

Hazards and Emergencies

Water hazards including river crossings

Water is a killer. If you look at accident statistics on school trips, water and transport top the list of dangers. We're talking about fast flowing or deep water. Bogs are rarely a great threat to us, more an inconvenience that can be avoided. Should you stumble into a bog you can usually reverse out, pride hurt, but we are not in the realms of quicksand here.

Cold water swimming

Swimming can be a brilliant thing to do on a hot day. Many upland lakes are shallow, the water warms up nicely and they are very safe. On a hot, summer day there is nothing more refreshing that a swim in a fresh, mountain lake. It's part of the long history of mountaineering. However, I'd tend to avoid reservoirs. They never seem to warm up and there can be some weird currents where water is extracted – plus it is drinking water!

Geoffrey Winthrop Young wrote, in his 1920 book, *Mountain Craft*: *"… when the main effort of the day is past, and the body has no fear of calling on its last reserves, the bathe on the descent is an indescribable delight and refreshment."* He goes on to say: *"… at such natural moments of interruption the bracing impetus of a bathe will help to regulate our circulation anew and to store mind and nerves with new energy for the new commencement,"*

Legions of contemporary 'wild' swimmers' would see the utmost sense in Young's sentiment. Let's say the cold-water swim is our equivalent of the athlete's ice bath. It is highly likely that you will have someone who enjoys the benefits of outdoor swimming in your group given its growth in popularity.

Considerations for outdoor swimming

- Is the water moving?
- How deep is it?
- Can you see the bottom?
- Is the bottom, muddy, gravelly or rocky?
- Does it look clean?
- Is it easy to get in and out of?
- Does the swimmer have a plan to change and have appropriate after wear?
- Is the swimmer experienced at cold water immersion?

People, and especially mountaineers, have been open water swimming for years. It should not be dangerous. Be very careful of any currents. Be aware that mountain lakes often drop off steeply and therefore get colder sooner (is it a corrie lake or a ribbon lake?). Experienced swimmers will get in the water slowly and acclimatise gradually, they do not jump in. Jumping in comes with a whole new range of problems associated with cold water shock and the depth of the water, avoid this if you can. Finally limit the amount of time in the water.

In group situations people often stay in longer than they should. There can be a euphoric feeling as the water works its magic, but if you stay in too long then the blood flow to the limbs will slow down to protect the core. When the blood flow returns to the limbs, they will cool the blood and as this cooler blood returns to the core you experience the 'afterdrop'. Limiting the amount of time in the water will reduce the possibility of an 'afterdrop' but should someone in your group experience this, then make sure they have changed, had a warm drink and move them slowly to a safer place. On reaching safety they should allow their body to warm slowly. Having a shower straight away is not recommended as this increases the rate of blood flow to the core and can actually increase the effect of the 'afterdrop'.

If you have members of your group who want to swim, then ask them if they are aware of the 'afterdrop'. Make sure any such swimming is well controlled and ideally near the end of your route. If this all seems like a strange world for the Mountain Leader, then think about the 'afterdrop' as an early stage in the onset of hypothermia. Remember, uncontrolled shivering is a danger sign and should be treated as moderate hypothermia.

You will find that open water swimming features high on any list of risky activities, but then so does hillwalking! You may find that without a

Open water swimming is very fashionable and irresistible for some. Rather than a blanket 'no', it's important that the Mountain Leader can ask the right questions about the activity. While the Mountain Leader remains in charge, the experience of the individual should be respected.

Hazards and Emergencies

lifeguard of some sort you are actually prohibited from allowing your group to swim, depending on the organisation they are from. A school group, for instance, may well be very unlikely to have permission to swim. With a group of youngsters, you'll find issues of drying and changing clothes to be troublesome too. I hate to say it, but if you take a group of youngsters swimming you could find yourself in 'hot' water.

Flooding

Flooding does provide a real hazard for us, especially in the remoter parts of Scotland where river crossings can be the norm. You need to be aware of the effects of heavy rainfall on your chosen route and any necessary river crossings, and pay even more attention than normal to the weather forecast.

Other aspects of flooding to consider are the impacts on areas of floodplain, particularly if you are camping. Make sure you understand what a floodplain is. Floodplains are there to flood, and they will flood in heavy rain.

A group caught out by rising river levels in the Nant Francon, Eryri.
Photo: Alan Pritchard

River crossing

River crossing is potentially a hazardous business. Anything that is around knee depth, if it's moving, is getting into the realms of being able to knock you off your feet. It is worth going well out of your way to avoid this type of crossing. In fact the rules of river crossing can be remembered as the three 'D's. **Don't do it, Delay or Detour**. A delay is often much simpler than you might think, most of our rivers are quite 'flashy' this means they rise quickly, but they also recede quickly too. If you wait an hour, things might look different, if you camp and try again in the morning then all maybe well. A detour to a safer crossing point may well make a lot of sense. Typically, if you go upstream there will be less water in the river, and with every tributary you

THE MOUNTAIN LEADER

This may be the easiest way to cross some water, keep your boots dry and just head across in bare feet.

cross the river will have less water in it. Conversely, sometimes if you go downstream the river may get wider, shallower and have some islands due to braiding which make it easier to cross. Be very careful of river bends, the water is usually deeper, and faster flowing on the outside of the bend and the bank is often steeper.

When, and if, you do have to cross a river, it is not always bad news. The tough decision is whether or not you can do it in your bare feet or whether it'll be safer to keep your boots on. If you think it's over boot height, and you can see the bottom, and the bottom looks OK to walk on, then there is absolutely nothing wrong with crossing the river in your bare feet. I've done this many times, and it's a lot nicer having wet feet that dry pretty quickly before putting your boots on again, than having wet boots on for the rest of the day. If, however you are not sure about the riverbed then keeping your boots on will be safer. Helen Howe of Snowdonia Mountain Skills recommends carrying a pair of sandals when walking in Scotland for this very purpose. Wet feet in wet boots are not the end of the world, it's just a bit uncomfortable for a while, not too bad if you're leaving the hill, but if you are at the start of a multi-day journey than it would not be what you want. Wet feet sat in boots that aren't drying can lead to blisters or, over several days even trench foot.

One school of thought is that you should loosen off your rucksack straps and undo your waist belt before heading into the water. The thinking being that you can abandon your rucksack easily should you need to. Don't however, be too hasty to completely get rid of your rucksack, if you do find yourself off your feet and floating downstream then your rucksack is actually going to be pretty buoyant, given that it is filled with waterproof, sealed bags. You may not however, want it strapped to your back. But, if a river is flowing with such velocity that you are having a discussion about what to do with your rucksack, then it is probably not safe to cross.

Hazards and Emergencies

Crossing a river as a three, each person takes in turn to move supported by the other two, the groups tend to rotate as the river is crossed.

Crossing in a line is great for those not at the front!

Crossing in a triangle means weaker people can be protected from the current, it takes a great deal of coordination though. Here you can see the leader using a pole for extra support and balance on the rough riverbed.

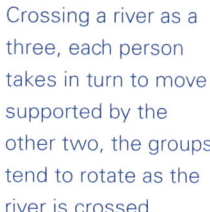

There was a time when ropes were used for crossing rivers by Mountain Leaders. Ropes are not now, part of the Mountain Leader syllabus for river crossings. Ropes and water are dangerous mix. Anyone tethered to a rope and caught in moving water has a tendency to be dragged under the surface; not at all ideal, I'm sure you will agree.

On your Mountain Leader training course you will have been shown some alternative ways of supporting each other as your cross a river. These are all useful to know and I find that some people prefer one way while others prefer another.

You need to be able to adapt your technique depending on the river. One of the trickiest aspects of river crossing is the riverbed, a rough or uneven bed will throw the best organised line crossing completely out of kilter straight away. While a smooth, easy to walk on riverbed will leave the triangle method feeling rather over the top.

In fact, choosing the best place to cross will be the key to success. You may reasonably expect a river to be deeper on the outside of the bend or that it will be shallow the wider it is, though not all rivers play by these rules, all the time! It will be a micro-decision in the end, as you study the intricacies of the spot you find yourself in. Rocks will, typically, be slippery when wet, but this can vary with the geology. Nice dry rocks protruding from the water could give good stepping stones, a walking pole will greatly aid this process. Just be very aware of the sloping, wet stones covered in lichen or moss. Take a look at the 'run-out'. What would happen if someone slipped? Where would they end up? Is there a waterfall or a pool below your crossing point? How likely are they to slip?

The removal of the rope from river crossings is to be applauded. It might be argued by some that the rope *could* be set up to use as a handrail. It is hard to envisage a realistic scenario where this might be better than the team supported methods already mentioned. It may well be that the Mountain Leader has to 'bite the bullet' and get in the water to support others, but do not put yourself in unmanageable danger.

THE MOUNTAIN LEADER

I once felt having a rope was a useful thing on a river crossing when we were traversing one of those old rock slab bridges. Under it the water course was deep and fast flowing, but narrow. On the bridge the water was about a foot deep. It would have been all too easy to have slipped and been washed into a very hazardous current. We used a rope, handheld at on both banks as a handrail and the support it gave, probably mainly psychological, was most welcome by the group. Should you encounter such a scenario, please be very mindful that you will be operating outside the remit of the Mountain Leader qualification.

I remember ... using the rope to aid a river crossing

I was leading a fit and relatively experienced group of teenagers who I had taken for an overnight journey one Scottish winter, below the snow line, with a planned over-night in a bothy. After a long day's walk, we got to the bothy, and just had to cross the river to get to it. I'd done a good map recce of the crossing and alternatives, spoken to friends who had been there before and read everything I could find online about it. All the evidence suggested it should have been a simple ankle-deep crossing, a fine way to end the day.

When we got there, an hour before last light the group were tired, it was drizzling and the river was up, really up, much more than anything I'd researched, and the weather would have suggested. I spent a bit of time checking out upstream alternatives while they snacked in their bothy bag, but it was no better. Faced with the option of crossing or a long trek out at night and the objective hazards that go with that, I committed to the former.

We crossed individually with them downstream of the rope to hold for support and me behind them putting on my best poker face. It was one of the hardest nights I've worked in the outdoors but the training, prep, rehearsals on the home bank and crucially, the rope paid off. I made sure we debriefed it in the morning after a great night around a fire that someone had kindly left built in the bothy: they were amazed that I thought it was a dangerous situation, it appeared totally seamless and practised to them.

Graham Hassall

Author's note: When using a rope in this manner it is crucial that the rope crosses the river diagonally, and that people cross starting from the upstream end, on the downstream side of the rope.

Hazardous animals

While we don't have any particular 'killer' species of animal in the UK and Ireland, we do have some which demand respect. Cattle can present a serious threat to your wellbeing and ticks can carry very serious, debilitating, disease. Midges are in no way life threatening, but they are perhaps the most deplorable of our creatures, certainly the most annoying. The leader should also be aware that there may be group members who are scared of some animals, simply through a lack of having ever encountered them.

Adders

It is hard to get bitten by an adder. Most bites seem to be to scientists actually getting up close to study them. Adders will be aware of your presence long before you see them and they will slink away, causing no threat. In a minority of cases, however, the bite can be a problem. Between 1876 and 1975 there have been 14 recorded deaths due to adder bites in the UK. It is worth noting that adder bites are rarely fatal. Those most at risk are the very young or the very old, or those with underlying health problems.

A pair of lovely adders, male and female, during the spring breeding season. While adders are our most common snake, it's very rare you see them as they keep a low profile.

Adders are found across England, Wales and Scotland but are not present in Ireland (having been chased away by St. Patrick). They can be locally common on moors and heathland, and if you are lucky you might see them warming themselves up in a sun trap on warm early summer days.

If you are unlucky enough to get bitten and subsequently feel unwell then do go to hospital where they can treat you. You may have some teeth marks and redness around the site of the bite. There isn't really anything you need to do in terms of first aid, the advice is to stay calm, most adder bites are not at all serious, but do monitor yourself, or whoever has been bitten over the next few hours.

Cattle

I don't remember cattle ever being an issue as a young walker in the seventies and eighties. I can't help but think that something has changed, and that modern cattle are bred differently making them a bit more nervous. Maybe there is just more reporting, maybe there are more people walking or maybe, as some studies are suggesting, it's the change from feeding them on hay to feeding them on silage and keeping them indoors for longer periods of time that is making their behaviour more challenging.

Let's start with the facts. In the five years between 2015 and 2020 twenty-two people lost their lives in attacks on them by cattle. The majority of those people were working with those cows. In the same period there were also

THE MOUNTAIN LEADER

Young cattle can be very inquisitive and are best avoided. Fortunately these weren't on a public right of way.

65 attacks by cattle on members of the public, which resulted in injuries serious enough to be reported to the Health and Safety Executive. We have no idea how many near misses or unsettling episodes there have been. The Wildlife and Countryside Act 1981 actually bans bulls of recognised dairy breeds (Ayrshire, Friesian, Holstein, Dairy Shorthorn, Guernsey, Jersey and Kerry) in all circumstances from being at large in fields crossed by public rights of way. Bulls of other breeds must be accompanied by cattle. This is not however a problem with bulls, it's a problem with cattle. The danger is most prevalent in lowland fields, but these might be the fields you pass though as you head for higher ground. The breeds of cattle we are likely to encounter 'on the hill' are typically very gentle and should not be feared. The Welsh Blacks and the Highland Cattle in particular are very docile breeds.

Cattle with calves present the most danger and you must try not to get between the two. Cattle are also inquisitive and they will be keen to investigate any dog you may have. I have personally been in a field where cattle have run over to us, skipping and bucking, and it felt very threatening. I brazened it out, but I'm not ashamed to say we exited that field smoothly, quickly and calmly and that involved changing our route.

The Ramblers Association and the BMC have issued guidance for walkers. The National Farmers Union has issued guidance for farmers and support the guidance given to walkers by the Ramblers Association which I reproduce here:

Do

- Stop, look and listen on entering a field. Look out for any animals and watch how they are behaving, particularly bulls or cows with calves.

- Try to avoid getting between cows and their calves.

- Be prepared for cattle to react to your presence, especially if you have a dog with you.

- Move quickly and quietly, and if possible walk around the herd.

- Keep your dog close, on a short lead, and under effective control.

- Remember to close gates behind you when walking through fields containing livestock.

- Report any frightening incidents or attacks to the landowner, the highway authority, the Health & Safety Executive (HSE), and also the police if it's of a serious nature.

- Keep us informed of any problems you experience.

Hazards and Emergencies

Welsh Black cattle on the path into Cwm Idwal, these docile cattle present no threat and are important for good upland management.

Don't

- Don't hang onto your dog if you are threatened by cattle – let it go as the cattle will chase the dog and not you.

- Don't put yourself at risk by walking close to cattle.

- Don't panic or run – most cattle will stop before they reach you, if they follow just walk on quietly.

I think that's quite a lot of advice. It's certainly easier said than done to not panic and not to run. Do let go of your dog, it will be better able to avoid the cattle than you are. I'm a former dog owner and I can remember three occasions I had to let her go in fields of cattle, she simply ran in a massive loop around them and met me in the next field.

Midges

There are many, many horror stories about midges out there, most of us have one. Mosquitoes, flying ants, even horse flies have nothing on midges. Yes, ticks can carry life changing diseases, but midges simply drive you mad.

The midge, *Culicoides impunctatus*, finds perfect conditions for its life cycle in the glens of the western Scottish Highlands. I remember bad midge episodes on Stanage Edge in the Peak District, in Dentdale and the Duddon Valley, you'll all have your own horror stories, but it's the Scottish Highlands where the midge dominates. The very thought of midges puts off many travellers, and stories of utter, midge misery dominate far too many contemporary accounts of highland holidays. Perhaps, it hasn't always been this way. Alasdair Roberts, in his classic wee volume *Midges*, asked why are tales of old not fully replete with the 'highland curse'?

> **I remember ... midges**
>
> No one can prepare you for the horror of a bad midge episode. From being a kid camping in Dent with Mum and Dad, to standing in Stromness Bus Station with my wife to be, I've danced the bloody midge dance. As soon as one appears I'm on edge. But the horror show was an overnight in Glencoe. Fortunately, were we sleeping in a van, but as ever, you need a wee in the morning. It was still dark, or so I thought. Dark is good, the midges go away in the dark; so I fumbled towards the door and released the handle. Light flooded in; I was confused. I looked again at the windscreen; it was dark. Then I realised why it was dark, the windscreen was completely blacked out by resting midges. Never before had I seen so many midges in one place. It was like a scene from a horror film. I aroused my companion who shared my revulsion to midges, I think most people do. A plan was made. I slipped into the driver's seat and started the van. I drove briskly down the road for a mile. This cleared the midges fairly quickly and we knew it would take them a few minutes to find us if we stopped. We stopped, we dashed out for our wee then leapt back into the van and cleared off. Pastures new were calling.

There are other midges in other parts of the world, but here we have enough on our plates with our very own Highland midge. They are tiny; 1.44mm long. It is the female that bites for she needs a stomach full of blood in order to lay her eggs. This blood can come from any mammal, so humans will do nicely. The first midges to emerge in spring are the males, these don't bite, and indeed the female can lay her first batch of eggs without biting. From May to September, but especially in July and August the female midge will be on the hunt for blood. She bites the skin, then injects something that stops the blood clotting so she can lap it up till she's full, or squashed. She's most active at dawn or dusk.

Historian Alasdair Roberts observed the lack of midge misery in stories that preceded the arrival of the great Victorian Shooting Estates. He suggests that with more people on the land and more varied farming going on, (in particular before the clearances) the conditions which midges love were less prevalent.

As walkers, our worst nightmares will come true on still evenings, with little cloud cover, no rain, bogs nearby and a lack of movement. Think very carefully about that riverside wild camp in the summer months. You should be OK in April, May, September or October, you might get away with it in June. I'm told, tongue in cheek, that the key date for their arrival is May 23rd!

Hazards and Emergencies

My advice is to camp high or on the coast. Above 500 metres there are few midges, while on the coast the seemingly constant breeze keeps them at bay. They don't like direct sunlight and they can't cope with wind of more than 5 miles an hour so, stand high, look for knolls or just keep moving. Do have a midge net to hand, just in case you blow it. It's worth being ready to start walking too, what I mean is that you typically park in a glen which could be midgey. Make sure that you are ready to get out of the car and go, faff time around the valley bottom car park is an invitation to breakfast for midges.

Dressed to cope with midges on a Scottish camp.

Some people swear by certain repellents, eating marmite, smoking or smoke, I'll take a good breeze every time! You can always go indoors and the secret of a successful summer vacation maybe to hire a cottage rather than camp. Either way, when you understand how midges behave you can begin to skirt around them. You're unlikely to avoid them completely but knowing what they like and what they dislike means you can still have a nice time in the Scottish summer.

Ticks

The only other animal that really presents a threat in the UK or Ireland is the diminutive tick. Ticks are actually one of the greatest hazards facing us in the outdoors today. While the prevalence of disease carrying ticks is low in the UK and Ireland we, as Mountain Leaders, are highly likely to come into contact with them.

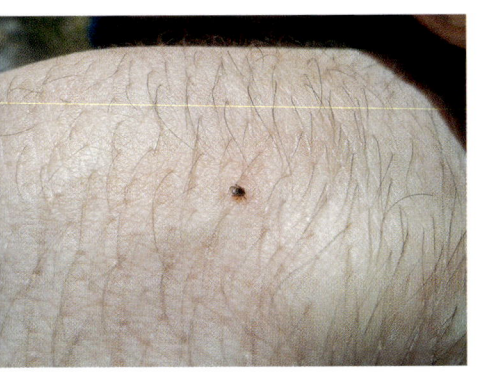

There are about twenty different tick species in the UK and Ireland, the commonest being the sheep tick. While not all of them carry Lyme disease it would be very difficult to identify which species of tick you had and from which animal it came. I suggest you treat all ticks as a potentially serious problem and deal with them in the same way, i.e. remove them as soon as you possibly can. Ticks are common from March to October, but are not unknown outside this period. If they are removed within 24 to 36 hours there is little chance of them passing on any disease to you.

A tick found during a walk on someone's leg. Fortunately we spotted this one before it attached itself to the prospective host.

The principal disease they carry is Lyme disease and this is a really difficult disease to deal with. It is a bacterial infection which can be hard to spot and can be seriously debilitating over a period of years (see box).

In July 2020 Public Health England confirmed the diagnosis of a case of babesiosis and a probable case of tick-borne encephalitis in England. This was the first record of a UK-acquired case of babesiosis and the second case

THE MOUNTAIN LEADER

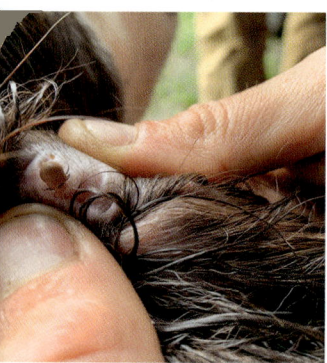

An engorged tick feeding on someone's dog. It needs removing before it can pass on any disease.
Photo: Luca Celano

of tick-borne encephalitis being acquired in the UK. Babesiosis is caused by a parasite which infects red blood cells while tick-borne encephalitis is a viral infection that affects the central nervous system. Both are rare and currently, highly unlikely in the UK.

Tick removal

Do not underestimate the threat posed by Lyme disease to you or your group. We must be very aware of ticks and brief our groups about the importance of prompt removal. They can be avoided to some degree by avoiding walking through deep bracken or long grass. You might wish to tuck your trousers into your socks, wear gaiters, apply insect repellent and choose light coloured clothing so they can be seen easier. Try to remove ticks within 24 hours of getting them on you. Look out for them in warm, moist places like your waistband or the tops of your socks. Do not put anything on them. Always use a tick removal tool to remove them. These tools are designed so that you can remove the tick without squeezing its body.

There are a range of tick removal tools available. The leverage fork works well and has no moving parts so is a good tool to carry around in your first aid kit. There is tendency to break the tick's body from its head with this type of tool and, while this shouldn't be too much of problem, it is a little unpleasant and can lead to a septic spot. The lasso type is little more expensive but does reliably remove ticks, complete with their heads. This type of tool contains moving parts and will therefore need checking from time to time.

There are several types of tick removal tools. The lasso ones probably work best, but the bent fork style has no moving parts and is cheaper.

A good first aid course will cover tick removal techniques.
Photo: Snowdonia First Aid

Hazards and Emergencies

Lyme disease

Lyme disease is an infectious disease caused by the bacterium *Borrelia burgdorferi*. Which can be passed into humans by the bite of an infected tick. It can be difficult to diagnose Lyme disease as symptoms overlap with those of many other diseases. Early symptoms might include headache, fatigue, fever, facial palsy and a skin rash. If you experience any of these within a couple of weeks of a tick bite then you must see your doctor, antibiotics can clear up any infection at this stage. You may have heard of a target rash around a bite site, while this shouldn't be overlooked it isn't a reliable sign of Lyme disease. The illness caused by Lyme disease can affect many parts of the body including eyes, joints, heart and brain. If inadequately treated or treated late, it may be difficult to cure and will remain debilitating for years.

Lyme disease was named in 1975, after a number of cases occurred in Old Lyme, Connecticut, USA. It is not a new disease and the bacterium was carried by Neolithic 'Ötzi the Iceman'. First reported in the UK in 1985 Lyme disease-carrying ticks, typically hosted by deer, can be found throughout the UK and Ireland in urban parks and gardens as well as in the countryside. There is much that we, as yet, do not know about Lyme disease.

Other animal hazards

There aren't any. Goats, sheep, bees and wasps really do not present a threat. If you are allergic to stings then that is a different case. But, for most of us, we need to just get on with our walk. Herring gulls can be a bit of a pain as they protect their nest sites, but while I've come across this on the coast it's rare in the hills. I always give farm dogs a wide berth too. These are working animals not pets. With any dog, let it come to you, don't go to it, it might well feel intimidated and they can give a nasty bite.

I always check the length of chain a farm dog might be on and give a wide berth.

Hazards created by people

There are a number of these hazards that we need to be aware of.

Mines and quarries

I like mines and quarries; aged, disused ones that is. I find them fascinating places, resonating with history, and hosting ghosts of the past. There are plenty of hills that don't have mines or quarries on them, so those that do should be considered to have special qualities. In terms of safety management they vary enormously. I doubt you'll be entering mines on a typical hillwalking day, however tempting they may look. You might get close to some of the slate caverns and while they may be regularly used, they are not regularly inspected, and it is very hard to judge how solid they are. Yes, the risk of collapse while you are there is minimal and you'd be very unlucky to get squashed in one of these places, but it is not impossible. Have a visual inspection. If it looks solid it probably is, if it looks loose then it probably is. I'm loath to say you mustn't visit these places and I'd be hypocritical too, but be wise, think about it, how important is poking your head into the slate caverns today?

Quarries vary enormously too and you need to be very careful near edges. Natural edges have usually weathered quite nicely, but a quarried edge can be abrupt and un-weathered, and therefore loose. Some quarries are so old and weathered that you'd hardly know they were quarries, some have normal routes passing through them, others are evil places. Typically, by their very nature, quarries lead to dead ends but it can be interesting to sneak up to the entrance and have a peek around. Again, it's a judgement call. You probably shouldn't be there, but it's better you control the group as they take a sneaky look, that you point out the dangers and that you

Some quarries are so old and weathered that you'd hardly know they were quarries. This is the old manganese quarries on Moel Ysgyfarnogod in the Rhinogiau.

Hazards and Emergencies

Beware of abrupt and loose edges around disused quarries.

are clear about what is OK and what is not OK. We are all inquisitive and this should be encouraged, but do take the opportunity to teach risk assessment skills too.

Landowners have an obligation to fence off disused quarries and mineshafts, so crossing barriers of this nature when leading a group does need to be considered carefully. That you'll remain within your own operational guidelines is extremely doubtful.

Stiles

Stiles come in all shapes and sizes, and people crossing stiles come in all shapes and sizes. Sometimes stiles are high and slippery, sometimes they are loose and rickety. Sometimes they are wet stones protruding from a wall. You'll soon come across someone in your group who struggles with stiles; look out for them, you might well need to do some spotting.

A traditional stone stile. Great care is needed not to pull on the top of the wall. Is the top of the wall secure, do you need to spot people and if so, on which side?

A typical ladder stile, but spot the broken step.

Heuristic traps

Heuristic traps are something we often associate with avalanche terrain. Put simply, it is the thought that if you have been there before and it was OK, it'll be OK this time too. We need to make dynamic risk assessments; we need to be aware of changing conditions and we need to think about the route and its suitability for the different groups we might be leading. Just because you've done this route before with one group doesn't mean it'll work for the next group. Repetition breeds familiarity and can engender a slackness of response to changing situations and conditions. Think, please.

> **I remember ... benighted**
>
> I was a young instructor. I was camping with a group in the Moelwynion. I thought it would be fun to take some of them in a slate mine, a slate mine I knew well. It was fun and the mine was a great place to be on a rainy, low-cloud evening. It must have been nigh on midnight when we exited the mine to a drizzly evening. We headed back to camp, a route I knew well. Or at least I thought I did. We went wrong somewhere and after spending some time wandering around in the dark, in the low cloud looking for something vaguely familiar. I had to admit defeat. We sheltered under a boulder, all huddled up together to wait for daylight. At first light I recognised our location and we wandered back to camp in surprisingly good spirits, it had been an adventure after all. My Chief Instructor, however, didn't quite see it that way. He'd heard the gossip about our emergency bivouac and sought me out. Ouch! If you do cock it up, the first thing to do is admit it to your line manager and make sure you have learned the lessons. My lesson: never go anywhere without a map and compass!

Top tips from Mountain Leaders

Just remember that it's always worth mentally checking before making a decision and ensuring that you're actioning based on the facts in front of you, rather than a set of facts that might have been true in the past.

Adam Betts

HAZARDS AND EMERGENCIES – ROPEWORK FOR MOUNTAIN LEADERS

We often say ropework for Mountain Leaders, but we should be careful here. This is most definitely unplanned use of the rope for Mountain Leaders.

Unplanned use of the rope

It is often said that a Mountain Leader only needs to do ropework once, and that is on their assessment. By and large, for the vast majority of us that is true and the rope sits comfortably below your first aid kit in the bottom of your rucksack. Ropework is very much the last resort. From time to time however, it can just save a day. You should really try to avoid any potential ropework scenario, you should have planned the route with the group in mind and you should have checked out the group's ability. The undeniable truth is that on most occasions, if you feel the need to use the rope something has gone wrong, you have got lost or you have been caught out by someone in your group. These things do happen though, and someone may be weaker in descent compared to ascent, someone may have picked up an injury during the day or maybe there has been a landslide on the path. On the other hand, you could be on an unfamiliar route and a quick bit of rope work, just for your peace of mind, might well be a wise thing to do. It is most unusual that the Mountain Leader uses the rope within the scope of this qualification.

Perhaps you are out in the hills, with a group newish to this environment, perhaps you have some heavy rucksacks, perhaps it is nearing the end of a long day, perhaps there is a rock step, with a poor run out i.e. a great big drop, perhaps it's a rock step that normally you pop up and down with barely

This rock step is quite lowdown on the east ridge of Pen yr Ole Wen and it has the potential to catch you out. Usually it's an easy scramble. In descent, however, it could be very challenging for some people in poor weather, carrying rucksacks. This is just the sort of place you might consider using a rope, at the very least for your peace of mind.

a second thought. However, if there is any hesitation, if you start to think, hang on a minute, there is a risk of a slip here, and the consequences could be pretty nasty, if the lemons are lining up, change things. Change the route, stop and review the situation with the group. As a last resort, when all other options have been considered, then you might get the rope out.

You'll need to have a good, easily remembered system. If you can do everything with an overhand knot, you're unlikely to get it wrong or forget how to do it. The systems you'll have been taught on your training are designed to be as un-technical as possible so that you can 'sort of' work it out, should you need to. It will be inevitable that it's ages since you did your training and assessment so you will be scratching your head a bit. If you were taught overly-complex systems, then you'd be pretty stressed about using the rope. If your system is simple, however uncomfortable with ropes you are, it should work.

Take your time. Getting the rope out really slows things down. Flip back to your leadership skills, brief your group, get them to put another layer of clothing on, get dry things on, have something to eat. Inform them that what you are doing isn't particularly dangerous but given the prevailing conditions you think it's worth being a little cautious and you're going to put the rope on for this step down because climbing down is tricky and made harder by the rain, fatigue and their loads. So, reassure them that this is perfectly normal (even if it is far from such), and that you know what you are doing. This will be all about the group having confidence in you, this is not the time for macabre jokes, this is the time to step up and live up to your name as a Mountain Leader.

A couple of Mountain Leader trainees learning the ropes in Cwm Idwal.
Photo: Stu McInnes, Wet and High Adventures

Hazards and Emergencies

> **I remember ... when having a rope made the day**
>
> I once led a group of 6 teenagers on a continuous journey on foot across the 4,000ft mountains of Scotland from east to west. We made a mix of long, single days and some overnighters. One of these mini expeditions was from Corrour Station to Nevis Range taking in Aonach Beag and Aonach Mor, with an overnight camp just south of the Aonachs.
>
> We climbed up the slopes to the Bealach between Stob Coire Bhealaich and Sgurr a Bhuic, it was easy going until we hit a short, easy, grade one section of mixed rock and grass about 20 metres long and not far from the top. The decision was either to retreat down and find another way round or even go all the way back to Corrour. I elected to protect the group (they were pretty strong after all) up the short, exposed, section. The ground was not difficult, but the consequences of a slip were significant, especially as we had expedition packs on as well. I had brought a 30 metre length of rope with me as I was unfamiliar with the ground having not been there before, a decision I was glad about as I had procrastinated over it before departure.
>
> I used standard ML ropework and had a clearly defined area for them to wait at the bottom and a clear gathering point at the top where, fortunately there was a good spike anchor. Once everyone was up, we packed the rope away and continued on easy ground all the way to the top gondola station where the guy operating it told us to 'jump in' as there was plenty of room – result!
>
> Alistair Othen

Which rope?

Well, it depends. Are you actually intending to use it? Or are you carrying it just in case? Within the scope of the Mountain Leader qualification, we are definitely not intending to use the rope. So, we'll question ourselves as to whether or not we should actually bother carrying one. Therefore, we are more likely to carry it if it's not too heavy. You'll soon get fed up with carrying 30 metres of 9mm rope around I can assure you. So, will 25 or even 20 metres suffice? Probably, yes. Remember, we are not carrying a rope to ascend or descend cliffs of the same height as your rope is long, but it is handy to have a little extra rope so you can go further back to find anchors.

How thick should the rope be? Well, for handling purposes as thick as possible. For carrying purposes, as thin as possible. An 11mm diameter rope will handle nicely. A 9 or 8mm rope will cut into you and hurt. A 7mm rope will be very hard to grip. Would it be best to take at least a 7mm rope, rather than not take a rope at all? Good question, and the answer is to practise with the 7mm rope, see how it feels, see if, with a pair of gloves, you can actually waist belay with it. If you are someone who has the skill set and knowledge to use a sling and karabiner and you can put an Italian hitch on, try this too. It's not easy holding a 7mm rope, with a person's weight on it through an Italian hitch. However, always remember, this is not a free-hanging in space person, this is someone who has slipped on steep ground, on a small, gentle angled clifflet.

There are some trainers and experienced Mountain Leaders who like to carry a long sling of the type used by climbers. I am not amongst their number. A 240cm or 16' sling is very light and easy to carry, they work quite well for confidence roping, but I'd only recommend them to climbers as you'll need to potentially use a tricky knot, like a sheet-bend, to make it work well. Slings also have different properties to ropes, they can be damaged easily by melting, they are slippery to handle and they do need to be inspected regularly. If you're carrying a sling you might want to carry a karabiner too and before you know if your rucksack is filling up again. The chance of a sling being the best piece of kit to use is so low that it is hard to justify carrying one.

To put it in context

On a Mountain Leader training or assessment course, we spend quite a lot of time looking for the perfect spots to train and assess you in the skills required to use a rope in a Mountain Leader context. Should you be required to use the rope in an entirely unplanned fashion, the chances of the location mirroring the locations used on your training and assessment course are slim. In fact, as trainers and assessors we walk past a lot more little cliffs, that won't do, than ones that will do. We're always looking for cliffs of the right height, at the right angle, a bit broken but not loose. At the top we need a selection of anchors to tie on to. Ideally there will be some poor anchors and some good anchors, and maybe a few in between, so we can teach, then later assess, anchor selection.

So, how does the Mountain Leader manage a group up, or more likely down, a cliff that was rejected as a suitable location for training and assessment, but just happens to be the cliff that is in the way? What if it has no anchors at all? You may need to be able to belay without an anchor. You would need to be able to sit down, as low as possible, with your heels dug in and waist belay your group. You'll need to keep the rope extra tight as any slack will put a dynamic force on you. Wow! Dangerous eh? Not, perhaps, as dangerous as you might think, but there are still factors of topography to consider. Anchorless belays will only work on flat topped cliffs, where you can get back from the edge and use friction over the edge. It is deadly if you sit too near the edge, it is deadly if you are on a slope down to the cliff edge and it's no good if the rope isn't kept tight. It is this sort of thought

Hazards and Emergencies

process that leads some trainers to think that unplanned use of the rope is not appropriate for Mountain Leaders.

Nonetheless, it's in the syllabus because there have been enough occasions where the alternatives were far worse.

> **Note for Trainers – why bother?**
>
> It is very easy to argue against the use of the rope. I have used the rope as a Mountain Leader, but I'm not convinced I really needed to, and I was probably using it because I could.
>
> Take that scenario and apply it to someone who has very little experience of using ropes and you can soon imagine a potentially dangerous scenario. Even climbers tend to place too much faith in the system and are not fully aware of what actually happens when someone falls off unexpectedly, it could be a lot worse for walkers. I've heard it said that you can confidence rope an injured person off a mountain. I'm afraid this is more likely to be 'short-roping' and that requires a skill set that is challenging for Mountaineering Instructors never mind Mountain Leaders.
>
> So why do we do it? The reasons are probably lost in time, but they revolve around the qualification being one for mountaineers, they respect the variety of mountainous terrain in the UK and Ireland, they recognise that the weather can change fast, they recognise we don't always get our decisions right and they hark back to a time when mountain rescue was a self-organised exercise. But every now and then, on very rare occasions, it can save the day and enhance the teams experience, if done well. To be done well, it should taught well; simply, memorably and properly consolidated.
>
> As a slight aside I tend not use the word 'climber' or say things like 'climb when you are ready'. It's a walking qualification, not a climbing one.

How to carry the rope

I always recommend that the rope is carried in a rope bag. Not one of the big sport climbers' bags, just a small stuff sack. Flake the rope into the bag, as you would flake the rope out after uncoiling it. If you flake it in well then you should be able to pull the rope out as you need it. I always put a knot at each end just so I can find them easily.

A leader's rope flaked into a stuff sack, ready to be deployed.

THE MOUNTAIN LEADER

The overhand knot. This simple knot can be made by anyone without specialist knowledge or training, yet it is safe and can be used in many different ways.

Appropriate knots

We need to recognise that if the Mountain Leader is to use the rope then the system they have been taught needs to be very memorable. It needs to be simple and safe but, above all else, memorable, so that even if it's a bit hazy when, and if, they ever need to use it, they can work it out again. Of course, anyone with climbing experience will have no problem using the rope in a safe way, but if you are a genuine walker, with no interest in the vertical world, with no other use for a rope, then trying to remember how to use it could be quite stressful.

This is why there is no point in using any knot other than the overhand knot, not even the slider knot, leave that for the climbers to play with. If you do this knot, the slider knot, then make sure you have three wraps, not two, and a long tail. It will work its way undone and needs checking every time it's used.

Selecting anchors and belaying

You were probably shown several ways of anchoring your ropes on your training course. You will have been shown how to select good anchors. I like the four S's – size, shape, solidity and stability. Make sure you can rethread your overhand knot if the best anchor requires threading.

Some of you may have been shown how to use a direct anchor, that is a rope around a rock spike using friction to belay. I do not teach this as a matter of course. I will discuss the use of a direct anchor with people who have some climbing or mountaineering experience as it's something they may have come across. The difficulty with teaching it to someone without that experience is that it does require a high level of judgement. If the person belaying is 'in the system' and sat down using a waist belay, all lined up nicely, then actually very little load goes on to the anchor. If that same person is direct belaying i.e. holding the rope around a rock the force of any slip by the person descending (highly unlikely to be ascending) will come directly onto the anchor. To counteract the force of the load the belayer needs to apply the same force on the other side of the rock and, indeed, if the slip is a sudden one and there is any slack in the rope then the force is greater. What this means is that any direct anchor needs to be able to withstand the weight of up to four or even six people pulling on it rather than half a person. Even when more, or less, friction is included this is a significant matter to consider. Be very careful, if in doubt, get in the system and sit down, with your ropes all in line, nice and tight.

Hazards and Emergencies

The four S's of anchor selection

Size – How big is the anchor? One square metre of water is a metric ton, a square metre of rock is therefore much heavier than you and will be difficult to move.

Shape – Is the rock of a suitable shape to put rope around. Will it sit behind the boulder? Will it go through the thread? Will it stay in place if moved? Are there any sharp edges, if the rope isn't moving it should be OK, but it's also no big drama to pad it out with something like a glove or your rope bag.

Solidity – Is the anchor part of the mountain? Is it attached to the cliff? Is it bed rock? Is there any movement in it? Is it likely to break off? Be careful pulling on rocks to test their stability. It's possible to kick a rock and not see the movement yourself, so the best method is usually to put one hand on the rock and with the other hand bash the rock with the side of your fist, can you feel any vibration in your flat hand?

Stability – How stable is the rock? If it's a big boulder it will take your weight if it is sat on something flat at the top of the cliff. If it is on a slope there is chance it could slide down the slope. Soil is lubricated by lots of heavy rain, but it's also loosened by dry weather. It's surprising how easy it is to move a very big boulder, which doesn't have a good attachment to the surface it is sat on when you've got gravity on your side.

A direct belay with all the force coming onto the anchor.

An indirect belay. The belayer will absorb most of the force and transfer it to the ground through his body rather than on to the anchor.

Using the rope on its own

We should have established by now that the Mountain Leader is in no way shape or form planning to use the rope. Indeed, it's probably only carried on a minority of occasions as a quick risk assessment usually would conclude that there's no point carrying it. If you do choose to carry the rope and you have the skills and knowledge of how to use a sling and karabiner, given that these days they weigh next to nothing, who's to argue that you shouldn't carry one if you want to? But remember, this is beyond what most Mountain Leaders will be comfortable with.

Should I carry the rope today?

Why might you need the rope?

Perhaps to safeguard a rock step in ascent or descent?

Have you chosen the right route for the group?

Should you reconsider your route?

Perhaps to use as a confidence rope?

Why do you think someone in your group might not be confident enough for the route?

Is it the first time you've met this group?

Are you going to steep mountains with this group?

Is there significant exposure at any point on this route, don't forget the descent?

It's entirely possible that you won't have met your group before going into the mountains with them. Taking a rope in these circumstances could be wise. A 7 or 8mm rope would be fine.

Perhaps to assist with an emergency carry?

What is the likelihood of needing to do this?

Is that likelihood increased by the nature of the group?

Is that likelihood increased by your intended location?

Is that likelihood increased by poor weather or ground conditions?

Can you improvise a carry without the rope, should it be required?

Hazards and Emergencies

> Carries with the rope are actually of limited use in practice compared to using a group shelter, helping someone down or calling for help.
>
> Might I need the rope to help a pony out of a bog? I know one Mountain Leader who has had to do this once!

Managing a group on a short rock step in ascent or descent

This is the essence of your Mountain Leader ropework. Once you've worked out what a good anchor is and how to secure yourself to it, you'll now be in a position to use the rope to safeguard your group down the tricky rock step. You'll need to think about where the members of your group are in relation to the edge or the base of the step. Ideally, they will be back from the edge and you can throw your rope to them, then ask them to step into the loop you've created and get them on belay before they reach the edge. There are various ways of tying people on to the rope. A simple loop made with an overhand knot works best. It doesn't really need to be adjustable, get people to stand in the loop then pull it up their legs so it sits under their rucksack. You might be surprised to find, when you make this loop, that people are actually slimmer than you might imagine, so it doesn't need to be a very big loop – experiment! It's up to you to keep the tension right so that the rope doesn't slide down their legs. At the bottom, they can just step out of the loop and you can pull it up for the next person.

The belayer has sat in a loop formed with an overhand knot. In this case, the belayer left the rope to the anchor slack, then, when in position, shuffled back a little, took up the slack and tied off the bight with another overhand knot, on shuffling forwards again they end up tight to the anchor.

It's really quite important that you are tight to your anchor. This is something that it takes climbers a lot of practise to get right. It would be unreasonable to assume walkers would get the hang of this after one, relatively short, session on a Mountain Leader training course. The best trick I've come across, is to deliberately leave slack in the rope between yourself and the anchor, then get in position and shuffle back a little. Next, take up all the spare, slack rope in a big bight and tie an over hand knot between you and the anchor, then shuffle forward again and you should be nice and tight.

Gloves can be insisted on by some trainers and ignored by others. I think you need to be able to belay the rope with gloves on, even if it's just to keep your hands warm. If you wear gloves your technique will be very important as most gloves are a bit slippery on the rope, I don't think this is a bad thing to be honest, and bringing your locking hand in towards your stomach should be seen as more important that just tightening your grip on the rope. There's

Different gloves – which would you chose for ropework, which are you likely to be carrying?

no doubt, however, that everything is easier without gloves and the chances of a rope burn are not too great, as long as you have good technique and keep the rope snug. It may well be worth practising with different types of gloves and different thicknesses of rope. You wouldn't want to box yourself into a position whereby you always need to carry a certain pair of gloves just in case you need to do some rope work. Which brings me back to where we started, by saying it's probably not a discussion to waste too much time on, as, after your training and assessment, the chances of you needing to do this type of unplanned ropework are very low indeed. Pretty close to zero.

What do you do with your rucksack? Ultimately you will need to wear your rucksack for your descent of the rock step. You'll need to be able to abseil with it on. The South African abseil lends itself nicely to this as you can undo the waist belt and tuck the rope up into the small of your back, leave the waist belt undone though so it doesn't restrict the rope. If you are belaying, try it with the rucksack on too. If you tighten up your shoulder straps so the rucksack isn't pulled round to one side then it creates a nice cushion to run the rope on and saves the rope cutting into your back.

> **I remember ... a story from a friend**
>
> After a day out on Moel Siabod with a group of teenagers. The leader got back to the layby where the minibus was parked, put their bag on the wall and the van keys fell out of the lid and onto the steep grassy slope above the river. It was easy enough to get down the bank to the keys, however a slip would have been very serious! The leader belayed one of the more confident group members down the bank to retrieve the keys successfully. Upon returning to the centre, the group members were more excited about this event than the mountain day!
>
> Anonymous

> **Note for Assessors – take it easy**
>
> This can be a very stressful part of the assessment for some candidates. It is well known that use of the rope, in a Mountain Leader context is a rare thing. Make sure you choose a location with a good chance of success. The key elements are: can they tie on to a sensible anchor and can they waist belay. They may have had some confusing input on training, this isn't the candidate's fault, just keep it simple, look for these key basics and don't be averse to a bit of coaching, you should be looking to pass people unless they really are not taking this seriously, haven't practised and can't tie an overhand knot.

Hazards and Emergencies

Types of abseil

I always think the syllabus line 'types of abseil' is rather dramatic. I'm quite sure it conjures up some very differing images in some people heads. We're not really talking about abseiling here. We aren't leaping out of helicopters or descending alpine mountains, we're not approaching a sea cliff or just taking, what to a climber is, the easy way down. We're actually just showing a bit of respect to our group, in particular the ones who we've just put a rope on to descend a rock step.

The South African abseil
Photo: Stu McInnes, The Climbing Company

If you've deemed the situation serious enough to rope your group down, highly unlikely I know, then if you just solo down the rock step it might be perceived as showing off. It may of course also be the case that the rocks are slippery and wet and it would be a wise precaution to use the rope. Typically, a wrap around the wrist will be all that's needed on the terrain in question, you could wrap it around both wrists and let it run along your back for a little better grip (known as the angels' wings). If you need to use the South African abseil then I'd be worried about where you are and how you got into this mess. The South African abseil is, however, a very neat trick and it's one you should practise so that, should you need to do it, as you probably did on your assessment, then you should be able to do it slickly. Be very careful, practice on a grassy slope where it doesn't matter if it all goes wrong.

One of the advantages of the South African abseil is the potential to be able to retrieve your rope. The chances of finding a suitable spike around which you can place the rope to abseil down and then pull the rope down is, however, incredibly unlikely. What you're more likely to have to do is cut the end of the rope off to make a separate piece of rope that can be placed around the anchor and tied to make a sling. You pop your rope through this loop then you are more likely to be able to pull it down afterwards.

There is one other type of abseil that you may get introduced to and that is known as the classic abseil. It's a very uncomfortable way of abseiling, it worked fine back in the 'classic' days when everyone wore tweed, but it's to be avoided these days if at all possible. It can, however, be very useful if your anchors are far back from the edge of where you are descending. Unlike the South African abseil, you can do this on one strand of rope, so rather than seeing it as good way of abseiling further, which in exceptional cases it may well be, see it as coping with a small rock step that has the best anchors far back from the edge. You will need to fix the end of the rope, I'm afraid you'll have no chance of retrieving this rope, you'll have to leave it, but this is an emergency situation after all.

The act of holding an elbow gives someone the confidence to balance on one leg while they take a stride.

Confidence roping

As part of your Mountain Leader competencies you will have been asked to demonstrate how to give someone confidence using a rope. You need to have a clear view of the context in which you are working here. If you think someone is lacking in confidence then getting the rope out may not be the best way to reassure them. There is much you can do before you need to use the rope.

People, typically, lose confidence around exposed areas with big drops. There are those who struggle on uneven ground or walking across slopes, usually through unfamiliarity with the outdoor environment, but you are unlikely to get far enough up the hill for a confidence rope to come in to play! The overriding factor when employing a rope for confidence reasons has nearly always been the fact that there is a big drop within this person's eye line. They will tend to lean away from the drop, this will mean them trying to use all fours to progress, it shifts weight away from the soles of their boots and left unmanaged they will end up sitting down and shuffling along. It is rare to see these behaviours in ascent. I have seen it on ridges, quite broad ridges even, but ones where the drop sneaks into the corner of the walker's eye. It's most typical in descent when someone who has been fine all day in ascent and walking along the tops, turns and faces straight down a slope, they lean away from the drop, i.e. backwards, and end up on their bottom.

Using a confidence rope should be the last resort. Most of the time in this situation, walking alongside someone, simply hiding the drop, will help. You can chat to them, guide their foot placements, you can even hold their elbow, and this will make a massive difference. What worries these people is the action of standing on one leg each time they take a stride. They always want to retain two points of contact and each time they lift a leg to progress by walking they feel the need to reach down to the ground with a hand, this puts them off balance. If you simply take their elbow you are providing that second point of contact, it really should be no more than that. If, however, you are committed and maybe the step, or exposed section isn't terribly long, then maybe a rope could be used.

The action of using the rope is no more than to give that extra point of contact. It just means you can't really progress by holding the elbow. When holding the elbow, you will be downhill of the unconfident person, you will be hiding the drop, you will be on hand to 'spot' any stumbles. This is what paddlers call, the position of most usefulness. As soon as you switch to using the rope to provide confidence you need to be up hill of the unconfident person. This changes everything. You are no longer hiding the drop. Do not ask the unconfident person to look straight down the hill and walk straight down the hill. Make a descending traverse, get them to look where they are putting their feet and focus on the strides they are taking. The rope should be kept tensioned at all times as if you are replicating

Hazards and Emergencies

holding someone's elbow. If they stumble, you need to be able to support a little more firmly with the rope. The rope needs to be constant, reassuring and present. See if you can come up with your own acronym for that. We are not preventing falls, merely slips.

Confidence roping can only take place in locations where it really wouldn't matter if everyone fell over, it's about confidence rather than a safety technique which the previous uses of the rope is considered to be. If you descend on a diagonal so that the unconfident person isn't looking straight down hill, you will need to change direction at some point. To do this, ask your unconfident person to turn in to the slope, i.e. to face you. You will be facing out, they will be facing in. You then slide the rope around to their uphill hip, having the rucksack waist belt undone will aid this process.

I remember ... confidence roping

As a Mountain Leader, I once confidence roped a 12 year old boy on the upper slopes of Cnicht, who was otherwise was too afraid to get off his knees. I had a group of 10 young people, about 11 / 12 years old. All went well climbing Cnicht until on a steep slope near the summit. The youngster turned around and looked away from the slope and for the first time fully appreciated the height and what, to him, was exposure. He became very nervous and immediately took to his knees. After some discussion and reassurance, he was able to continue with the help of a confidence rope, in order that he and his friends could achieve the summit. After this, in descent he was much more confident unroped.

Stuart Halford

Confidence roping

To knot or not

Some people recommend adding a knot to the rope, in front of yourself and a fixed distance from the person you are hoping to give some confidence to. I'm not keen on this as the static length of rope is rarely the perfect length. You can find yourself with too little rope out so you pull uncomfortably on the other person or you have to lean forward into a less powerful position than is optimal. Alternatively you can have too much rope between the pair of you in which case it's harder to keep the rope taut. If you are walking along a broadish ridge, where the drop can be seen on both sides, and this is the issue, then a knot might help to give you a firmer grip on the rope, but generally I find it unhelpful.

Note for Trainers

The action of walking requires us to balance on one foot each time we take a stride. It is this moment that concerns unconfident walkers. The feeling of balancing on one leg in between strides can be exacerbated by exposure. Most people who need a confidence rope are simply scared of heights. Work through a series of confidence giving steps before getting the rope out. As described above, walking below someone holding their elbow works well. Once the rope is out it is all about keeping a constant pressure, not too hard, not too soft, this is the most important aspect of confidence roping and we sometimes get a bit too carried away with stance and elbow shock absorbers.

Note for Assessors

Look for the constant, reassuring, presence of the rope above all else. Look for candidates turning the less confident person in towards the slope, make sure the person being confidence roped is never facing completely downhill. The person being assessed should be talking to the person in their charge constantly, about what is going on, where to stand and generally being reassuring. These things are more important than adopting a 'short-roping' lookalike stance.

HAZARDS AND EMERGENCIES – EMERGENCY PROCEDURES AND FIRST AID

It actually came as a bit of a surprise to trainers and assessors when a survey revealed that this was an area candidates felt weak in. I guess, we haven't all given it enough attention. I think the 'mechanics' of looking after everyone and calling 999 are fairly straightforward, but what might be underestimated is the emotional aspect of any such situation. Let's take it one step at a time.

Dealing with an incident

If you come across an incident, or you are unlucky enough to have one in your group, you need to provide leadership. It's you, the Mountain Leader, who needs to take charge of the situation. You need to remain calm, calm and serious, not calm and flippant. Avoid 'gallows humour' and making promises you can't keep. You need to be reassuring, while being realistic. This is where your training should kick in. Not only the instruction from your Mountain Leader training course but the exercises you should have experienced on a good quality, outdoor, first aid course. In a first aid scenario, it is the first aider (probably the Mountain Leader) who is the most important person.

I do like it when I have other first aiders in my group, or even medical professionals, however, we need to assume that this is not the case. You will need to administer important first aid and take stock of the situation. If you need help from the rescue services, you need to recognise this quickly. If there are other people around, they could be useful. They might be able to make the 999 call, they might be able to reassure the casualty, they might even be required to manage onlookers.

4mm closed cell foam pad. It is easy to carry and makes excellent insulation from the ground. You can also use it as a sit mat. About half a metre square will do the job.

Usually, the first thing to do is pull out an insulating mat and ask the casualty to sit on it. It's rare the casualty can't manoeuvre themselves onto an insulating mat. But it may be that they need assistance. Insulation from the ground is really important as the ground will drain heat from anyone, especially someone who is not well. As long as they are not insulated from the ground, in first aid terms, they remain at D for danger, danger of getting colder and heading towards hypothermia. I use some 4mm closed cell foam, it's easily purchased online. It's light and compact so will easily fit in my bag and isn't a pain to carry. A quick primary survey of the casualty is the next step.

Primary survey

This really is quick. You will need to return very briskly to looking after yourself and your group and potentially calling for help, but before that you need an idea of what you might be dealing with.

1. Check for danger – assess the situation, can you, or will you be able to approach the casualty, will the casualty need moving (e.g. away from an edge or out of the wind)?

2. Is the casualty responding to you? – Let them know everything will be under control and that you will look after them.

3. Is the casualty's airway open and are they breathing? – It usually will be. The casualty will typically be breathing and tell you what the problem is. On the occasion when this isn't the case, you need to take control and move quickly.

4. Are there any signs of significant blood loss? – This will need stemming as soon as possible.

5. Breathe.

You should now have a good idea of what you are dealing with. So, lets deal with it.

Action points

1. Are you comfortable? Do you need to put on an extra layer? Get dry gloves and a dry hat on?

2. Your group will be looking to you. Get them to put extra layers of clothing on and fresh gloves, get them to pool their food, get them to stand by with the group shelter. Maybe one or two of them can identify the nearest sheltered spot. Give them jobs, be clear and directive with your instructions to them.

3. Let the casualty know what is going on and undertake a secondary, more detailed, assessment of their condition (see DrABCDE on p260).

At this point you have to decide: Can you walk the casualty off the hill? Can you carry or support the casualty off the hill? If you have two 'no's' then you need help.

Hazards and Emergencies

If you need to call for help:

4. Start your accident report card.

5. If possible, delegate giving first aid and reassurance of the casualty.

6. Call for help or delegate calling for help using the accident report card.

7. Make sure your casualty is as warm as possible, insulated from the ground and wrapped up in a 'Blizzard' bag or blanket as soon as you can (or occasionally, sheltered from the sun). Then, with the whole group inside bring the group shelter over your heads and tuck it in well. Make sure everyone is insulated from the ground too.

8. Look after your casualty, evaluate your first aid so far and start to monitor the casualty.

9. Be prepared for a long wait.

Accident report card

You should make your own accident report card. It will help you to explain the situation on the telephone. It might also help if you can send someone else to get assistance and they can take it with them. It should be a laminated sheet, ideally A5, and it should be in your first aid kit with a pen that will write on it. By making your own form, you will remember what it contains better than just copying someone else's. Include the following:

- Your name and date of birth, you'll be asked this first to prove your identity.

- Location, grid reference and description.

- Your phone number.

- Number in group and how they are being looked after.

- The casualty's name, nature of injuries, and time of incident. Do they have any medical conditions or allergies? How old are they? Can they walk or not? Are they warm?

- What is the weather like at your location (in particular wind and visibility)?

- You should also have a casualty monitoring form where you regularly record the casualty's vital signs.

THE MOUNTAIN LEADER

The most frequent need to call mountain rescue is for lower limb injuries, there are nearly as many of these as everything else put together. Heads and arms come next and are typically due to minor tumbles that have resulted in a damaged limb or a bang to the head.

If we work carefully with our groups, coaching them how to walk more efficiently and where, and how, to place their feet, if we take our time, if we make sure they are fed and warm, then we reduce the risk of any incident occurring. Sadly, mountain rescue also gets a significant number of calls to cold casualties, this should not be our group.

It can be difficult getting into a group shelter on a windy day, make sure you've practised this before you need to do it for real.

Key first aid concepts and actions

Most modern, outdoor first aid courses aimed at Mountain Leaders and other outdoor instructors will follow a clear plan like this one – **DrABCDE** (Doctor ABCDE).

D – Danger, is it safe to approach the casualty? Is the casualty in further danger of injury? Is the casualty sheltered from the prevailing elements?

R – Response, what is the casualty's level of response? Are they alert and talking to you, telling you what is wrong with them? Can they tell you what their name is and where they are from? Have you asked them about allergies or medical conditions? Ask them what you can do to help them. Are they not alert?

Alert is conscious.

Descending levels of unconscious are: voice responsive, pain responsive, unresponsive.

Ideally a casualty will ascend through these levels. You need to be mindful that it is possible a casualty will descend through them. The scale is known as A/VPU and Level of Consciousness is a key first aid concept.

A – Airway, is it open or closed? Can you open it by tilting their head? Are they choking? Are they having an allergic reaction to something? Is it an asthmatic issue?

B – Are they Breathing? You will need to get in close and look, listen and feel (hand on their abdomen). Normal breathing is gentle, rhythmic and typically around 12 to 18 breaths per minute. Monitor this throughout the scenario.

C – Circulation. Are they bleeding? You'll need to apply direct pressure on the wound. Do everything you can to stem the flow.

D – Damage. Is there any other injury? Typically breaks, dislocations or strains. It doesn't really matter whether it is a break, a dislocation or a strain. Be guided by the casualty. Can they walk off? Can you help them off? Do you need to stay put? Seek shelter and wait.

E – Emotion, Evacuation, Environment and probably most importantly, Evaluation. Everyone will be stressed and emotional, you need to show leadership and calm everyone down, you need to hold the casualty's hand and look after them, but if you are with a group, be very aware of how they are responding to the situation too. Hopefully a mountain rescue team will be working on an evacuation plan, but it takes time. You need to be prepared for a long wait. Have you dealt with environmental factors, bright sun and midges can be unwelcome, but cold and wind can be life threatening? Probably most important of all is to evaluate, and keep evaluating. Have you done everything you can? Have you missed anything? Is everybody comfortable, are your group well, do they have sweets? Revisit your DrABCDE and start to monitor the casualty, things like their breathing rate, pulse rate, level of consciousness, temperature and colour.

The first aid kit

In this section I'm going to relate the things you should carry in your first aid kit back to the first aid protocol of DrABCDE. This approach was first brought to my attention by Tim Cain of medicREC. We sometimes talk about a personal first aid and a group first aid kit. They shouldn't be very different. If you're carrying a group first aid kit, you aren't carrying enough kit for everyone in the group to need first aid. The key items will still tend to be those which help you keep the casualty warm.

D for Danger

Carry enough warm kit to remain static by the casualty's side for extended periods. This is your belay jacket, your extra gloves and hats, put them on before you do anything else. Make sure the casualty is insulated from the ground. Get the group shelter ready for your group, ask them to get into dry things and put their extra layers on.

R for Response

You're going to touch the casualty – examination gloves, these will usually be nitrile medical gloves but could be rubber washing up gloves.

THE MOUNTAIN LEADER

A for Airway

You will need to get close to the casualty to listen and feel for breathing – gloves.

B for Breathing

You may have to breathe for the casualty – CPR Face shield. You should record the breathing rate and collate the accident details. Accident report card and monitoring card with pen.

You may need to deal with a heart attack – 300mg Aspirin.

C for Circulation

You may need to cut clothing to access a wound – Tuff Cut shears.

You may need to apply direct pressure to a bleed – wound dressing.

D for Deformity / Disability

You may need to immobilise a fracture – improvised splint. 2 x 15cm crepe bandages, a triangular bandage. Strapping for a sprain – duct tape. Painkillers.

E for Environment, Evaluation, Emotion, Evacuation, Energy

Closed cell foam pad, blizzard bag, hot drink and food.

A typical Mountain Leader's first aid kit

Hazards and Emergencies

Suggested first aid kit

- Accident report card, monitoring sheet and pen
- Two 15cm crepe bandages
- One wound dressing
- One triangular bandage
- CPR face mask
- Gloves
- Painkillers
- Aspirin
- Shears
- Plasters / plaster strip
- Tape (zinc-oxide and duct)
- Tick removal tool
- Energy gel
- Burn dressing
- Tweezers

Plus:

- Blizzard bag
- Headtorch
- Group shelter
- Spare hat, gloves and jacket
- Closed cell foam pad (4mm ones are easy to carry)
- You can improvise splints with walking poles and laminated maps. You can make cheat triangular bandages with slings or belts. An absorbent cloth can help when applying plasters or cleaning around wounds.

Do an **outdoor first aid** course.

Calling 999

The UK rescue number is 999, this number is also used in Ireland. You can send a text to 999, but only if you have registered your phone number with them. This service was originally set up for people hard of hearing but could be handy if you have weak reception. To register your phone just text the word register to 999 and follow the instructions you receive back.

When you call 999 ask for police and mountain rescue. In some places you'll be talking to the mountain rescue team straightway, in others the police will take the details and get the mountain rescue team to ring you back. It's important that if you have had to move to get reception that you stay where you have had to move to, so that you maintain phone reception. You may need to bear this in mind if you have to leave your casualty to find reception, make sure they are warm and comfortable, and tell them this could take a long time. Once you call mountain rescue they have to assemble a team who are all volunteers. The volunteers then have to get organised, collect together and then walk up the hill to meet you. Even when they send a quick advanced party up to you this all takes time. We are very lucky that the Coastguard can assist this process with their helicopters and they will conduct the rescue if flying conditions and availability permit.

Mountain rescue set up

It's a bit surprising to find out that every mountain rescue team is a separate entity from all the others. This is not a national organisation in the same way that the RNLI is. It's an accident of history that different teams were set up at different times, in different places, and they have just kept their independence. This means that you'll see each team doing their own fundraising and some are better at it than others! There are umbrella representative organisations though, and it's fair to say that whatever goes on behind the scenes they all have the same purpose and the same drive to help people who are in trouble. To contact a mountain rescue team in an emergency call 999 and ask for police and mountain rescue. Technically, you should ask for the police and they decide whether or not a team of mountain rescue volunteers might be called upon. The reality is the police are only too glad of the assistance they receive from mountain rescue teams and are very keen to have them help out. Given the number of emergency calls the police receive it's worth flagging up the need for mountain rescue early on the in the conversation, hence asking for police and mountain rescue. While mountain rescue teams do remain voluntary, they are very impressive in the way they go about their business and they could be considered to be acting in a professional way. Each team will have a selection procedure, they will a have high level of training, organised amongst themselves, but also, often with external professionals contributing.

Personal locator beacons

Personal locator beacons (PLBs) have been part of the normal kit for sea kayakers and other ocean goers for some time now. Walkers, climbers and mountaineers heading into remoter places where there is no phone reception might consider carrying one. They are small, light and waterproof. You can buy one on a subscription service which enables you to communicate by pre-written text message to your own base. Or you can buy one as a one-off purchase which is purely for emergency use.

A PLB is a radio beacon which is linked to an international satellite system for search and rescue. This satellite system has global coverage. If activated, the PLB will transmit a message, which includes a code uniquely identifying the individual PLB. This code can subsequently be matched with the information you supplied when the PLB was registered on purchase. It will first check the likelihood of an emergency with your provided contacts. If it is likely to be an emergency, the local rescue organisation will be alerted.

Improvised carries

In the early days of the Mountain Leader qualification there were occasions when self-rescue was the only way to go about things, and improvised carries were explored with a view to evacuating a casualty from the hill. It is much more likely these days that you will be calling for assistance on your mobile phone (or your PLB or similar). Carrying someone off a hill is a major undertaking that requires a significant number of people.

What we might need to do is move a casualty out of further danger. This will really only be the case if the casualty is in an exposed position. Think of the difference between sitting on a windy summit and tucked in below it, in the lee. So, moving a casualty could be a vital part of any incident management. Getting them out of the wind and into a more sheltered location could make a real difference to them. If you can ascertain that they are breathing and not losing significant amounts of blood then getting them to a sheltered location will quickly become more important than any physical injuries such as broken bones. I know this is easy to say (even though a conscious casualty will be able to help themselves somewhat) but the danger of hypothermia is real and a human being in an exposed, cold location will deteriorate quicker than you might expect. Get them out of the wind, into a Blizzard bag and into a group shelter with the rest of your group. If you just do this, you will save lives and make a big difference to the situation. On arrival at hospital a warm casualty can be treated for their injuries, whereas a cold one has to be treated for hypothermia before their injuries can be considered.

THE MOUNTAIN LEADER

Improvised carries are hard work, and sustaining them safely over any significant distance is a long way from being easy. Keep it short, plan where you are going to go, make sure everyone has a role, don't rush, keep a constant dialogue with the casualty.

Without doubt, getting the casualty to move themselves is the best way and if they can, they must. If they can hobble away with your assistance, even crawl, this will be a great help, as soon as you lift someone you put yourself in danger of an injury. Take your time, make a plan.

It's relatively easy to move someone a short distance on a group shelter. The more hands the lighter work, but do not underestimate the importance of moving a casualty to a sheltered location.

If someone is wearing waterproofs, handles can be improvised by bunching up the material so that they can be picked up and moved a short distance.

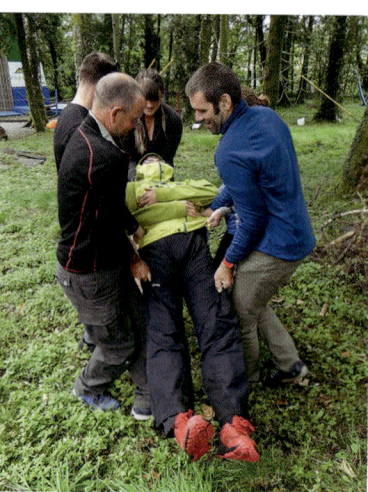

Note for Assessors

There is an impossible amount of 'what if's' and 'yes but's' in this part of the syllabus. Of course, it's highly unlikely that any of these things will ever happen but they do happen, and you need to be confident that your candidates can manage such a situation. You can definitely ask them a question on their home paper, you can give them scenarios on the hill. You could get them to work as a group to move a casualty to shelter. You'll find it hard to build robust evidence to defer or fail someone though.

The other thing to never forget is that you remain in charge. If a member of the team is doing something dangerous then you will need to intervene. The timing of this intervention is crucial. If you pre-empt a poor decision, they may suggest that they weren't going to do what you thought they were. If you step in too late, well, it could be too late.

Emergency bivouac skills

It is not beyond the realms of fantasy that you might, in an emergency, need to spend an unplanned night in the hills. Finding shelter from the wind and rain is key. There are plenty of nooks and crannies on a typical British mountain. The sheep and goats will have found them before and they will have used them as a toilet, but they will be the best locations. We used to carry plastic bivy bags, those big orange ones and this is when they came into their own; you could slice them open and use them as a ground sheet. I'm afraid you'll just need to crack on and forget the poo. If it's about survival then a bit of sheep poo is not going to hurt you. Your modern, mountain gear is all very washable.

If there is no rocky, cave-like area then a night in the open is still to be avoided, work that bit harder and get yourself to shelter, anywhere out of the wind. You'll be able to sit the night out in a group shelter. It won't be perfect, but you can make things better with walking poles holding the shelter up above your heads. It'll be noisy if there is wind, you'll get condensation, you might even get the unpleasant aroma of sweaty bodies. All this can be survived, a cold wind can't.

Inside a group shelter is a great place to be, it lifts spirits instantly, but it can get uncomfortable after a while.

Post scenario

If you haven't called in the mountain rescue and you've dealt with the situation yourself, well done, but do talk to somebody. Find a mentor and talk through what you did, how you felt, how your group were etc. It is important to talk about these situations to properly deal with them inside your head. If mountain rescue has been involved, despite being volunteers they are really good at this. If they offer you someone to talk to, do not 'tough' it out, talk to them. You will not be 'all right'; the events and your actions will flow around your head for years to come. Talk about it now, it will help.

Scrambling on Tryfan

A final reflection

The author of the following story has gone on to be a very successful mountaineering, climbing and paddle sports coach and a successful teacher. He now advises and runs workshop events for Mountain Training and is a joint author of the acclaimed *Coaching Adventure Sports*. Being a reflective learner is key for any development to occur as a leader. Read this story and consider; is it a story that convinces us of the importance of ropework? Or is it a story that makes us think more about decision making and judgements, and how our pre-conceptions can affect our decision making while leading? It's a story that works well with the Lemons Theory. Can you spot the lemons that lined up?

I remember – should I use the rope?

Internally I was struggling. Externally I was trying my hardest to look like I was in control and be as calming as I could be. The pressure was starting to build. You know the analogy of a duck swimming – serene on the surface with feet paddling like mad under the surface? That's how I felt. It was my own decision making that got me to this point and now my thought process was at conflict with itself – do I use the rope or not?

The couple of days had been going well. It was the autumn term of my second year of teaching (and second year of holding my Summer Mountain Leader qualification). Along with another teacher (Rupi) we had taken a group of disaffected Year 8 students to North Wales on a three-day residential visit. Over the previous couple of days, we had been rock climbing, enjoyed a short mountain day and for the final day had decided to head up Y Garn via the Devils Kitchen.

We had a slightly later start than planned but were soon heading into Cwm Idwal. Telling stories based around folklore, looking at the glaciated terrain and relating it back to their geography lessons. We had started to slow down on our approach to the Devils Kitchen, partly due to the student's lack of fitness, but also due to one or two of them struggling with the exposure of the 'path' up to Llyn y Cwn. The weather was wonderful, better than forecast and I judged that we had made good time, so I gave the students the choice, we could continue with our planned journey to Y Garn or we could ascend the slightly taller (and more impressive) Glyder Fawr. Naturally, the collective opted to change the plan.

That is when it started to go wrong. Three of the students started to struggle on the steep, initial climb. It took us, as a group, nearly 2 hours to get to the summit, by which point the weather had started to deteriorate, the wind had picked up and the clouds had started to come in. Not wanting to turn around and retrace our steps, I selected to descend via the track close to Y Gribin (which, as a direct route I thought would be faster ...). We had a quick snack in the small shelter cairn at the top. Just as we finished the clouds closed in. I quickly discussed with Rupi where I wanted her to be in the group and to work with two specific students. I made a quick phone call back to school to say that we were going to be late back – we were just leaving the summit at the time I had planned for us to start the drive home!

I had been up and down that section of ridge a handful of times over the previous three years, so knew that I needed to look out for a few features. I remember thinking that I was pleased that the clouds were in so the students wouldn't feel just how exposed our route was. We were slow and careful with our descent; spotting was employed in a couple of places and then we got to a section where we needed to down-climb. It was no more than 8 metres tall, with a ledge roughly halfway. I decided to spot the students down, one at a time. The first three students must have taken several minutes each to get down. At this point, predictably, we started to noticeably lose the light. While I was moving around loads, being very active and keeping warm, everyone else was stationary and getting cold. One or two of the students started getting vocal about how cold they were (let's not forget the makeup of the group at this point – they were disaffected 12-year-olds. Vocal doesn't quite do their complaining justice ...).

In my mind, I would have failed in my role as a Mountain Leader, if I was to use the rope. General consensus with my peers was that if I used the rope, I had 'failed'. Yet here I was, in a situation where use of the rope would dramatically speed up the process for managing the group down this rock step.

I chose to deploy the rope, and we were on the move again.

The rest of the group were down in less time than it had taken me to spot the first three students down. There were smiles from all the students, with a few 'can we do that again' comments. The first three students down were jealous and wanted their go. The rest of the journey went well, but I still felt as though I had failed by using the rope.

Reviewing the visit with the students afterwards, one of their standout memories of the trip was being lowered, and not for any negative reasons. They enjoyed it. It took a few reflective discussions with other teaching colleagues (and fellow Mountain Leaders) before I accepted that I did the right thing by using the rope. As I reflect now, I can see how the use of the rope changed the group dynamic, enlivening them into enjoying a new challenge as well as speeding up our descent, encouraging me in future to be much less hesitant in deploying my rope.

It was this experience that led me to realise that the people we are leading in the mountains have no understanding of our world, the qualifications that we hold and the experiences that we have. They just expect us to look after them appropriately (and dare I say it entertain them!?) in any given situation. All that was left to address was the decision-making errors that had led up to that point ...

Paul Smith of Rock and Water Adventures

A discreet high mountain camp near Rhinog Fach.

How we lead overnight trips

Expedition Skills

Camping, wild and free in the mountains has long been one of the best bits about walking and climbing in the mountains. On a fine summers evening, when you can share food, maybe a wee dram, sit around and watch the sun set, then look to the stars hoping to see a shooting one. Perhaps you can enjoy a swim, maybe even a skinny dip, in a clean, fresh lake. These are the simple pleasures in life that so many of us aspire to and provide such a therapeutic contrast to the constant rush, strains and pressures of modern, urban life. As Mountain Leaders we get to do this with people; we can lead them here, look after them, inspire them, help them, heal them; what a privilege. Walk, eat, sleep, repeat. It might be, however, that your first wild camp when leading a group is not on a gorgeous summers evening, you might not have permission to swim and having a tot from your hip flask may be inappropriate.

Unlike the lovely pictures on Instagram of sexy, wild camping, sometimes it rains. Unfortunately, our lives are so controlled and programmed that we will tend to choose a weekend for wild camping far in advance, long before we know what the weather will be like. You will have learned how to camp in the rain and cope with the wind. You will be prepared for spending long hours in your tent. You might need reminding sometimes, that when we go camping on the hill it is supposed to be fun, because it might not always be

THE MOUNTAIN LEADER

An idyllic high mountain camp. Looking towards Errigal, from the Derryveagh Mountains, County Donegal, Ireland. Photo: Bren Whelan

a wonderful experience. I would always try to have an alternative plan when trying to wild camp with a group, I really don't want to put them off for ever. You'll be aiming to give those whom you lead an amazing, lifetime memory and you might need to be the jolly, positive, optimistic one, you might need to emphasise the joys and gloss over the wet bits.

Camping with the Duke of Edinburgh Award Expeditions

Many Mountain Leaders will predominately camp with D of E groups. The D of E philosophy is:

"Wild camping can be an exciting, memorable and highly rewarding experience for young people. It is well suited to D of E expeditions and can give teams an unsurpassed sense of independence and isolation."

In camp at different times of the year

Managing the day will vary at different times of the year. This is particularly apparent on Mountain Leader courses, where you have a programme to follow. If you are out for fun you do just walk, eat, sleep, repeat and the simple rhythms of life are one of the absolute joys of slow travel. If you haven't done a multi-day trip then do pull out all the stops to experience one.

As regards the Mountain Leader courses, camping in the summer means a long wait for the dark. You'll tend to camp around teatime, eat, have a break and a chat then go for a walk in the dark to experience some poor visibility navigation. In summer this could include an ascent of a peak and can be quite a magical experience, and one which you may look forward to sharing with others once qualified. On the other hand, it could be raining and a fairly short point to point course covering all the required techniques will be the order of the night.

In the autumn there is less 'down' time as you get to camp, eat, go for your night walk, then back to bed. This is a good time of year for this sort of activity, it means you don't have too many lonely hours in the tent and you still have plenty of time for a good night's sleep, unlike summer where you could be walking into the early hours. This length of daylight obviously repeats itself in the spring too.

In winter it might be that you chose to 'walk into dark'. The early onset of the night means that to get to camp before darkness can be a bit of a rush, depending on where you are heading of course. The nice thing about this way of doing things is that once you are in your tent that's it, you don't have to emerge again until the morning. Your trainers and assessors will have had this down to a fine art and will have suddenly appeared, despite your suspicions, at the appointed time all dressed, fed and watered, ready to go! To be this slick requires reflective practice.

Typically, with groups, we want to be out in the best of the weather so summer is the most common time to camp out. Don't rule out the other seasons though, especially if you can walk in the dark to some sort of built shelter.

Wild camping

So called 'wild' camping has become very popular in recent times. There is controversy and we were taken a bit by surprise when criticism started to pour forth on so called 'wild' campers. We couldn't understand why our 'dusk till dawn' remote, truly wild camping might cause a problem, we leave no trace of our passing, we toilet wisely, so why the issue? Disappointingly, the term 'wild' camping became apportioned to roadside free camping. We do this too, not necessarily in the context of being a Mountain Leader, but when we've driven far and camped by the car as a start to our explorations.

Unfortunately, the festival mentality of buying cheap gear and leaving it on site has spread across our land. The term wild camping was used for this. Some people now call it fly camping as in fly tipping, others just call it free camping, some still call it wild camping. Whatever you want to call it, it's not how we do things. Unfortunately, it has brought in restrictions which can affect us. For instance, if you are heading north don't be tempted to break your journey with a camp by Loch Lomond, a new by-law prohibits this, unless you obtain a permit. When you see the mess left behind by 'fly' camping it's hard to argue against the need for this restriction. We should maintain our low impact style and move on elsewhere.

THE MOUNTAIN LEADER

An inappropriate camp on private land, close to the road and in a national park. An unnecessary fire, beer cans strewn around, organic waste and poor toileting behaviour complete the picture. Unfortunately, this sort of camp gets us all a bad name. Note, the picture was taken at 11.00 am and one camper was still in the hammock. This is the antithesis of our dusk till dawn, leave no trace, style of wild camping.

In Scotland there is the right to camp. It came in with the Land Reform Act (2003) and it comes with some responsibilities that we would not think unreasonable. There is one unalienable fact however, that hovers over wild camping, and that is that, in England and Wales we have no right to wild camp. We have been tolerated for years and as long as we demonstrate impeccable practice, I have no doubt this will continue. We must leave no evidence of our passing, we should adopt a dusk till dawn principal, we should seek out of the way areas and try to keep a low key approach.

The Scottish Access Code and wild camping

In Scotland your access rights extend to wild camping. Wild camping is defined as lightweight camping, done in small numbers and only for two or three nights in any one place. You must avoid causing problems for local people and land managers by not camping in enclosed fields of crops or with farm animals in them. Keep well away from buildings, roads or historic structures. Leave no trace by:

- taking away all your litter

- removing all traces of your tent pitch and of any open fire (follow the guidance for lighting fires)

- not causing any pollution

On the lighting of fires, the code says never cut down or damage trees. Use a stove if possible. If you must have an open fire, keep it small and under control and remove all traces before leaving.

On going to the toilet the code says that if public toilets aren't available, carry a trowel and bury your faeces well away from open water, rivers and streams.

Expedition Skills

Camping and the current Law in England and Wales

In 2021 the Government have proposed to make certain types of trespass a criminal offence. While the proposed law is aimed at particular groups of travellers there is a fear they it may well be used to target bona fide outdoor people. We are most definitely potential victims of poor behaviour by significant numbers of fly campers. In all our national parks new signage has sprung up prohibiting camping, sometimes claiming that it is illegal to camp outside of a campsite

Currently there isn't a law prohibiting wild camping or trespass, so you can only be asked to move on unless the landowner wants to bring a civil injunction. This has worked well for many years. The argument against making trespass illegal is that anyone leaving a mess and causing damage is breaking other laws which are criminal offences anyway, and making trespass illegal could have a detrimental effect on peaceful, thoughtful, enjoyment of the countryside.

The concept of land ownership is considered by some to be artificial given that the land has always been there and will be there long after humans have gone. The law, however, doesn't see it this way.

No one wants to damage or interfere with legal activity taking place on private land, but we do want to pass freely without hinderance and, from time to time, rest overnight. We can do this responsibly and cooperatively. On a couple of occasions, I have been approached by gamekeepers while on discreet wild camps. Having a civil conversation has allowed me to stay overnight on the condition I scare away any foxes!

There is one notable exception to the lack of laws on wild camping and that is on National Trust land. Rule 13 of the 1965 by-laws for land owned by the National Trust states:

13. No unauthorised person shall pitch, erect, or permit to remain on Trust Property any tent, booth, windbreak, pole, clothes-line, building, shed, post, fence, railing or other erection or obstruction whatsoever.

It should also be noted that the CROW act of 2000 also makes it clear that there is no 'right' to camp. *"Section 2(1) (...this Act...) does not entitle a person to be on any land if, in or on that land, s/he engages in any organised games, or in camping, hang-gliding or paragliding."*

There is provision for wild camping on parts of Dartmoor, but that is currently under review so please do check the position locally.

> **Overnight camping is nothing new**
>
> People have always walked. We spread around the globe by walking. It is only in relatively recent history, the last 1,000 years, that UK and Irish land has been enclosed and owned privately. Even then, throughout this period, the commonest form of travel was walking. Many people couldn't afford a horse or a boat so travelled on foot. Sometimes quite long distances across the country would be covered, maybe to trade, to seek harvest work, to move livestock or on pilgrimage. Inns were great places to stay, but not everyone could afford them and then, as now, people would have camped rough, or 'wild' to save money and stay on their route
>
> Scott's Pine's are aften associated with travellers as they were used by drovers to waymark their favourite inn or a safe river-crossing in a manner which could be seen from a distance. They are fast growing and evergreen and would stand out from the native trees in Wales and England in particular. According to legend, drovers from North Wales took pine-cones with them and planted them in clumps of three or five near the inns they wanted to recommend. Railway companies used the same system to mark their stations so walkers could see them from afar.

Equipment for camping

The basic kit needed for camping is a tent, sleeping bag, mat, stove and few other sundries. Personal choice will dictate what type of kit you are selecting, it'll depend very much on the time of year you are camping, how often, whether going solo or with groups. Your budget may well be the overriding factor.

Tent or tarp?

This is a question that has come up from time to time in recent years. I've met people wanting to use bivvy bags as well. I'm afraid that if you are leading a group, you need a proper tent. Your tent could be a key item in any emergency that you may have to work through. Imagine someone in your group loses their tent, you need space in yours, imagine you need to make an improvised shelter, a tent will be better than a group shelter. Even if you look at it from a selfish point of view, you need to be warm, dry and comfortable yourself to continue as an effective leader. Your tent is a fantastic refuge from any prevailing bad weather. If you are going on an overnight excursion yourself, then take what you like. I love to sleep under a tarp in good weather, I like a night under the stars in the bivvy bag. All too

Expedition Skills

A tarp in use in ideal conditions down by the sea.

often though if the weather isn't great, you need to be in a bivy bag if you are underneath a tarp. In fact, given the choice, I take the tent and a tarp, this works well when sea kayaking, but adds to the weight when walking. I don't believe a bivvy bag, ground sheet and a tarp will give you any significant weight saving over a modern tent. There are many brilliant tents out there that are amazingly light.

When buying a tent, I'd look for one made in wet and windy countries. By this I mean some tents have flysheets that don't go right down the ground, this is an invitation for the wind to enter. The other important aspect for camping in the British hills is to have a tent that either goes up inner and outer as one, or the outer, flysheet, first. I'm not the only one who has had to pitch camp in the pouring rain, and I can tell you, doing it inner first is not to be recommended, as everything can get wet!

You should be able to get a tent weighing around one kilogram, that doesn't break the bank. How much you intend to use it might just sway you on how much to spend. It's typical when leading a group, in the mountains on an overnight expedition, that you use your own one-person tent. You probably did this on your assessment too, which is perfectly understandable. I've been a little jealous from time to time of those who've shared a tent. The camaraderie can be excellent and tent's being soundproof means they can have right, good old natter. I guess, having your own tent just makes it easier for you to be in control and do things as you would like them to be done. Besides, you can hear everything going on because you've actually worked out that tents are not really soundproof!

A selection of well-pitched tents on a great campsite in Eryri.

It's highly unlikely you will be buying the lightest of tents for a group new to wild camping. It is perfectly possible to use cheap tents from the high street brands. These tents might not be as light as yours, as long lasting as yours or quite so well made as yours, but they do make wild camping accessible.

Tent organisation is important. You'll soon learn where you want to put things, I think developing good organisational habits will really help you. What goes in the flysheet porch entrance? What goes on your left side? What goes on your right-side? What can be dismissed away down to your feet? We know we have to teach how to pitch, and how to strike a tent, but do you give thought to tent organisation? I'm sure, like me, you've seen someone leave their boots outside their tent, slept with their feet pushed against the wall of tent, or got their kit wet through sheer lack of organisation. People need to learn how to get out of their waterproofs as they enter their tent in the rain! You need to teach these skills.

Having a tent in which you can sit up makes a real difference. I am quite tall too, so it's always a bit of a compromise between the size of the tent and its weight. Getting in and out of the tent can be the tricky bit when it's pouring it down. You need to be able to strip off your outer, wet, shell layers in the porch area, so a good sized porch is a must, I end up doing a sort of forward roll, in slow motion, stripping as I tumble into the tent. This process is then reversed upon exiting the tent. You'll need to be good at this as, on a multi-day expedition, like your assessment expedition, you can be in and out of your tent several times in daylight and in the dark, and it might be raining for all of them – Yuk!

Expedition Skills

Sleeping bag

Whatever choices you make with sleeping bags the following are the criteria you should be working to:

- You need to be warm.

- We all have different comfort levels.

- You need to be able to carry your chosen sleeping bag.

- You need to be able to keep it dry.

The first question often asked is should I buy a 1,2,3 or 4 season sleeping bag? The answer is, it's up to you. The thing is though, each manufacturer will have slightly different versions of the above. If I talk about a two-season sleeping bag being the bag I use, pretty much all the time, then that only works for me and the particular type of sleeping bag I am using. I also possess a three-season sleeping bag which I've used more than adequately well below 0°C. In the UK, a regular four-season bag would, typically, for the average person, be too much. A three-season bag will work well for most people, most of the time. In summer the three-season bag may well be too warm. I'd always advise a full length zip for ventilation or turning the bag into a quilt. A good two season bag should cover most people's needs for camping in the UK, but not everyone's! I should add that a three-season sleeping bag will be heavier than a two-season sleeping bag. You will have to carry which ever bag you choose. The purchase of a new sleeping bag can be a frustrating business and they are tricky to try out, none of them feel cold lying on the shop floor!

The other big factor to consider is synthetic or down. The die-hards, like me, will always say down. It packs smaller than anything else and it weighs less, for the warmth provided, than anything else. If you get it wet, however, it is completely useless. You must keep it dry. You need to be very careful with it, you'll need to keep it in its own dry sack. It can be done, most of the time anyway. I've only had dampness when I've camped on a slope and slid down the hill so my feet have been forced into the end of the tent. You should, with practise, be able to keep your down bag dry. There is also a worry about washing down bags. I certainly don't rush to wash mine and, if you do, it needs to go into the tumble dryer, with some balls. See box on next page.

When working with groups the likelihood is you'll be using easily washed synthetic bags and they'll be heavier sleeping bags than yours. You must take into account that this extra weight will have an influence on your route length and choice.

How to wash a down sleeping bag

Professional sleeping bag washing services are available, but you can do this yourself, if you really must!

Machine wash

What will I need?

- A large tumble dryer is advisable as air drying takes a long time and you will have to constantly agitate the down as it dries to ensure that it does not clump.

- A bath or large capacity washing machine (10kg).

- Down wash.

- Clean tennis balls (or spiky down washing balls provided by manufacturers of down washing soaps).

Using the large capacity front loading washing machine.

- Try to remove all soap residue from the machine by flushing it through with an empty wash and clean out the soap dispenser.

- Set the water temperature to 30°C and fill the soap dispenser with the manufacturers recommended quantity of Down Wash (this depends on the weight of the bag).

- After the wash cycle is complete, remove the bag from the washing machine and rinse the bag thoroughly, or use the washing machines rinse cycle.

- Rinse until the water runs clear.

Hand wash

If you share a house with other people be considerate and negotiate a time slot for taking over the bath as this process takes quite a bit of time.

- Fill your bath with lukewarm water mixing in either pure soap flakes or down cleaner.

- Place your sleeping bag into the bath and gently press it down so it is submerged.

- Agitate it a little and then go away for a brew.

- After an hour or so, let the water drain from the bath and refill with fresh water. Gently massage the bag to remove the soap from the down, use the shower to help with this bit.

- Keep going, be patient, until all the soapy water is removed. Gently push down on the down bag to remove as much water as possible.

Important: Do not wring or squeeze the bag, this will damage the down.

Drying your sleeping bag

Now, what are you going to do with that soggy mass of feathers? Take care when lifting your bag, it will be heavy. If you have a tumble dryer, set it to the lowest heat option. Throw in the clean tennis balls with your bag. As the bag dries these will break up the down clumps. Large bags will require quite some time before they are dry, so hang around and check your bag's progress every half hour or so.

OR

No dryer? Lay it opened in a clean, dry, and shady area to dry. Massage and separate the drying down until completely dry (this is a painstaking process and not recommended at all). Air drying a bag can take days! If your bag is left unattended the down will clump together and it will not be nice and fluffy. Don't throw your bag over the washing line and leave it to drip dry.

The downside of down

Down is bird's feathers, the softer feathers which grow underneath the coarse outer feathers, the ones you see. Down, therefore comes from birds (geese or ducks) which are commercially produced. These geese can be the same ones force fed to produce pate foie gras. The down feathers can have been harvested from live geese as a by-product of the foie gras industry. Clearly this is not acceptable to most hill goers and the companies that create our down-filled garments have investigated supply chains and signed up to the Responsible Down Standards, which traces the down from source to manufacturer. The industry leader has been Mountain Equipment with their Down Codex system.

On the other hand, down is biodegradable and it is renewable, unlike synthetic fill materials, which are composed of oil-based non-renewables, though some are made from recycled material and can be recycled again.

Please check how the down in your garment was sourced. Down is really long-lasting and only needs to be fluffed up to keep its loft and its insulating ability. Keep your down items for ever, these are not fashion items, they are functional. A vintage down jacket should have extra cachet.

Options

There are some really impressive synthetic bags available these days, so the choice is not as clear cut as it might once have been. Synthetic bags will have a 'down-like' filling, e.g. PrimaLoft or be made of fibre pile. Both are very forgiving if they get wet. They can be washed easily and will remain warm if you do get wet on camp. If tarps are your thing, then the fibre pile bags go really well with these. I'm afraid, however, they are bulkier and heavier than down sleeping bags. So, is ease of washing and forgiveness to damp more important to you? Or is being able to lift your rucksack up and have space for other items in it too?

There are some other options. There are super-lightweight quilts and short sleeping bags with which you need to wear a belay jacket. If weight is the big issue, these are worth considering. One other thing to think about is a liner or not. If you are using a down bag, having a liner reduces the need for washing the bag, and the liner can easily be washed. A silk liner is nice, it's warm and easy to wash, but it isn't very robust. A cotton liner works well, for many people they are worth a try and are very easy to wash. They feel nice too. I've used a cotton liner quite a lot. In winter it has given me a bit more warmth in my three season sleeping bag, while in the summer it's been nice to be in the liner and use the sleeping bag quilt-style. I think it's worth experimenting with a liner. It's only when I'm trying really hard to keep the weight down that I decide not to take it.

Are you a pillow person? For most of us a pillow makes a real difference to our night's sleep. You can buy some neat little camping pillows and there are some inflatable ones. Most of us will tend to use what we have. Traditionally this is the rest of your clothes. A great little trick is to use a dry bag, pop some of your spare clothes in in it, tuck it inside something, ideally a shirt of some sort, and you have pretty good pillow

Sleeping mats

Sleeping mats have evolved quite significantly over the years. I remember starting out without one, then discovering Karrimats, a closed cell foam pad, and thinking I'll never be able to do without this again. I now think the same about the Thermarest and its copycats. Insulation from the ground, and the associated loss of heat, is absolutely fundamental to your comfort and a good night's sleep.

Expedition Skills

A selection of sleeping mats

For most of us this will mean an inflatable mat with insulation inside; a lightweight sleeping mat, typically self-inflating. In the same way a vacuum cleaner is known as a Hoover, 'Thermarest' has become a generic term for these lightweight sleeping mats. Thermarest invented them, others have copied. They come in varying lengths, thicknesses and weights. A threequarter length one used to be the choice, it kept the important part of you insulated from the ground and was lighter than a full length one. Nowadays, there are a range of full length mats available from a range of manufacturers, including some very small, packable, mats which you need to blow up yourself. Supplying groups with lightweight inflatable mats is rarely done. They'll be on a closed cell foam pad, they'll be warm, but won't sleep as well as you do. Closed cell foam pads do come in a range of qualities and the cheaper ones will tear easily.

> **Do self-inflating sleeping mats self-inflate?**
>
> Yes. They do. I know I'm not the only one who can be a little impatient, but honestly if you leave it alone for about ten minutes it will self-inflate. You might need to top it up a little with blown air, but minimising blowing air in is good, as when you blow into the mat you will exhale moisture. Don't blow it up as hard as you possibly can though, it'll actually be a little more comfortable if it has some 'give' in it.

Other kit

One other little bit of kit I've found useful when out on camp is a pack towel. They are really light, easy to wash and quick drying. When packing your tent it's best to stuff it into a stuff sack in a fairly unruly way. If you fold it neatly then you'll create weak points along the folds (like on your maps). If you grab your tent at its apex and stuff it into the stuff sack, you should be able to pack it away without the inner getting wet. If you do have a few splashes on the tent floor it's easy to wipe up with your pack towel. It also means you've got no excuse for not going for that wild swim as well!

> **Top tips from Mountain Leaders**
>
> Keep a microfibre cloth with your tent to dry the fabric before putting it in your bag. This ensures your tent is dry when you put it up and allows you to pack the inner and outer together further reducing pitching and packing away time.
>
> Al Topping

Other kit needed will be a mug (thermos mugs are great), a spoon (I just take one from the kitchen draw at home), means to light your stove (lighter), and an extra water bottle to reduce trips to collect water. I would also recommend ear plugs to reduce wind noise or to block out snoring neighbours.

Using camp stoves

One of the joys of wild camping is spending time outside. A nice spot with a good seat and a view of the sun setting will be the best place to cook. You will have learnt how to cook under your flysheet porch for your assessment, in case it was raining solidly for the three days of the expedition. Think about this space when buying a tent, it is crucial. The porch area needs to be big enough for you to strip off in, leaving your boots and waterproofs behind. You might need to leave a wet rucksack in here too and it's a dry space for cooking in. When introducing people to wild camping

Cooking on a gas stove, nicely set up away from the tent.

Well organised cooking close to the tent, but not under the flysheet.
Photo: Bren Whelan

they need to learn how to use camp stoves. In the early days you'd cook well away from the tent. Getting to the stage at which you are teaching someone how to cook in their porch should be the culmination of a structured progression. I do think it's important to consider this as a goal, some of the people you lead will want to go on and become Mountain Leaders themselves, so they should have these skills. The key skill required is to risk assess the cooking location as I know I'm not the only Mountain Leader who's seen a tent go up in flames or had to treat camp stove burns.

Risk assessment consideration for cooking in camp

Risk assessments should not be downloaded and printed out, they need to be worked through practically with the leader and the learner. Here are a few of the things you might need to consider:

- Is it windy?
- Is it sheltered?
- Is it raining?
- Is there enough light?
- Is the ground solid and level?
- Is there any flapping material nearby?
- Have the stove users been taught how to use that particular stove?
- Can they light and extinguish the stove?
- Can they place a pan safely on the stove?
- Can they remove a pan safely from the stove?
- Will they need to refuel and can they do this safely?
- Do they know how to treat a burn?

Modern gas stoves are brilliant, efficient and stable. Even the ones that look a bit tall can be made to stand upright, and because they have a secured lid it's not the end of the world if they do fall over, depending on where the flame goes obviously. If you are cooking in your porch the stove needs to be as central as possible and as far away from your tent as you can get it.

It's useful to be able to get organised with water and have everything to hand and be able to cook in your tent porch, even when the weather is good. You'll be laying down and resting your body for the next day's activity. It's a must when it's raining.

Trangia are really good stoves to use outdoors. They do have some special risks though, refuelling needs managing very carefully. Often, a leader will not authorise youngsters to do their own refuelling but, as with everything, this will need teaching at some point. These stoves, when using the traditional fuel of meths, work better out in a breeze, away from the tent porch. Those converted to gas can be used pretty much anywhere.

Trangia stoves, with their built in wind shield are brilliant stoves for new people camping in the wild. I use a gas Trangia set up when sea kayaking and it works really well. Unfortunately, it's too heavy for me to carry when walking, though it works well for groups. I've got a Jetboil type stove ('systems stove' or 'all-in-one') which has seen many years of use and I'd wholly recommend this style of stove. It is designed for simply heating water up, quickly and efficiently; this works very well for lightweight backpacking. Currently I've also got the tiniest pocket stove imaginable, it's gas and I use a titanium pan on it, it really does keep the weight down, but it does need to be sheltered from the wind. Life will be easier if you restrict your stoves to boiling water, no need for washing up, no need to get food stuck in the pan. We'll look at how to achieve this in the food section.

Not many people will opt for the multi-fuel pressure type stoves in this country. If travelling abroad, or on an extended expedition you do need to think about them if only for the cost of the fuel. Gas is quite expensive, meths can be hard to find while petrol is actually dirt cheap (honest!).

Expedition Skills

Top tips from Mountain Leaders

I've only had to deal with two injuries in all the leading of walkers I have done. Both injuries involved accidents with stoves. (I'm not counting blister preventions, or people I wasn't leading who I was able to help). There are a number of ways we can improve safety in this area:

- Teach your group how to use their stoves before setting off – have a practice brew.

- Consider spending a first night camped by a bothy so they can cook communally and you can supervise.

- Insist that, if possible, they cook outside (consider taking a tarp to create a sheltered cooking area).

If it is pouring with rain and cooking in the tent porch is the only option:

- Make sure that no one is in their sleeping bag while cooking is taking place.

- Tie tent flaps securely.

- No one should enter or leave the tent while the stove is lit.

- Never leave a lit stove unattended.

The Mountain Leader will have to give good briefings to cover these points. While they are cooking, put your waterproofs on, squat in front of each entrance in turn, chat with the members of your group and check that they are following your guidelines.

Franco Ferrero

In the days when people smoked cigarettes, as long as you had a smoker in your group you'd be sure that they would have a light. These days you need look after yourself. An old smoker would have a least two lighters in waterproof bags and a set of matches hidden away. You can have great fun with turbo lighters, waterproof matches and flint striking kits. Two cheap disposable lighters will work and it'll be a long time before you do need to dispose of them so they are not as bad as you might think for the environment. Matches are more environmentally friendly (according to the manufacturers anyway) and you could use a refillable lighter. Rubbing two heather stems together won't work.

THE MOUNTAIN LEADER

Note for Trainers

Don't presume everyone has experience of camping in the hills. You may still get people on a training course who have not experienced it. They may well think 'wild' camping is just camping, but not on a campsite. Many will have had their last experience of camping on their own D of E expedition and will be tuned into carrying very heavy rucksacks which contain all sorts of stuff you now know is unnecessary.

Teach them, show them what you use, how you pack your bag, show them and tell them your top tips. They may well be worried about going to the toilet, about how much food to carry and what spare clothes they should take with them. Assume nothing, but do look for experience within the group and try and get them to share their experiences too.

Remember it's fun! I know it might be raining, but that's just the luck of the draw with your calendar. Extol the virtues of camping, it's not to be endured, it's to be enjoyed.

The exponential growth of fire pits

Led by poor role modelling on TV shows it's become very fashionable to 'Insta' yourself, settling down over a fire in the great outdoors. It is possible to have a fire and leave no evidence. Below the high tide line of a beach works well, removing, then subsequently replacing a turf works fine inland. Leaving a burnt circle is not fine, though if it were just one burnt circle it wouldn't be so bad, but they do have a habit of multiplying. I found fourteen at one Eryri beauty spot and this was a location you had to walk to as well. I'm going to really upset some of you now and say that, actually, cooking on fires is a bit of a pain too. It leads to filthy pans and half-cooked food. If you do it, wait for the embers and use some of the old scouting techniques like foil-wrapped potatoes in the ashes. A barbecue grill can be passable, but you aren't going to carry one of those on your lightweight, camping expedition are you?

An opportune and appropriate fire. On the beach, below the high tide mark.

High in the Moelwynion someone has burnt whatever was laying around, mostly heather stems and a fence post, and left their mess behind. A most inappropriate fire in an inappropriate place.

They are allowed in Scotland. The Scottish Access Code says the following:

- Do not light fires in forests, on farmland, on peaty ground, in very dry conditions, near cultural heritage sites, on Areas of Special Scientific Interest, or near buildings and roads.

- Keep fires small, under control and supervised at all times.

- You may be liable for major damage caused by a fire.

- Remove all traces of an open fire.

Expedition Skills

This is the scarring a disposable a barbecue leaves behind when used directly on the ground. The scar will last for two or three years.

This disposable barbecue was found near the summit of Tryfan. It'd probably been taken and left there by people, possibly licked clean by a dog, or washed clean by the rain.
It could have been moved here by a raven though. Either way, as Mountain Leaders, we need to remove this kind of waste.

The curse of the disposable barbecue

- As they are portable, they may be used in unsuitable locations such as under trees or near long grass, bushes or fences which may easily catch fire.

- The bottom of the barbecue is foil and gets extremely hot, so damages the ground underneath.

- They can easily tip over.

- They may take several hours to cool down and so are often left while still hot.

- If they are placed in a bin before they are completely cool they may set the bin or rubbish bag alight.

- Barbecues produce carbon monoxide which is toxic and using them in a non-ventilated area, even a tent, can be fatal (this is true of camping stoves as well).

- Don't use them.

- Disposable barbecues are deeply hated by the farming community too. It is good to see moves to ban the sale of disposable barbecues in and around some national parks, led by the Co-op. The BMC has campaigned against their use too. On the BMC website is a template to aid your letter of objection against the continued sale of disposable barbecues.

Water

Before we look at food, everything is dependent on water. Carrying sufficient water for even an overnight camp would be very heavy and we don't need to do that. But can you drink the water?

Yes. We are lucky to live in the British Isles, it's a land of plentiful rain, our warm, wet climate means we never have water shortages (well not in the hilly bits anyway!). There may be a shortage of water in the places urban Britains need it, but that is not in the hills, where the streams, quite remarkably, continue to run well and clean. However, you do have to be mindful of one or two traps. The first story you will have heard is: *"What if there is a dead sheep upstream".*

Well, there hardly ever is. Sheep do not go to streams to die; they just don't do that. They do get washed into streams and over the years I have seen one or two dead sheep in streams, it's not nice, but it does happen, usually they have been washed in by heavy rain, but it's rare. So, in heavy rain, when you'd think this would be the best time to drink from a stream, and it probably still is as the water is straight from the sky, the odds of disease from a dead sheep are slightly increased, but it's still an uncommon sight. On the other hand, if there is a drought and anything unpleasant in the water may become concentrated, you need to make sure that you are as near the source, the spring, as possible; this is good practice anyway. Always seek out the highest water on the hill, make sure it is flowing well. When you find water flowing from underground in the mountains it is pure, clean, sweet and a real thrill for people to drink. I don't like drinking stationary water. If I have to drink from a lake when camping I make sure I boil the water, you just keep a bit of rolling boil going to fill up your water bottle. You'll usually pass another spring source when you move on the next day.

Top tips from Mountain Leaders

A simple briefing goes a long way. When I get to camp, one of the things I cover with the group is the importance of maintaining a clean water supply. Key points are to pick an obvious feature on the river and make clear that:

- Drinking water should only be collected upstream of that point.

- Water for rinsing pans or people should be collected from downstream of that point.

- Water used in washing should be emptied well away from the stream.

- Any toileting should take place downstream of the chosen point and at least 50m from the stream.

Franco Ferrero

Probably the biggest dangers are locations below human habitation and agricultural run-off. Below human habitation there is always a risk of something unsavoury in the water. Perhaps not so bad as in less developed parts of the world where you would never drink the water, but enough to proceed with caution. Agricultural run-off can lead to growth of bad bugs too due to the fertilizers in the water. So, drink high, drink beyond human habitation, get your fill when you can, and enjoy it, it's one of the thrills of wild camping. In my experience, young people actually get quite a thrill from drinking spring water, they can take some convincing though, so take them through your risk assessment procedure and how you choose where to drink from.

Expedition Skills

The Falls of Tarf. High up Glen Tilt in the Cairngorms. This is fast flowing water straight off the hill, above any human habitation, but would you drink it?

If you are worried, or you believe you have a delicate stomach then don't be averse to filtering your water, there are some really good lightweight filters on the market now, some even use UV light. Of course, don't forget boiling, boiling is a brilliant way of making sure your water is free of harmful life-forms such as bacteria that can cause illness.

Treating the water

Boiling – You have a stove, it works, it's low cost, it's chemical free, it kills everything. But it does take time, it's tricky if it's windy, a faff if it's raining, and the water does need to cool.

Chemical treatment – Chlorine and chlorine dioxide are the most common (iodine now outlawed). This is lightweight, compact and low cost, but it does leave a strange taste and needs 10 to 30 minutes to work.

Filtration – Effective systems have a pore size of I micron or less. This is relatively quick and simple, reliable and removes debris too. But it is expensive to buy initially, it is bulky, the filters will need cleaning or replacing and it doesn't remove viruses.

Ultraviolet light – Tools like a steripen deactivate bacteria by disrupting the DNA with ultraviolet light. This is therefore free from chemicals and it sterilises the bacteria so they can't reproduce and cause harm to humans. But it doesn't remove all the pollutants, it requires battery power and it's very expensive.

Is water 'on the hill' safe to drink?

Yes, well probably, but possibly not!

Generally, the higher you go, the faster flowing the water, the safer it is to drink. Drinking from water sources, springs, in the mountains of the UK and Ireland should pose you no threat at all. However, you will have heard of some water-borne diseases and you should not be ignorant of the threats that could be posed.

Giardia intestinalis – Protozoan parasite that settles and reproduces in the small intestine, causing diarrhoea, stomach cramps, and foul smelling-gassiness, illness can last for months.

Avoid by washing hands, boiling water, filter or disinfect.

Cryptosporidium – Protozoa covered by a hard shell which protects it from disinfectants like chlorine. Infection symptoms include watery stools, stomach cramps, nausea and vomiting.

Avoid by boiling. UV and chlorine dioxide will also inactivate it.

***Escherichia coli* (E coli)** – Bacteria found in the lower intestine, some occur naturally and others cause poisoning characterised by diarrhoea that can turn bloody, stomach cramps and fever.

Avoid by boiling, filtering or disinfecting.

Camp food – what should we eat?

Over the years I've fluctuated between dehydrated food and boil in the bag food. Some people will swear by one brand or the other. Recently, there has been a growth in smaller providers producing some excellent dehydrated and freeze-dried food, and if it's for one or two nights I usually choose these. Occasionally, I do some longer trips and you then start to notice the cost of these items so if you are on a budget have a look in your local supermarket, you'll be surprised what there is lurking in the ready meal, dehydrated section. Even if it's just noodles or instant mash you can have a pretty good meal without too much stress. I like porridge for breakfast. I pre-prepare it in a plastic jar, oats, with dried milk, brown sugar and dried fruit. I then just add boiling water, cover and leave for a few minutes, as it cools to a temperature whereby you can eat it, it hydrates to form a lovely porridge.

Whatever you do choose, try to eat good, natural healthy food and don't forget to tick your food groups: carbohydrates, fats, proteins, vitamins and minerals. They all have a role to play when you are physically active. The gold

Porridge made simple. Use the cheaper smaller oats, just add boiling water, leave for 5 to 10 minutes and you'll have delicious porridge to suit your taste. I make it in the plastic jar and carry rations in plastic bags for subsequent days.

standard is probably to buy a dehydrator and make your own dehydrated meals, although this is slow and needs carefully planning. When teaching groups how to wild camp this is a major area to consider and cost verses convenience will come into play. For one night, you can get away with pretty much anything, but as soon as you are teaching people how to wild camp for consecutive nights, more serious consideration needs to be undertaken. For two, three or even four nights the commercially produced camp food is probably the best option, beyond that, which is rare in the UK to be fair, alternatives, including visits to a café or pub, might need planning for.

Snacking is handy when you are on a trip and again for a short trip, I'm not too bothered what I eat, any energy bars, chocolate bars, breakfast bars or a malt loaf. Some people like a trail mix, this is a good option, particularly if you make it yourself. Just fill a bag with dried fruit, sweets such as jelly babies and some nuts to suit your taste buds.

You will need to think about your daily, calorific intake. Some commercially produced dried meals or camp foods do not provide as much as you might think. On a normal day you need 2,000 to 2,500 calories, if you are out in the mountains for the day you can probably double this quite easily. If I'm organised, I'll prep some flapjack to take with me. Fruit filled syrupy flapjack will take me a long way (it's quite heavy though)! Bread can be a bit of a pain, some people take pitta breads, but I think I prefer squashed bread myself. Sweets, chocolate and biscuits for in the tent nibbling are good too. Salted peanuts (or other nuts) are good for arrival at camp, high energy and salt replacing yumminess. I miss fruit, fruit is too heavy to carry, and on return to a valley I usually have a craving for orange juice. You can buy dehydrated orange juice, but it's very expensive.

Top tips from Mountain Leaders

If people are joining you on a trip where they have to supply their own food, you might consider sending them an outline of what makes suitable camp food and some sample menus, including quantities.

Franco Ferrero

Where to camp

We shall leave the legal aspects, discussed previously, aside for now as we consider where to actually camp. Out of sight, out of mind will be important, high in the hills is best. If you are on your own you can plan to have enough water and camp pretty much anywhere. It's quite 'Insta' fashionable to camp on summits. This is unlikely to be the best place to camp with a group. We will need to look for sites which are level, and have a water source, ideally it will be sheltered from the prevailing winds and the ground will be dry. There are many places like this, but there are a whole load more that aren't. A flat little oasis of sheep-cropped grass, not exposed to south-westerlies and next to a stream of fresh, running water is the dream, this is your nirvana! You may need to compromise. I've spent ages trying to get the head end of my tent uphill if there's gentle slope only to get into bed and swear blind my head is downhill! As soon as you pitch your tent a rock or a lump will appear where your hip needs to go. You'll find your porch is full of sheep poo and then you'll realise you can't even see the view that you so carefully pitched by! Be mindful of flooding, camping next to a stream can be hazardous. I'd tend to avoid old quarries too, there can be loose rock and unprotected cliff edges. Heed these lessons and build them into your teaching. Having a discussion with the group about *"What makes this a good campsite?",* is a good way of passing on this knowledge.

It always seems to be a bit of a compromise. You soon give up looking for perfection and make do. But as soon as you do take the decision to stop and camp, to make your home for the night, to pitch your tent and settle in, it becomes home. You want to stay there and departure is always a little sad in the morning, you linger and then you vow to return. When you are leading groups, don't forget to reiterate the rules about not polluting water, where to go to the toilet and not leaving any trace of your visit.

Top tips from Mountain Leaders

Try not to move rocks when camping; each rock has its own undisturbed ecosystem underneath. If you do move rocks when pitching a tent on a wild site, always replace them when you leave.

Derek Clarke

Campsites often feel odd on arrival, it takes a while to settle, they then become home for the night and you can be reluctant to leave in the morning.

Expedition Skills

Washing

I don't wash. There, I've said it. No soap will touch me when out in the hills, I might take a toothbrush on a two night camp, but not on a one-night camp. I might rinse myself in a lake or a stream, particularly if it's hot, but not with soap. I find it best not to go overboard on the bodily products all together; they shouldn't be introduced to the natural environment at all. In normal, British conditions, it takes two or three days before you actually start to smell. What I do, is shower where I can, so on longer journeys I will visit a hostel or similar in the valley, but, for a two-night camp, I can cope. I hate wet-wipes, they are an eco-disaster and should not be used.

That's all well and good for me, but what about a group? Most will be fine for one night, but some will need a lot of convincing not to take soap and cleaning products. Most will actually enter into the spirit and enjoy their night away from soap, but you do need to prepare people for this. A splash or even a dip in a stream can be brilliant in the right conditions and with the right group, but I think it might be the exception rather than the norm. If you get the opportunity to teach people who will be embarking on several nights under canvas then you'll need to break down your own habits and make them appropriate, and teachable, to this new audience.

Sphagnum moss, nature's wet-wipes

Sphagnum moss is really good at purifying water, but this is not an instant process, water needs time to pass through the sphagnum bog. Rainwater held in the moist moss will be safe to drink, but it can't be used as a water filter to kill bacteria instantly. It actually changes the pH of the water over time to inhibit competition from other plants. The way it rots down and traps carbon has come to be recognised as of crucial importance to our planet. It is also really handy stuff for us. In war times it was dried out and used to dress wounds as it is superabsorbent and has antiseptic qualities. A sphagnum bog is a good place to use as a toilet, as your excretions will be sent through the bogs natural filtering systems and clean water will flow from the bog, but only in limited numbers and definitely not repeatedly in the same place. It's great stuff for washing with too, rather like nature's wet-wipes, but again this must be very limited.

Sphagnum should not be abused as it is an important ecosystem, and we cannot afford to damage our sphagnum bogs, so go carefully. It'll cope if we don't all use the same bit, so instead of going near camp, wait till you have travelled some way and then take a little time out to use nature's wet-wipes. Coniferous plantations often have good stands of sphagnum within them.

Toilets

Going to the toilet. We are actually quite lucky here in the UK, in that our warm wet, temperate climate can deal quite well with human waste. Anything buried will decompose relatively quickly. Temperatures need to be above freezing, hence in the Scottish winter, carrying out is recommended and the Cairngorm Poo Project has been widely applauded.

The Keep Cairngorm Snow White project

Generally known to climbers and walkers by its original name, the Cairngorm Poo Project has had some success in keeping human waste off the mountains. There was a problem with people going to the toilet, particularly in winter in similar locations. The good snow-holing sites soon get known and act as a bit of draw. Because of the low winter temperatures, human faeces was being preserved through the winter and spring would be greeted with piles of thawing poo. The rangers base at Cairngorm can supply you with a poo-pot which you bring down to a disposal point in the car park there.

Make your own poo-pot

You can of course make your own poo-pot. You just need some bio-degradable dog poo bags and a solid, leakproof container to seal it in for the journey down to a disposal point. Top tip is to have a sheet of newspaper in your dog poo bag, fold this out, poo on it then fold it up and pop it in the dog poo bag. This is much easier than aiming for the dog poo bag while you are trying to hold it in the right position, keeping your trousers out of the way, balancing on your toes, with the wind blowing, the snow threatening, with raven and grouse cackling at you ... In summer you can just dig a hole, keep a trowel handy.

Now, try teaching your group how to do that ...

In hot deserts and mediterranean climates, spreading human waste onto rocks is the recommended method, the sun then breaks down the waste. Here however, shallow burial away from water sources works well. Of course, there are some caveats in that large amounts can accumulate in 'hot spots'. There have been issues in the both the Lake District and Eryri where poor toileting has affected water quality below popular camping spots.

Best practice for going to the toilet, for number 2's, in the UK and Ireland, outside of any season where temperatures are consistently below 0 degrees, is to make sure you are 50 metres away from any water source.

This can be difficult in wet weather in some of our uplands. If it's this wet, let's hope there will be extra dilution.

Remove a turf and dig a small hole, 6" deep, you can probably get away with burying some toilet paper, but many have impregnations of plastic or perfume. You should burn it, carry it out in a dog poo bag, or better still use leaves or moss, nature's wet-wipes (don't ever use wet-wipes). Sanitary towels should be carried out too.

Wash your hands. Evaporating bio hand-gel works well, as does sphagnum moss.

Dressing for dinner

Dress for dinner, what a bizarre idea! Well, don't rule it out completely. On a one or two-night camp I will take no spare clothes. I might have a spare pair of socks and a spare pair of wicking underpants. Beyond this, I don't need anything. Modern fabrics are quick drying, many are odour suppressing too. There really is no need to carry anything extra for a one or two-night camp. We are not all the same though, taking a spare base layer is really light and can make a difference to your warmth and comfort in the evening. Beyond this, it becomes worth considering for everybody, especially if you're on a journey where you rub up against civilisation. So, if I'm sea kayaking then I'll take a change of clothes to wear in camp in the evening, but in this context, weight is much less of a problem. If I'm bike-packing, weight is nearly as critical as when backpacking on foot, so while I will take spare clothes, (mainly for pub visits!) they will be very lightweight. You can get some really lightweight flip flops, lightweight summer trousers and a lightweight shirt. It's amazing how smart you can end up looking with just a little thought. If I'm walking though, I really want to avoid this if I can, but do not dismiss it out of hand. As I say, for a three-night plus expedition it is well worth thinking about. If you are somebody who already takes a spare set of clothes, for camp, then consider ditching them as this is a really easy way to save a bit of weight.

> **Looking after the group in camp**
>
> It's easy to forget on your ML training and assessment that you are being assessed with a view to looking after a group on a wild camp. This is not a race to get the best pitch for your tent, you will be helping the group to choose a pitch and make sure they can put their tent up well. You'll be discussing where to get water from, if it's from a lake or a tarn make sure they boil it. You need to look at how they are going to cook, you'll have done lots of preparation for this beforehand, but you still need to check that any rules you have put in place are being followed. You'll need to make sure they eat and they rest. Make sure any schedule is clear. You sometimes have to tell people what to do,

collect water now, eat now, go to the toilet now, etc. Make sure they know when they need to be ready in the morning and they've thought about how long it will take to get ready. Make sure they don't pollute any water, that they don't wash up or wash themselves with any kind of soap. Watch out for discarded food, everything brought in must be taken out (however yuk it is!).

Camp routine with groups

Time – allow plenty.

Finding camp – can you involve them in the decisions?

Pitching tents – they may well have practiced before but you need to keep an eye on them at this stage. They can be heavy-handed, lack wind awareness, ignore stony ground, fail to put pegs in properly and be half-hearted about the shape of the tent.

Water – where are we getting it from, are we safe from flooding, where is the toilet area?

Eating – check that everyone eats well.

Change of clothes – is it necessary?

Footwear – do you need a change?

Chatting – not too late into the night please.

Lights – everyone has a torch on their phone these days, but a head-torch will be much better in camp.

Tent management – make sure everyone is organised in their tent and that kit will be kept dry.

Time in the morning – It will always take longer than you think to strike camp and get everybody ready for departure.

Multitasking – is it possible to teach some movement efficiency and get some of your youngsters doing more than one thing at a time?

Hygiene – check for waste food, check for toothpaste, make sure everyone is as clean and healthy as they can be and no trace has been left behind.

Litter – double check your site before leaving.

Expedition Skills

Use of huts, bothies and other shelters

I love bothies. They are not everyone's cup of tea. Some bothies are incredible places, on fantastic sites, in fantastic places. For me, the remoter the better, and if I can go midweek in school term, I know I'll have a lovely time. There is just a risk that your chosen bothy can be full, particularly at weekends, particularly during the school holidays. You need to be confident not to take your tent and to rely on there being space in the bothy – that's the other thing, other people. Some people go 'bothying'. They may well walk to the bothy, but the bothy is the object of the trip, not wandering over mountains as we might do.

This has pros and cons. Bothiers carry coal, alcohol and a generosity of spirt. Chat, join in and make friends, these will be some of the best people you'll ever meet. There are a few oddballs though and don't think just because you've gone to bed early the revelry will die down. All the Mountain Bothy Association owned (actually they only own two, the rest have private owners) or managed bothies require volunteers to look after them. Bothies are free, you should consider joining the MBA, it's really very cheap. Whatever you choose, you should aim to leave the bothy in perfect condition. Leave no rubbish, sweep the floor on departure, make sure the door is properly closed. If there are any problems with the bothy you can report them on the MBA website, if it's a problem with excess rubbish how about making the removal of such the object of your next trip?

Bothying is not really for groups. There is a limit on six people in one group visiting a bothy. It could be handy to camp near to one in bad weather, but you'll be hard pushed to stay out of it if the weather really is bad. For personal journeys though, I can't recommend them highly enough, they really do make winter trips much more pleasant.

Ben Alder Bothy, it's a hillwalkers' favourite.

THE MOUNTAIN LEADER

Bothying at its best a roaring fire in the wonderful Cadderlie bothy.

The Bothy Code

The Mountain Bothies Association manages bothies on behalf of bothy owners. They have an established code of conduct applicable to all who stay in bothies. To maintain the use of these bothies it is imperative that we abide by the code.

Respect other users

Please leave the bothy clean and tidy with dry kindling for the next visitors. Make other visitors welcome and be considerate to other users.

Respect the bothy

Tell us about any accidental damage. Don't leave graffiti or vandalise the bothy. Please take out all rubbish which you can't burn. Avoid burying rubbish; this pollutes the environment. Please don't leave perishable food as this attracts vermin. Guard against fire risk and ensure the fire is out before you leave. Make sure the doors and windows are properly closed when you leave.

Respect the surroundings

If there is no toilet at the bothy please bury human waste out of sight. Use the spade provided, keep well away from the water supply and never use the vicinity of the bothy as a toilet. Never cut live wood or damage estate property. Use fuel sparingly.

Expedition Skills

Respect the agreement with the estate

Please observe any restrictions on use of the bothy, for example during stag stalking or at lambing time. Please remember bothies are available for short stays only. The owner's permission must be obtained if you intend an extended stay.

Respect the restriction on numbers

Because of overcrowding and lack of facilities, large groups (6 or more) should not use a bothy. Bothies are not available for commercial groups.

Note for Assessors

You just need to be clear about the programme of events. You may well be used to being a bit vague about where you are going. You don't need to hide anything, you'll soon see who's ready and who isn't. I give a rough route outline of where we'll be heading and where we'll be camping. I tend to suggest we'll do some night navigation on both nights, I'd rather do two shorter chunks and use the day well, rather than one big one that eats into the day's journeying.

While this isn't intended to be a route march it's not unreasonable to include one or even two quality mountain days on your expedition. You'll be looking for them to set a good example in the wild, to eat well, keep hydrated and go to the toilet. You will not be looking for them to just survive. They need to look like leaders, like role models, they need to appear to be enjoying themselves and should be able to answer questions about group management well.

Entertainment

The evenings in camp can be long. If you ended up doing your Mountain Leader training or assessment at certain times of the year you would have been holed up in your tent for a significant amount of time. In summer, there will be a necessity to wait for it to go dark. Ideally this time will be spent sitting around outside engaged in convivial chat, maybe having a swim or just enjoying the fresh air and watching nature go by. In the autumn and spring, you might have time for a meal then go out for a walk in the dark. On return it'll be bedtime so there is less down time in these months. In the winter, when it's dark early, you could have completed your night navigation tasks quite early in the evening and you could be looking at (particularly if the weather is poor) a 14 hour stint in your tent. At times like this a book is worth its weight in gold. A second-hand paperback that you are not too precious about is probably the best choice because, with the best will in the world, they can get wet. Maybe a thin book, rather than a heavy book.

Of course, these days you do have other choices and as many people as take a book probably load a film onto their mobile phone to watch in the evening, hopefully they'll have the manners to wear earphones. You can also get quite a lot of books downloaded onto a mobile phone. Whatever you choose to do, for me, an evening of guilt free reading is another joy of camping.

On reflection

One of the most important exercises after a camp is to think about what you have used, what did you really need and what could you have done without. Some things you'll always have to take whether you use them or not, such as your first aid kit. Other things may have turned out to be superfluous and next time you should try without them. Likewise, you may have thought of something you'd like to have brought, bring it next time. Here's a few I've played with: try taking an extra, empty water bottle, then once filled up you can stay in your tent without needing to get back out for water. If you are in a situation where you want to stay in your tent then you need a system for going to the toilet. Blokes can use an empty boil in the bag food bag. For females you might need some sort of bowl or to experiment with a female urinating device such as a Shewee. How about a hip flask with your favourite tipple (obviously, not if you're leading a group)! Can you manage life without milk? I bet you took too many tea bags, and do you really need to carry that fancy coffee maker?

While many Mountain Leaders rarely camp after their assessment expedition it is greatly enjoyed by many others. It is quite fashionable, very rewarding and will appeal to many people. Do not underestimate the need to prepare, you'll be surprised at what people get wrong. Dissect what you do and how you do it then build this into a series of lesson plans to be used when teaching expedition skills.

> **Top tips from Mountain Leaders**
>
> On a Duke of Edinburgh Award expedition (or any expedition with young people), the rucksacks will often be too heavy and too big relative to what they actually need. They will have two of everything they don't need but only some of what they do need. Get them to unpack their rucksack before setting off. Don't take their word that they have packed a lunch / waterproofs / sun cream / water etc. You need to actually see it.
>
> Paul Sanderson

Expedition Skills

Camping with young people

There are Mountain Leaders who choose not to undertake camping with their groups. On the other hand, there are plenty that do and camping, particularly with young people, can be a very rewarding experience for all concerned. It is not easy work and appropriate skills and an awareness of safety needs to be built up progressively. When done well, it is an experience of a lifetime for many people. These pictures show young people from Bloxham School building up their organisational, cooking and teamwork skills. They start in Year nine and build their skills and knowledge each year. They move from practice expeditions on campsites to proper wild camps in later years.

Progression in camp skills at Bloxham School.

Walkers on Helvellyn.

What else do we need to know?

The Development of Hillwalking and its Representative Bodies

The origins of, and the development of, this wonderful pastime of hillwalking should probably be more important to us today. The legacy that has shaped how we 'play the game 'and how we influence others who use the same spaces has been developed in many places, by many people over many years. It is hard to pinpoint lead figures and locally influential voices, in the same way that climbing and mountaineering can. But the 'rules' of the game and our code of ethics have evolved to produce a low key, gentle and rewarding pastime. This includes a long standing distaste of waymarking, a love of maps and a leave no trace approach. It is a pastime with a conciliatory, and considerate tone, but when threatened can rise to make itself known, politely but strongly.

Exploring ring contours in Eryri.

A potted history of the development of hill-walking as a recreational activity

It's quite lucky, in some ways, that the idea of hillwalking for hillwalking's sake grew from a minor Victorian interest in mountaineering. It took some time after the beginnings of Alpine mountaineering by, amongst others, the British upper classes to realise that the smaller mountains of the British Isles would give some good 'sport' in preparation for travels to the so-called greater ranges.

To actually go for a walk 'over the tops' for fun was probably not an idea that would have occurred to most people before the Industrial Revolution. People spent their time walking to live, walking everywhere was part of daily life, so walking on a day off, especially over the hill tops would not be something that might have had any role to play in the lives of most people. I suspect this is true of most of the world's population, even today.

The idea of walking somewhere just to see the view seems to have been suggested for the first time in print by Thomas West in his 1778 volume *A Guide to the Lakes of Cumberland*, Westmorland and Lancashire. The Romantic poets William Wordsworth, his sister Dorothy, and Samuel Coleridge are now credited with the idea of visiting the Lake District and going for a walk for pleasure. John Keats went walking in the Lakes, Ireland and Scotland in 1818. George Borrow wrote about long walks in Wales in the mid 1800's. Robert Louis Stevenson famously travelled, on foot, with a donkey, through France in 1879.

The first walking clubs did begin to appear in the late 1800's. Sheffield and Manchester were some of the earliest places that saw the establishment of clubs. Some of these clubs were mountaineering and climbing clubs, others focused on walking, or rambling as it came to be known. The moors between these two cities were closed to visitors, even those on foot, as they were the preserve of the landed gentry who had started using them for shooting grouse. It wasn't until the 1930s when the ordinary working people were rambling in sufficient numbers and starting to put pressure on the landowners to let them have bona fide access to the uplands that rambling and walking became accepted pastimes of ordinary people. Prior to this, mountaineering in all its forms was undertaken by people who owned the land, were friends of those who owned the land or, because of their social status, they didn't care who owned the land. But, in the 20th Century, the working people started to get out walking, climbing and cycling. Pressure grew to allow access rather than tolerate it, or in some cases actively discourage it.

The Development of Hillwalking and its Representative Bodies

The Kinder Trespass

In 1932 a group of young walkers decided to take on the establishment and organised a mass trespass over Kinder Scout. Under the charismatic leadership of Benny Rothman hundreds of walkers approached from three different directions and met up on the summit plateau. Here there were waiting gamekeepers who tried to repel the walkers and violent scuffles broke out. Though trespass was, as is today, a civil offence some of the walkers were arrested and imprisoned, none of the gamekeepers were.

Though there are some discrepancies over the actual events of the day and some went on to argue that the event put back access privileges, there is little doubt that is one of the most celebrated events in the history of hillwalking. It must have led, at least indirectly, to the formation of the national parks, the Pennine Way and even the CROW act of 2000. The Kinder Trespass put walkers on the map, so to speak, and it raised an awareness of the desire of ordinary people to enjoy the hills.

The Winter Hill and Darwen Moor access campaigns

While The Kinder Trespass is the best known demand for access to uplands there have been other, even bigger events. In 1896, on Sunday the 6th September, up to 10,000 people from Bolton marched on Winter Hill. They went again the next weekend and again the next weekend. They were incensed that the landowner, Colonel Ainsworth of Smithills Hall, had locked a gate (SD 675132) preventing access to the hill. The local people claimed this was an ancient right of way. They pulled down the gate and continued over the hill and down to the village of Belmont.

Despite a strong defence claiming the track had been in public use for many years, Ainsworth won the court case against the march's ringleaders. The gate remained locked for many more years and it wasn't until 1997 that the track was officially declared as a Public Right of Way.

An even older protest took place just a little north of Winter Hill on Darwen Moor. In the 1870's the Lord of the manor, the Reverend William Arthur Duckworth, blocked ancient rights of way over the moor. Hundreds of local people campaigned against the Lord of the manor's actions. There were some bloody skirmishes between the protesters and gamekeepers. In July 1878 a writ was issued against the protesters led by John Oldham. On this occasion the court found in favour of the Freedom movement and the landowner was ordered to open up twenty-five acres as 'urban common' and allow the public use of all footpaths and tracks, resulting in access for all to 300 acres of moorland.

Walking ethics

The early walkers laid down the code of ethics we follow today. Obviously, it would be abhorrent to leave any litter in the hills and that has always gone without saying. A leave no trace, take only photographs, leave only footprints approach has always been central to our pastime. Litter could extend to some less obvious things and one of those is waymarking. To preserve the challenge in our small mountains, waymarking has been discouraged. With the fabulous maps available from the Ordnance Survey and compasses, readily available as ex-army offerings in the early days, waymarking has never really been required by the serious rambler or walker. The ability to read a map went hand in hand with going walking in our hills. Of course, tracks developed on the most popular walks and people have always trusted to their luck when following these, but the ethic of no waymarking and reading the map soon became well established.

There are, of course some waymarks on our hills. There are the 'finger stones' on Yr Wyddfa. The National Park actually consulted quite widely before putting these in place. They did consult with the BMC who you might expect to be quite opposed to waymarking in the hills as they attempt to protect the heritage of British Mountaineering, but even this group could

Slate trail signpost.

Yr Wyddfa finger stone. At the Snowdon Ranger and Llanberis path junction.

It's hard to imagine anyone thinking that it's OK to do this. Even biodegradable paint takes a long time to fade and is frowned upon by most event organisers. This graffitied way marker was one of several which appeared on the north ridge of Tryfan a few years ago.

The Development of Hillwalking and its Representative Bodies

Temporary trail race markers. The best race practice is to remove these as the last runner goes through.

see that Yr Wyddfa was a different case, and that to oppose signs on a mountain which doubles as a tourist attraction would be folly. I think it's fair to say that traditionally hillwalkers have been reluctant to accept more signposts and way marks in the hills, but being a fairly tolerant bunch, they've accepted them creeping in. There are signs on all of the highest hills in England, Wales, Ireland and Scotland and all have some sort of justification. We accept, and even encourage signposts on long routes such as the national trails like the Pennine Way or the recently waymarked Llwybr Llechi Eryri / Snowdonia Slate Trail.

One of the trickier types of waymarks are cairns. There has, in some places, been a bit of a proliferation of cairns. The John Muir Trust have removed some on Ben Nevis and, every now and then, I have come across walkers who are vehemently opposed to cairns. Cairns are waymarks and as such, reduce the challenge in our little hills, or so their argument goes. I suspect we're all quite happy to see a summit cairn though and there are some, such as those on the north ridge of Tryfan or along the summit ridge of the Glyderau, that many of us have been glad of on a misty day.

As Mountain Leaders we need to introduce these as topics of discussion within our groups. No one will achieve a blanket ban on waymarking. Many people would love to see more, and they are more common in other countries. What the right level is will always be up for discussion. I do see a lot of sense in clearly marked and signed footpaths in some places. Many people do not read maps, do not devour guidebooks, do not trawl the internet for routes to walk. Many people drive to a car park in the countryside and go for a walk, along the obvious paths. I think this is fine, but I also think the summits should be kept free, to maintain the challenge and adventure of hillwalking, where do you draw the line between the two? Well, that's the discussion.

This cairn on the north ridge of Tryfan reminds walkers to come back to the crest. I think this is an example of a useful cairn in complex terrain.

309

Representative bodies

I think being part of a representative body is important and I think you should contribute positively to it yourself. It will bring you various advantages like discounts and access to huts, but it's really all about representing hillwalkers in terms of access discussions or our general interests to government. So, you could argue, this background knowledge is essential and what's more, you could get involved too. Mountain Training has a close relationship with the BMC and many of you will be aware of The Ramblers as well.

The BMC

The British Mountaineering Council was formed in 1944, inspired by Geoffrey Winthrop Young who visualised a representative body for all climbers and mountaineers. The 'council' initially had 25 member clubs, today that number is around 300 and there are over 80,000 individual members too. From its first professional national officer in the 1970's, the BMC now has a busy office with a large staff team working hard on behalf of all walkers, climbers, mountaineers and boulderers. Within the BMC there is a specialist hillwalking committee and members views are always sought, these can easily be aired at one of the regional meetings. The BMC campaigns for access, nature and sound management of the uplands. It has run high profile campaigns to raise money for footpath repairs and raise greater awareness of plastic waste. The BMC employs full-time access and conservation staff who represent member's interests to the English and Welsh Governments.

Mountain Training is a sister organisation to the BMC hence the requirement for BMC membership on registration with the Mountain Leader qualification. While the BMC works in Wales and England, in Scotland the BMC's role is replicated by Mountaineering Scotland and in Ireland by Mountaineering Ireland.

The Ramblers

Following the establishment of a National Council of Ramblers Federations in 1931 the Ramblers Association was formed in 1935. By 1945 they had their first employee. Today, the Ramblers Association operates across Great Britain, with some authority devolved to Ramblers Scotland and Ramblers Cymru. The Ramblers are very active in promoting walking as an easy and accessible form of exercise. The association now has a membership of over 100,000 and around 500 local groups.

In Northern Ireland, a separate entity, the Ulster Federation of Rambling Clubs, performs a similar role, while in Southern Ireland, Mountaineering Ireland are the representative body. Since the 1930s, the activities of the BMC and the Ramblers have grown closer and it is good to see the two organisations working together in some areas, a combined voice would be a considerable one.

Mountain Training

The term Mountain Training is an umbrella term used to refer to the group of mountain training organisations. They are Mountain Training England (MTE), Mountain Training Scotland (MTS), Mountain Training Ireland (MTI) and Mountain Training Cymru (MTC) with Mountain Training UK and Ireland (MTUKI) being the coordinating body.

For most qualifications, including the Mountain Leader qualification, candidates register with their home nation organisation. For the Winter Mountain Leader qualification they must register directly with MTS. For the Mountaineering Instructor qualification, the International Mountain Leader and the coaching climbing qualifications registration is directly with the MTUKI.

There are two other organisations that come under the aegis of Mountain Training.

The Mountain Training Association is the support and development branch of Mountain Training, offering a range of workshops for trainee and qualified leaders and coaches across the disciplines, as well as great deals and discounts. It is open to membership for anyone registered on a Mountain Training qualification. (Mountaineering Instructors can join the Association of Mountaineering Instructors (AMI). International Mountain Leaders can join the British Association of International Mountain Leaders (BAIML). See next page).

The Mountain Training Trust (MTT) was set up originally by MTE, MTUK and the BMC to run Plas y Brenin, the then National Mountain Centre. It is now a separate body which continues to run Plas y Brenin (now the National Outdoor Centre) as its main interest, with the founder organisations represented on the MTT board along with a group of independently appointed directors.

The Mountain Training ethos

We believe in:

> The safe enjoyment of walking, climbing and mountaineering. We disseminate guidance on good practice and provide training and qualifications for participants, instructors, leaders and coaches.

> High quality training and assessment delivered by experienced and supportive practitioners.

> Developing independent walkers, climbers and mountaineers who practice and encourage, sustainable and sympathetic use of the outdoors by all users.

Supporting equal access to our sport for people from all backgrounds. We also believe that all people have the potential to develop leadership and coaching skills if trained appropriately.

Good leadership. Which is about more than decision making and technical skill; it is about supporting and developing individuals.

Inspiring people to enjoy walking, climbing and mountaineering with confidence and skill.

Representative bodies for Mountain Leaders and other leaders working in the British hills

The Mountain Training Association

The Mountain Training Association is the support and development branch of Mountain Training and provides its members with support and CPD (continuous professional development) opportunities. It now has over 6,000 members and has become the membership organisation for climbing, walking and mountain leaders in the UK and Ireland.

Key aims are to:

- Promote good practice and professionalism.

- Lead the way in providing quality personal development opportunities.

- Develop a growing supply of valuable resources.

- Provide a hub for communication and networking.

- Provide regionally focused communities of support.

- Build mutually beneficial links with other outdoor organisations.

- Provide a structure for members to contribute to Mountain Training.

To retain your membership of MTA you should do CPD. The recommendation from MTA is that every 5 years after achieving your Mountain Leader qualification you should:

- Complete 20 days of personal or group leading/supervision experience, ideally a mix of both.

The Development of Hillwalking and its Representative Bodies

- Gain a minimum of 2 credit points from a variety of accredited CPD experiences.

- Record your CPD online in the candidate management system.

"Promoting and developing a robust CPD culture raises the profile of the Mountain Training Association and allows us to confidently promote our members to potential employees, organisations and the public. It's also a great asset for a professional CV and highlights your dedication to enhancing your skills and knowledge. Commitment to CPD is part of being a full member of the association; it's a great way to keep your skills fresh and up to date and a means of demonstrating to others (including employers) that you are passionate about upholding good standards, good practice and professionalism. The records of full members who have held an award for 5 years are audited annually so it is important to keep your CPD record up to date."

From the MTA

The Association of Mountaineering Instructors

The Association of Mountaineering Instructors (AMI) is the representative body for professionally qualified Mountaineering and Climbing Instructors in the UK and Ireland. AMI was formed to represent the interests of the highly experienced mountaineers and climbers who have undergone rigorous training and assessment to qualify under the Mountain Training Mountaineering and Climbing Instructor Scheme. All full members of the Association are holders of the Mountaineering and Climbing Instructor qualification or Winter Mountaineering and Climbing Instructor qualification. AMI provides codes of conduct, CPD and many other services for its members.

British Association of International Mountain Leaders

BAIML represents the interests of its members, which are holders of the International Mountain Leader Qualification. BAIML represents the UK at UIMLA, the Union of International Mountain Leader Associations, which is the international governing body for International Mountain Leaders. BAIML works closely with UIMLA and Mountain Training to develop and promote a worldwide standard for training and assessment.

British Mountain Guides

BMG members work as Mountain Guides in the UK, Europe and further afield in the world's most famous climbing areas and high mountain ranges. Every BMG Guide has a solid base of experience, knowledge and skill. Collectively, they share a common passion for climbing, mountaineering and skiing, and a professionalism for leading groups in challenging and hazardous terrain.

BMG is a member of the International Federation of Mountain Guide Associations (IFMGA), which is the body that coordinates the standards and mutual recognition of the twenty-six national mountain guide associations. A British Mountain Guide is an IFMGA Guide, which put simply, means an internationally qualified guide with the knowledge and skills to lead parties in the world's most challenging mountain environments.

Other Mountain Training walk leader qualifications

The Hill and Moorland Leader

The Hill and Moorland Leader morphed out of the old Walking Group Leader. As its name suggests it's designed as a qualification for those leading in the moorlands and hills of the UK. The Irish haven't adopted this qualification. It has a three-day training course, a period of consolidation then a three-day assessment course. The key differences are that the leader doesn't have to operate on steep ground, they can walk around it, they do not cover unplanned use of the rope, due to the terrain they are in, and there is no overnight camp.

The leadership, environment and other aspects of the qualification are not greatly different to those covered in the Mountain Leader qualification. It is not about being a slightly less-good leader, it is about being just as good a leader but in different places. Many of the hills outside of the Lake District and Eryri, and big chunks in these places, in England and Wales are perfectly well served by the Hill and Moorland Leader qualification. In Scotland there are many smaller hills that would be covered too. It deserves to be more widely recognised and used.

Operating in Hill and Moorland Leader terrain.

The Development of Hillwalking and its Representative Bodies

Operating in Lowland Leader terrain.

The Lowland Leader

This qualification is for those leading walks outside the upland areas, it covers most of England and Wales and much of Scotland. Here, though things can get a little more complicated. Obviously there would be the same standard of leadership. Navigation can, in some people's eyes, get more complicated as we search out lowland rights of way, although in Scotland you can apply the Land Reform Act and walk almost anywhere as long as you follow the rights and responsibilities enshrined within that act. The environment is much more complex, being dominated by agriculture and a plethora of farmland, woodland and coastal birdlife and wildflowers.

The Lowland Leader requires only ten walks in their logbook before training as opposed to twenty on the other two walking qualifications, and the training and assessment courses are both only two days. The training course is pretty jam-packed. The big difference here is that you are following footpaths and you are rarely remote from roads and the other trappings of civilisation, help will generally be a mobile phone call away, so the environment is deemed as less serious for the leader. It's a great way to start off your career as a walking leader and I'm pleased with the growth of this scheme.

In Ireland, because there is no legal access to land the Lowland Leader will often be leading on national trails which are well signposted and waymarked. To be fair, the qualification does say it is for footpaths which are well marked on the map and on the ground, wherever you are in the UK or Ireland.

The Winter Mountain Leader

If you have completed your Mountain Leader qualification then the next step for many people is to consider the Winter Mountain Leader. There are

THE MOUNTAIN LEADER

Operating in winter conditions as a Winter Mountain Leader.

some days every year when the higher mountains of England, Wales and Ireland assume a winter mantle. These conditions can come and go in the blink of an eye and can change hourly through the day, it would be no bad thing to consider taking the Winter Mountain Leader qualification.

However, this qualification comes into its own in Scotland. In the winter, the Scottish mountains take on a much more arctic-alpine temperament. They can be unforgiving. They are our tallest mountains, they are furthest north and they have the shortest days and the most extreme weather. Winter can be in the Scottish mountains for long periods of time.

To travel safely and enjoyably in the winter mountains you will need an appreciation of snow and ice, to understand avalanches, and to be skilled with crampons and ice axes. You will need to be able to navigate for longer periods of time in more challenging conditions that in other parts of our islands. While I'm a great believer in using technology to navigate (outdoor specific GPSs are being used with great satisfaction in the Scottish winter), you still need to be able to walk for a kilometre or two, in white out conditions, buffeted by strong winds on a compass bearing. It is serious, but with serious, can come great reward and I can honestly say the some of my most memorable mountaineering days have been in the Scottish winter, warts and all.

Opposite page
A group exploring Cwm Idwal on a Nature of Snowdonia Workshop.

Appendix A
Teaching and Learning Skills

Teaching and learning skills are now part of the Mountain Training qualifications. For many years, Mountain Leaders have been teaching navigation and expedition skills to people who they were leading. It's good to see some recognition of these skills within the qualifications. I've picked out some key ideas here that will, I hope, have a positive influence on your teaching.

Inspire

First of all, a good teacher inspires learners to want to learn. If you are passionate, enthusiastic and appear competent then you will inspire your groups. People are good at copying, they can struggle to listen, but they are really good at following your example. Be a good role model.

Engage

In order to learn new skills, learners need to engage with the task in hand. The commonest failing in teaching is moving on before competence is established. Failing to revisit skills to check learning and progress means they won't be consolidated. Telling people how to do things is not teaching people how to do things. A new skill is only learnt when it can be done in different places, at different times, in different conditions with different people. There is no learning without remembering. There is little remembering without doing.

Structure

The nature of what we are teaching is typically practical. You will need to explain a task, demonstrate that task, then let the learners do that task. For this to happen you need to create a positive learning atmosphere. This will be friendly and supportive and it will involve you learning and using names and recognising people as individuals; it will allow for, and encourage learning from mistakes.

Make sure you have been heard and that what you have said has been understood, be prepared to explain again and to explain in different ways. Be prepared to demonstrate again and to demonstrate in different ways.

The bigger picture, the full story

It's important that learners understand what they are doing and why. They need to picture themselves doing whatever the task is for real, they need to see how it fits in to the bigger picture of hillwalking.

"Our brains privilege story"

Danial Willingham

Stories are really useful ways to help your learners remember key information and how everything fits together. Try telling the story of a day or a journey to see how new skills fit in and are useful. Use reminiscences as people will remember these stories including when and where they learnt something and what and how they learnt it. There are several stories of this nature throughout this book and you will all have your own too.

Assessment

Use targeted questioning to check learning and be sure to move around the group and select different people to respond. Observe new tasks being demonstrated more than once and in different locations.

Reflection

After every teaching session, take a few moments to reflect how it went. You'll usually feel good and have a nice warm glow if it's gone well. When you are working with youngsters, they'll often give you some honest feedback about the effectiveness of your teaching either verbally or by demonstrating the new task well (or less well.) Adults can often be a little too polite and aren't always good at honest feedback. Most people will have a nice time when they are out with us and they'll be loath to appear critical in any way.

Checklist for teaching

Before

- Have you created a positive, supportive teaching environment?
- Is the session in a safe environment?
- Is everyone physically comfortable?
- Have you got a clear aim for the session?
- How does the session link with the bigger picture?

During

- Are you communicating clearly and effectively with all learners?
- Are you checking for understanding?
- Can you change the way you are explaining or demonstrating a task to suit the range of learners?
- Are your demonstrations clear and effective?

THE MOUNTAIN LEADER

Towards the end

- Have the learners been able to demonstrate new skills (and / or knowledge) in different places, at different times, with different people?

Reflection

- How did your session go?
- How could you do things better next time?

The circular teaching and learning process.

Before

- Have you created a positive, supportive teaching environment?
- Is the session in a safe environment?
- Is everyone physically comfortable?
- Have you got a clear aim for the session?
- How does the session link with the bigger picture?

During

- Are you communicating clearly and effectively with all learners?
- Are you checking for understanding?
- Can you change the way you are explaining or demonstrating a task to suit the range of learners?
- Are your demonstrations clear and effective?
- Give space to experiment, to make mistakes, to learn

Reflection

- How did your session go?
- How could you do things better next time?

Towards the end

- Have the learners been able to demonstrate new skills (and / or knowledge) in different places, at different times, with different people?

Moderate yourself

I recommend you videoing yourself teaching. It's really easy to set up with your phone these days. You can then watch the film back and listen to how you are speaking. Listen for names, for clarity, for a clear start and end, for the checking of understanding. Time how long you are talking. Aim to reduce this and improve clarity (try limit yourself to 100 words as an exercise). Watch to see where you are looking, are you involving the whole group? Do you relate to males and females equally? Are your demonstrations as clear and as simple as possible? Listen for any repetitions, and fillers such as ums and ahs. Listen for variety in tone and pitch when speaking.

Teaching on the hill.

Teaching navigation on the hill.

Active learning in a classroom session.

Creating a positive learning atmosphere.

APPENDIX B
RUNNING FOR MOUNTAIN LEADERS

Compiled with enormous help from Alice Kerr and Kate Worthington

Running in the hills seems to currently be an ever growing industry and one that a lot of Mountain Leaders are not always fully prepared for. There seem to be trail running, skyline running, ultra-running and other types of running events in all our hills, every weekend. Head up to Bowfell and over towards Scafell on any weekend and you will see as many runners as you'll see walkers. Most will be well equipped with spares and look like they know what they are doing, a few however will be carrying nothing.

Running in rocky terrain. The leader needs to be able to support the faster and the slower runners.

Not all Mountain Leaders should be trained and assessed at working on the hill with runners, but those who choose to do such work might need to be made aware of a few issues that occur around running in the hills, especially when leading others. Mountain Leaders not involved with running in the hills will readily notice the apparent lack of equipment, the fact is that skilled and experienced mountain runners have honed down their kit over the years to the absolute minimum that they can get away with. Walkers can actually learn from runners in this respect. Particularly when it comes to camping, though an ultra-lightweight approach can include a level of discomfort that most walkers mightn't readily take to!

Mountain Leaders taking runners in the hills should consider themselves Mountain Leaders, first and foremost. They will be responsible for making sure the group has the right equipment for the day, that a proper risk assessment is done and that the route can be varied accordingly. There will be a higher risk of lower limb injures, or wrist injuries when hands are used to stop tumbles, when running.

With some cloud blowing around the leader needs to be constantly aware of the group's location. This tends to be more difficult when you are moving faster.

Running Mountain Leaders take people to all the places that we might go on a walking or scrambling day, to go trail or skyline running. They will often be heading into the hills with people from a running background rather than a walking background and they may not be as well-equipped as they would be if they were going hillwalking. The runners should all carry waterproofs, a spare layer and some food, but they won't have as much kit as people do when walking, with a larger bag, and it'll be the lightest kit available.

The leader has a responsibility to check that people have the things that they claim to have in their tiny, running bags. As with walking, the leader of the running group still needs to carry all the emergency kit in their leader's sack (First aid, Blizzard bag, group shelter etc) so they need to be able to run with a full 20 litre bag.

APPENDICES – Running for Mountain Leaders

Running in Eryri on a fine day. A trip however could have consequences.

Currently, there are no guidelines, for working using your Mountain Leader qualification on a running day. Be prepared to be underwhelmed by those that you lead; some will not be as capable as they led you to believe. You may have to change your route and to have to keep a slow moving, or even stationary runner warm. You'll need to pay extra attention to hydration and fuelling. The weather will have a greater impact on your plans than it will for walkers.

Just as is the case when leading walkers this role is all about people. Yes, an awareness of the place you are running through, why it is special and how we need to care for it (take your energy gel wrappers home) is very important. We are working with the most dynamic of resources: ourselves and others. It is always about yourself and your limitations, the group and their individual limitations. They will have goals, expectations, doubts, fears, interests and various physical and psychological needs. This can be a complex role and dealing with different people moving at different speeds with different visions of the day can be really quite hard work. You could find yourself being quite directive with your instruction, particularly around layering up and around route choice. Each runner will have their own goals, and the more you can align these goals when organising your day the better.

Some well equipped runners dealing with poor weather.

Top tips from Mountain Leaders

The Mountain Leader who thinks that 'running with clients' is mostly about running with clients will be very much mistaken! There's a lot of walking and managing, and some running and more management. More so than when I'm mountain walking with clients.

Kate Worthington

APPENDIX C
GAELIC, IRISH AND WELSH FOR MOUNTAIN LEADERS

I asked local experts for help with this section. They have chosen the most useful words for Mountain Leaders from their language. This is typically topographical words, but in some cases you can see that locations within the hills are named after colours, fauna or trees.

Special thanks to Kevin Woods, Gereldene Nee and Branwen McBride

Gaelic for Mountain Leaders

(Scottish Gaelic)

Hill names

Beinn (ben) – hill. Very common name across the Highlands, often anglicised to Ben.

Càrn (karn) – hill / pile of stone. Common in the Eastern Highlands and sometimes the NW Highlands.

Cruach (kroo-ach) – round hill / stack.

Maol (moo-il) – a bare head.

Meall (mee-al) – lumpy, round hill.

Mullach (moo-lach) – denotes the 'top' of something. e.g. Mullach nan Coirean (top of the coires).

Sgùrr (skoor) – pointed or craggy peak, particularly on the west coast.

Stac – stack.

Stob (stop) – protrusion or lumpy hill.

Topographical features

Aonach (oo-nach) – ridge/upland.

Bealach (be-ALUch) – pass.

APPENDICES – Gaelic, Irish and Welsh for Mountain Leaders

Ceann (kee-awn) – head. Often anglicised to Kin- (as in Kinlochleven, head of Loch Leven).

Coire (kor-uh) – corrie.

Creag (crek) – rock / cliff.

Druim (droim) – ridge.

Gleann (glown) – glen.

Leacann (le-achan) – broad slope.

Socach (socach) – snout, similar to sron.

Sròn (srone) – nose.

Stùc (stook) – pinnacle / peak.

Taobh (toov) – side, flank.

Water features

Allt (alt) – stream.

Abhainn (a-wain) – river.

Eas (eas) – waterfall.

Rubha (roo-a) – headland / promontory.

Caolas (koo-las) – narrows.

Loch – loch.

Inbhir (een-yer – English Inver) – confluence of waters, mouth of river.

Eilean (ellan) – island.

Colours

Bàn (ban) & Fionn (fyoon) – fair coloured.

Buidhe (boo-ee) – yellow.

Dearg (jerrack) – red.

Liath (lee-a) – grey.

Geal (gee-al) – usually denoting white.

Ruadh (roo-a) – red / rust-coloured.

Gorm (gorom) – blue, but sometimes green.

Glas (glass) – grey-green.

Odhar (o-ar) – brown.

Airgead (er-i-ged) – silver.

Description

Mòr (more) – big / great.

Beag (bek) – little.

Breac (brach-k) – speckled, spotted.

Caol (cool) – slim.

Fada (fata) – long.

Sean (shen) – old.

Ùr (oor) – new.

Meadhan (mee-an) – middle.

Fauna

Crodh (crow) & sprèidh (sprey) – cattle.

Bò (boe) – cow.

Damh (dav) – stag.

Fiadh (fee-a) – deer.

Laoigh (loo-ugh) – calf.

Madadh (mat-ay) – dog.

APPENDICES – Gaelic, Irish and Welsh for Mountain Leaders

Earb (err-ap) – roe deer.

Muc (mook) – pig.

Caorach (KOO-rach) – sheep.

Gobhar (goe-ar) – goat.

Eun (ee-un) – bird.

Fitheach (fee-uch) – raven.

Iolaire (ee-o-lair) – eagle.

Trees

Craobh (kroov) – tree.

Beithe (bey-e) – birch.

Feàrna (fee-arna) – alder.

Darach (darach) – oak.

Giuthas (gyoo-as) – pine.

Doire (dor-uh) & Bad (bat) – copse of trees.

Fine, if challenging, walking on the Isle of Skye.

Irish for Mountain Leaders

(Irish Gaelic)

Hill names

Binn (ben) – peak or pointed mountain. Can also be written as An Bhinn (on vinn) or Beann (be-yan). More often anglicised to Ben or Been.

Cnoc (knock) or sometimes (cruck) – hill. Sometimes just used for lower hills but not always.

Creag (crag) – crag or rocky outcrop. Can also be written as Creig (kreg), Screag (scrag) or Screig (skreg).

Cruach (crew-ach), Cruachán (crew-con) – stack or pointed peak. Anglicised to Croagh.

Maol (meel) – bald or bare. Usually written as 'Mweel' and can mean a smooth rounded hill or bald, bare hill.

Mullach (mull-ach) – summit. Often pre-fixed as 'Mullagh' (mull-ah) on mountain names.

Sliabh (sleeve) – mountain. Can also be written as Slieve (sleeve), Sléibhe (slay-ve) or Sléibhte (slave-teh).

Topographical features

Barr (baur) – top or summit.

Bealach (bal-yuck) – a road, way or pass.

Bearna (barn-ah) – gap.

Buaile (bool-yeh) – booley (a summer pasture).

Bun (bun) – foot or end. Can also mean the mouth of a river.

Bóthar (bo-her) – road.

Carn (kearn) – cairn. Sometimes anglicised to Carran.

Carraig (car-rig) – rock. Anglicised to Carrick.

Cloch (cluck) – stone.

Corrán (korr-awn) – sickle/serrated mountain. Anglicised to Carraun.

APPENDICES – Gaelic, Irish and Welsh for Mountain Leaders

Cúm (koom) – coom or corrie. Usually anglicised to Coum, Com or Coom. Sometimes also written as Coire (quir-eh).

Droim (drim) – ridge. Sometimes written as Drom (drum).

Dún (doon) – fort or castle. Anglicised to Doon.

Gleann (glan) – glen/valley. Often written as Glen or Glan.

Mám (maum) – mountain pass. Sometimes written as Maum.

Slí (slee) – path / way.

Srón (shrone) – nose like mountain feature.

Stuaic (stook) – pinnacle/peak.

Taobh (theeve) – (hill)side.

Móin (moan) – peat bog.

Water features

Abhainn – (ow-wan) – river.

Áth (awh) – ford.

Béal (bale) – usually mouth of a river.

Clochóg (cluck-ogue) – stepping stone.

Eas (ass) – waterfall.

Eisc (esk) – ravine / steep gully. Anglicised to Esk.

Inis (inish) – island.

Loch (lock) – lake. Can also mean sea inlet.

Oilean (ill-awn) – island.

Poll (pull) – hole / hollow / pond.

Rinn (rhinn) – headland.

Sruth (schr-uh) – stream. Sruthán (schr-uh-awn) – small stream.

Colours

Bán (bawn) – white.

Buí (bwee) – yellow.

Dearg (jar-ug) – red. Generally used for items which are painted or coloured red.

Rua (roo-ah) – red. Used to describe red hair or fur.

Donn (dunn) – brown.

Dubh (dove) or (doo) – black.

Liath (leah) – grey.

Geal (gyal) – usually means 'bright'.

Glas (gloss) – green. Usually means the green colours we see in nature.

Gorm (gor-um) – usually means blue.

Description

Ard (ord) – high place. This could be physically high but also a place of importance.

Beag/Beg (byug) – small.

Bogach (bog-ach) – soft. Origins of word bogland.

Fliuch (fluck) – wet.

Fuar (foor) – cold.

Gaoth (gwee) – wind.

Grian (gree-an) – sun.

Mór (more) – big.

Sneachta (snoc-ta) – snow.

Tirim (chirim) – dry.

Te (tay) – hot.

APPENDICES – Gaelic, Irish and Welsh for Mountain Leaders

Fauna

Bó (boh) – cow.

Caora (cweer-ah) – sheep (singular). Caoirigh (cwreer-ee) – sheep (plural).

Éan (ane) – bird.

Fiach dubh (fee-ach doo) – raven.

Gabhar (gow-er) – goat.

Iolar (ill-or) – eagle.

Trees

Beith (beh) – birch.

Caorthann (kware-thawn) – mountain ash.

Coill (quill) – a wood. Anglicised to Kill.

Crann (kron) – tree.

Dair (dar) – oak.

Fearnóg (far-nogue) – alder.

Fine open scenery, good walking country on Slieve Carr, Ireland's most remote peak, in the Nephin Mountains, County Mayo.
Photo: Bren Whelan

Welsh for Mountain Leaders

(Cymraig)

In Welsh most letters are pronounced phonetically, with this knowledge and special letter sounds described below you should be able to have a stab at Welsh words. Welsh is fairly consistent, but here are some tricky sounds for the English speaker!

A – use a "hard" a as in apple.

Ch – sound from the back of the throat as in Loch.

Dd – very similar to 'the' in English.

F – said as v.

Ff – said as English f.

Ll – tip of the tongue on the back of your front teeth and let the air hiss out through the sides of your mouth.

O – use a 'hard' o as in orange.

Rh – as in rhinocerous.

Th – sound from the tip of the tongue as in think.

Vowels: a, e, i, o, u, w, y

Often you say the word exactly as you see it.

Words and meanings can vary depending which part of Wales you are in.

Words may mutate, e.g. Bryn might appear as Fryn.

Hill names

Ban – summit / peak / top.

Bryn (br – in) – hill.

Carnedd (karn-edd) – pile of stones / cairn / cairn topped mountain.

Copa (ko – pa) – summit / crest.

Moel (mo-el) – bare / barren hill. Literally translates as a bald head.

Mynydd (myn – idd) – mountain / hill / unenclosed mountain land.

Topographical features

Bwlch – pass or gap.

Braich (Imagine you're saying the name Brian, Bri-ch) – arm / spur.

Cefn (ke-vn) – back / ridge.

Clogwyn (clog – win) – cliff / crag / precipice.

Craig / Creigiau – rock / rocks.

Cwm – corrie.

Dyffryn (duff – rin) – valley.

Esgair (esg – eye – r) – ridge/spur.

Glyn (gl – in) – narrow valley / glen.

Pen – head.

Trum / Drum – (tr – im) crest / ridge.

Trwyn (trw – in) – nose.

Water features

Afon (av – on) – river.

Aber – confluence of waters, mouth of river.

Ffynnon (fun – on) – spring / well / source.

Cors / Gors – boggy gound.

Dwr – water.

Llyn (ll – in) – lake.

Nant – stream / brook.

THE MOUNTAIN LEADER

Rheadr (rhe – adr) – waterfall.

Penrhyn (pen – rhin) – headland / promontory.

Ynys (Yn – is) – island.

Colours

Coch (slightly elongate the o) – red.

Brown (own as in "I own that") – brown.

Du (tricky! Imagine the word "dim" as in "dim the lights" without the m and elongate the i slightly. di) – black.

Llwyd (llw – id) – grey.

Gwyn (gw – in) – white.

Gwyrdd (gw – irdd) – green.

Glas (slightly elongate the a) – blue, but sometimes green, or even grey-green!

Melyn (mel – in) – yellow.

Cader Idris, or is it Cadair Idris?

APPENDIX D
NOTES FOR TRAINEES

Before you undertake your ML training, you should have completed 20 quality mountain days, in other words you'll be a hillwalker of some experience. The numbers quoted in the Mountain Leader qualification are always minimums, so it pays to have more than 20 days. The question about what is a QMD is, in my opinion asked far too often. I think the criteria are pretty clear, and my conclusion is that a QMD will ideally be going hillwalking somewhere you haven't been walking before.

> **Mountain Training's definition of a Quality Mountain Day (QMD)**
>
> In terms of experience, the quality of a mountain day lies in such things as the conditions experienced both overhead and underfoot, the exploration of new areas, the terrain covered and the physical and mental challenge. Such days make a positive contribution towards a person's development and maturity as an all-round mountaineer.
>
> Usually some or all of the following criteria would be fulfilled:
>
> - The individual takes part in the planning and leadership.
> - Navigation skills are required away from marked paths.
> - Experience must be in terrain and weather comparable to that found in UK and Irish hills.
> - Knowledge is increased and skills practised.
> - Attention is paid to safety.
> - The journey is five hours or more.
> - Adverse conditions may be encountered.
> - The ascent of a substantial peak would normally be included in the day.

No one expects you to be able to just pick up a strange map and find a good QMD on it. Especially as, particularly for those training in England and Wales, you'll be strongly advised to get as many QMDs in Scotland as possible. But how do you know where to go? This is where guidebooks and lists are useful. You should have heard of the Munros. The Munros tend be visited frequently by walkers and have good guidebooks, are regularly trafficked and will have paths on them. To find some quieter hills that might challenge your skills a little more take a look at the Hewitts or the Corbetts. Other lists are available, you could try the P600's, the Marilyns, the Murdos, the Grahams, the Donalds, the Furths, the Nuttall's, the Wainwrights or the Vandeleur-Lynams.

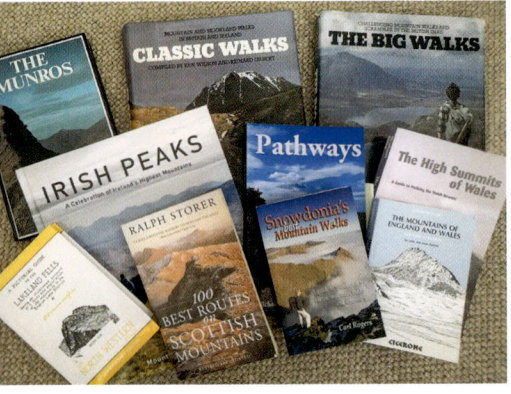

A selection of walking guidebooks.

If you stand on top of Ben Nevis you'll see lots of other mountains. Choose some, identify them from your map, now to find the best routes on them, this is where the guidebook comes in handy. It will help you with transport or parking arrangements, it'll help you find the best route and it'll give you an idea of how far and how long it will take. There is nothing wrong with using a guidebook, it's normal. Once on the walk you will need to use the map. To keep your navigation skills up to scratch just relocate a few times, and maybe try a different ridge for your descent to the one described, it's actually quite exciting experimenting with routes.

There are many classic guidebooks, but I know a lot of you will use online resources too and there is an abundance of these as well. The online guidebooks are usually started by some enthusiast with a grand vision for an online catalogue of the best routes on every mountain in the UK and Ireland. It's amazing how close they have managed to get, but they need to make a living. There is a constant dilemma between advertising on the site, asking for a subscription or donations, or selling out to one of the big, multinational web companies. Don't forget magazines either. Over time the articles will get a bit repetitive, but for a year or two they are a sound investment and you'll soon have plenty of routes to go at.

Walking guidebooks

For inspiration it's hard to beat the coffee table books produced by the late Ken Wilson, *The Big Walks*, *Classic Walks* and *Wild Walks* are superb. Everyone should be familiar with the works of Alfred Wainwright and Mark Richards. There are many, many lovely coffee table books and hundreds of detailed guidebooks. Far, far too many to mention here, check out Paddy Dillon though, with over 100 titles to his name he must be one of the most prolific. I should give an honourable mention to the *Irish Peaks* produced recently by Mountaineering Ireland, to *The Munros* from the Scottish Mountaineering Press, Mark Reeves's *Snowdonia Mountain Walks and Scrambles* and the very sexy *The Munros: The complete collection of maps* from Harveys Mapping.

APPENDICES – Notes for Trainees

Online route sources

There is currently a plethora of online route sources. Walk Highlands, UKHillwalking, Walkingworld and Mud and Routes would be four that spring to mind and that I have used with some success. I also look at routes on OS maps and Outdoor Active. You should be aware of AllTrails and Komoot, who don't use OS maps, but are very popular apps. This an ever changing field and apps will come and go. What is popular now may well disappear, new players could yet rule the roost.

Before you even go on your training course, make sure you are a hillwalker. You should have gained enough experience that you have a few stories to tell. This will mean that you have tested your kit, you know what works and what doesn't. You'll have worked out how to carry your maps, how big a rucksack you need. You should have been using some different maps, you should have made some wild camps and you should have travelled to some different hill areas. You don't need to have led groups, but spending time with them will stand you in good stead. You might have learnt some basic things like:

- How to keep the weight as low as possible for an overnight camp.

- To keep everything in your rucksack in dry bags.

- How to keep your sleeping bag dry.

- That rucksack covers usually blow off.

- That you need a proper compass.

- That laminated maps are better than map cases.

- Headtorches are a good idea if you end up walking in the dark.

- You can keep your phone dry when it's raining.

- You've got a copy of the book *Hillwalking*.

- You are interested in the upland environment.

- You understand what type 2 fun is.

- You know that Yr Wyddfa / Snowdon should never, ever be called Mount Snowdon.

THE MOUNTAIN LEADER

End of course briefings and action planning

A key time on the journey to becoming a Mountain Leader is the consolidation period between training and assessment. Candidates who have a good quality, structured, action plan, which is achievable, typically do well at assessment. Good habits formed at this stage on your journey should help you, post-assessment, to keep your skills up to scratch, to learn more, and develop your knowledge and understanding of the upland environment as well as reflecting on the leadership experiences you accrue.

How you design your action plan is entirely up to you. On the Mountain Training website there is one which is basically a syllabus tick list. Your training provider will help you with their own style of action plan.

You should keep some notes through your training course, it's good if you share this with fellow trainees. It's good if you work together to note down what has been covered. As you make these notes, think about what they signify and whether they lead to something that requires action on your part? You may need your trainer to help you to understand ways of learning more and consolidating new knowledge.

Before you go for your assessment, can you answer these questions: Most people struggle to give a clear yes or no. Think about a scale of – no – I'm starting to – I think I can – yes, or better still devise your own scale.

If you can do things in different places, at different times, with different people in different conditions, then you can answer yes.

- Can you navigate and relocate with linear features?

- Can you navigate and relocate with just contour features?

- Do you know how to get the weather forecast and how to plan accordingly?

- Do you know your responsibilities as a Mountain Leader?

- Can you talk knowledgably about the upland environment?

- Are you aware of different land uses and other interests in our uplands?

- Do you understand access arrangements in the UK and Ireland?

- Can you look after a group safely and manage a group appropriately in the mountain environment?

- Can you use a rope in unplanned situations?

APPENDICES – Notes for Trainees

- Can you give confidence with the rope?

- Can you pitch a variety of tents?

- Are you up to speed with stove safety?

- Are you happy advising others on equipment?

- Can you navigate and relocate in darkness or poor visibility?

- Can you look after others in camp?

- Can you walk & talk (navigate, environmental chat and group care all at the same time)?

Have you read and understood the syllabus?

To build up your confidence at answering these questions you may need to maintain a dialogue with your trainer. Your trainer will be keen to help and reassure you. They can suggest places to go and explore, they can give you navigation legs to do, they can tell you about different mountain ranges; pick their brains. There will be no substitute for getting out there and going walking though. Do workshops, walk with other leaders and trainees as well. Consider some solo walking.

> **Ropework between Mountain Leader Training and Assessment**
>
> Spend some time thinking about anchors when out in the hills, have a look around for some, test them. If you aren't going to use them just test them out with your four S's. This works well if done with a friend.
>
> Make sure you don't forget how to waist belay; if you forget this it's not really for the assessor to remind you. If you can't remember between training and assessment, what chance is there should you ever need to do it? Practise.
>
> Don't forget how to use the South African abseil. Practice in non-serious places, like small, short grassy slopes.
>
> Get organised with your rope, have it in a bag, make sure you can handle it with, and without, gloves.
>
> When confidence roping, keep the rope snug. Not too tight, not too slack. The rope has to be constant, reassuring and present. See if you can come up with a suitable acronym for this.

Habit forming

Successful action plans can only be completed by forming good habits. You need to have a routine of going out walking. If you live near the hills it could be every Sunday, if you live further away it could be every second weekend in the month, or whatever. These types of habits are as much about helping those around you, as helping yourself to achieve your goals. If your partner knows you go away every third weekend, or whatever, it makes their life easier for planning.

For your part, you must go, whatever the weather! Any action plan will be interrupted by life events so make a plan that exceeds the minimum. If you only go walking in the hills once a month, it will take a long time to accrue the appropriate experience. If you live away from the mountains logistics can be more challenging, but on the other hand each weekend you can go to different mountains. You will also need to commit some holiday time to this period of development. If you live in England or Wales you will be strongly advised to go walking in the Scottish Highlands, your trainer should be able to help with some sound, practical advice and suggestions about where to go.

When you pass

There is the danger that you will now get worse! You practised and prepared and worked through an action plan to get to your assessment week. How are you going to keep your skills up, what will your new habits be? You must keep walking, keep reading, keep learning. Only by leading and walking and attending CPD events will you maintain your standard. In time though, all being well, you'll actually get better. After all they do say you don't really know a subject until you start to teach it. Pob lwc (good luck).

Continuing personal or professional development (CPD)

CPD is crucial in any walk of life. It's no less important for the Mountain Leader. You need to keep your navigation skills well honed, you might want to develop your teaching of navigation. Picking the brains of experienced Mountain Leaders, not just those running the CPD, but those attending too, is really important. I'm very keen that we continually develop our environmental awareness and understanding. CPD should become a habit, a good habit.

> **Top tips from Mountain Leaders**
>
> My top-tip, particularly for those who don't live in mountainous areas would be not to underestimate terrain in their local area. I use Cannock Chase, a local area of heathland / woodland for navigation practice. Although I didn't hold out much hope for this at first, I soon realised that it was an excellent area to sharpen my fine navigation skills.
>
> Gareth Davies

APPENDICES – Notes for Trainees

Top tips from Mountain Leaders

When I was getting ready for my ML assessment, and living in Berkshire (not exactly mountainous or hilly), it was not always easy to get to Eryri, the Lakes etc. I did a lot of local orienteering. I would usually put on a rucksack and walk around the course (I found blue courses gave a good challenge). After a week or so, I would go back at night and do the course in reverse or just pick features on the map I'd never visited on the course. I actually found it was brilliant night navigation practice. I still do orienteering and I still 'walk' courses.

Doing it alone boosted my confidence for the assessment and got me familiar with my headtorch and using my rucksack at night. This would be one of my top tips for candidates getting ready for doing night navigation for the first time – I also think it is a lot safer doing it on your own in lowland woods etc. Once you get your confidence at night, I think candidates can then head for the hills. It's all about small incremental steps.

Steve Goodrum

Top tips from Mountain Leaders

Leadership – remember that a leader doesn't always have to be at the front. Leading from within your group can give you a much better insight, with regard to the capabilities of your group and may help with route choice, instruction and guidance. This is especially useful to a group not known to you. It also enables the speed at which a mixed ability group to be better regulated.

Navigation – keep it simple. Utilise obvious natural / man-made handrails as close to your objective as possible, even if this means extending the length of the 'leg' slightly. This is particularly pertinent in poor visibility. This reduces the margin for error considerably.

Ropework – Practice the basic ML knots and ropework at home. Get slick at setting up belays. Staircases are useful training aids! On assessment be over zealous with testing anchor suitability.

If you're overstressed about doing your assessment, then perhaps you're not ready? Knowing that you've done far more than the requisite amount of QMDs both solo or with others is a great confidence booster.

John Mainwaring

THE MOUNTAIN LEADER

APPENDIX E
GOOD LEADERS

Leadership spectrum

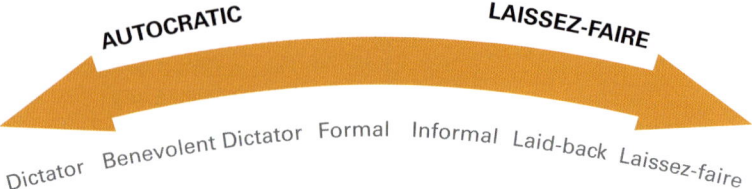

The INSPIRE Mode

Inspire and motivate your followers with a unified vision

Nurture an environment of team-focused goals

Set the example you want to see in your followers

Praise, and give constructive feedback to help your followers develop

Insist on setting high standards, relative to each individual

Recognise and respond to each individual's needs

Encourage followers to create and implement their own solutions

CLAP

Communication

Line of sight

Avoidance of hazard

Position of maximum usefulness

BIBLIOGRAPHY AND FURTHER READING

It's increasingly hard to be at one with your bibliography. No longer is there a list of heavyweight text books and learned papers. Today's research takes place online as much as anywhere else. We use Wikipedia a lot. Wikipedia has overcome its early criticisms and is littered with references that can all be followed. Writing a book of this nature has required constant refence to Mountain Training's own website and the BMC's. Most of the work in the book is mine, based on my experience and formed of my opinions. I hope they will at least provoke discussion. What you'll find in this bibliography are some places to go for further reading as well as sources I've visited for information. I included some quotes from *Mountain Craft* (1920), ed Winthrop Young.

You should be aware of Mountain Training National Guidelines. The intention of this book is to complement Mountain Training's own publication for their walking qualifications. I hope you will value my book alongside:

HillWalking, The official handbook of Mountain Training's walking schemes, Long, MTP (2018) ISBN 9780954151195

Many of these topics appear on YouTube or similar websites. They are mostly quite good though, as with this book, look for personal opinion and bias. Try to see who is providing the information. Is it an experienced Mountaineering Instructor or is it part of a college project?

Leadership

Coaching Adventure Sports, Paul Smith and Daniel Wilkinson, Adventure Sports Media House (2020) ISBN 9781838189204

Leading and Managing Groups in the Outdoors, Ogilvie, Ken C. (currently out of print)

Visit the Leadership resources on the Mountain Training website: www.mountain-training.org/campaign/leadership-resources#:~:text=MTA%20Leadership%20resources,-The%20Mountain%20Training&text=INSPIRE%20brings%20together%20seven%20key,of%20your%20clients%20and%20students.

Download the *Remote Supervision* PDF from Mountain Training: www.mountain-training.org/england/resources-and-downloads

There are several sources of codes of conduct for challenge events. Here are three of many:

www.snowdonia.gov.wales/wp-content/uploads/2022/02/Organised-Competitive-and-Charitable-events-document.pdf

www.thebmc.co.uk/bmc-green-guide-challenge-events-hills

www.ciof.org.uk/events-and-training/resources/three-peaks-challenge

Navigation

There are plentiful instructional manuals on navigation. Here's a sample:

Mountain and Moorland Navigation, Kevin Walker, Pesda Press (2016) ISBN 9781906095567

Navigation in the Mountains – The definitive guide for hillwalkers, mountaineers & leaders, Carlo Forte MTP (2018) ISBN 9780954151157

Teaching Navigation, Nigel Williams, Harveys (2018) ISBN 9781851376087

You also find tutorials on the Ordnance Survey website:

https://getoutside.ordnancesurvey.co.uk/guides/beginners-guides-map-reading/

Access and the environment

Type into your search engine 'Why is nature good for us?' and you'll find several articles. Most of them are based on the research by Professor Miles Richardson of the University of Derby and his team. His blog is worth following:

www.findingnature.org.uk

Books

Adventures of a Nature Guide, Enos A Mills, Temporal Mechanical Press, 2015, ISBN 9781928878414

Between Mountain and Sea Poems from Assynt, Norman MacCaig, Polygon, 2018, ISBN 2018 978-1846974496

Bibliography and Further Reading

Hostile Habitats, Mark Wrightham and Nicke Kempe, SMT, 2019, ISBN 9781907233258

Nature of the Brecon Beacons, Kevin Walker, Pesda Press, 2019, ISBN 9781906095659

Nature of Snowdonia, Mike Raine, Pesda Press, 2020, ISBN 9781906095680

Look out for the forthcoming *Nature of the Scottish Highlands* from Pesda Press

Rock Trails Series, Paul Gannon, Pesda Press

The *Collins Complete Guide* series are also very useful.

Apps

Google eye, iNature, PictureThis, or PlantNet.

Book App

Mountain Flowers, Alan R Walker

Hazards and emergencies

The NHS website is the 'go to' source for medical issues. I also found the following of interest:

Epilepsy.org

Asthma.org

Diabetes.org.uk

Lymedisease.org.uk

Mind.org.uk

Lightning

For a fuller read on lightning deaths in the UK go to:
https://radar.brookes.ac.uk/radar/file/9ba72fba-4d12-4c6f-94e1-f11de-a9b7351/1/fulltext.pdf

For more on drinking water

www.mountaineering.scot/safety-and-skills/health-and-hygiene/drinking-water

Equipment

Always check the manufacturers guidelines, but the best book on this topic is

Keeping Dry, Staying Warm, Mike Parson, Outdoor Gear Coach, 2020, ISBN 9781916283008

BMC Downloads available from www.thebmc.co.uk:

The Green Guide for Groups of Walkers

The Green Guide to Challenge Events in the Hills

Weather

While there are several excellent weather books, for most of us the Met Office and MWIS websites will have more than enough information. There is an eLearning module from the Met Office on the MTA website and a Weather for Mountain Leaders two-part eLearning module on my Patreon page Patreon/mikeraine.

Background knowledge

The history of the BMC is outlined here www.thebmc.co.uk/a-brief-history-of-the-bmc. There is also a book *The First Fifty Years* available from the BMC shop ISBN 9780903908078

There is a potted history of The Ramblers here www.ramblers.org.uk/about-us/our-history.aspx

I haven't seen a definitive history of hillwalking. It would be an interesting exercise, but much combing of many other texts would be required. You could try:

Wanderers, Kerrie Andrews, Reaktion Books, 2020, ISBN 978789143423

Risking Life and Limb, Judy Whiteside, Ogwen Valley Mountain Rescue Organisation, 2015, ISBN 9780993494901

Bibliography and Further Reading

Wainwright, the Biography, Hunter Davies, Orion, 2007, ISBN 9780752848525

The Way that we Climbed, Paddy O'Leary, The Collins Press, 2015, ISBN 9781848892422

A Century of Mountaineering, W.D. Brooker, SMC, 1988, 9780907521211

Or just grab one of John Burn's humorous books such as:

The Last Hillwalker, John Burns, Vertebrate Publishing, 2019, ISBN 9781912560455

Midges

Midges, Alistair Roberts, Birlinn, 2005, ISBN 9781841583860

This little book is essential reading!

Symbols

5 D's, the 62
999, calling 264

A

abseiling 253
access 104
access, England 100
access, Ireland 103
access, Scotland 102
access, Wales 100
accident, dealing with 257
accident report card 259
adders 233
AdventureSmart 174
ALAA (Adventure Activities Licence) 195
allergies 180
AMI (Association of Mountaineering Instructors) 313
anaphylaxis 180
anchors 248
anchor selection 249
animal hazards 233, 239
AONB (Areas of Outstanding Natural Beauty) 127
apps, environment 93
apps, hiking 47
apps, mapping 36, 46
aspect of slope 63
ASSI (Area of Special Scientific Interest) 130
asthma 178
atmospheric hazards 223

B

BAIML (British Association of International Mountain Leaders) 313
barbecues, disposable 289
base layer 21
bearing, taking 56, 59
bearing, wallking on 59
belaying 248, 251
belay jacket 25
birds, knowledge of 87
bivouac, emergency 267
blisters 183
Blizzard bag 176
BMC (British Mountaineering Council) 129, 310
BMG (British Mountain Guides) 313
books, environment 90
boots 18
boots, looking after 19
Bothy Code, the 300
bothys 299
boxing (navigation) 63
bracken 118
breathability, clothing 23, 24
briefing, group 151
Buff® 28
butterwort 98

C

Cairngorm Poo Project 296
Cairngorms Connect 120
calling for help 264
Campaign for the Protection of Rural England / Wales / Scotland 129
camping 271
camping equipment 276
camping food 292
camping, where to 293
camping, wild 273
camp routine 298
cards, timing 63
carries, improvised 265
carry, what to 34
Caru Eryri 108
cattle 233
charity events, working on 192
charts, synoptic 76
checklist, leaders 209
CLAP 200
clothes, spare 30, 34
clothing 20
clothing, group 33
coaching 204
compass, using 55
confidence roping 254
consent form 143
consent, informed 144
conservation 124
contour features 41
contouring 41
contour interpretation 51
cooking in camp 285
Countryside Code 105
cows 233
CROW (Countryside Rights of Way) Act 101
cuckoo 96
Cwm Idwal 130

D

DBS (Disclosure and Barring Service) 195
DDT (direction, duration, terrain) 62
deer stalking 114
diabetes 181
direct anchor 248
direct belay 248
disposable barbecues 289
dog-legs (navigation) 63
down, downside of 281
down jacket 26
DrABCDE 260, 261
drinks 140
Duke of Edinburgh's Award 183
duty of care 205
dynamic risk assessment 147, 214

E

eLearning, environment 93
England, access 100
environmental hazards 216
Environmental Protection Agency (Ireland) 126
environmental responsibilities 147
environment, apps 93
environment, books on 90
environment, courses on 92
environment, eLearning 93
environment, inspiring others 95
environment, knowledge of 85, 89
epilepsy 179
EpiPen 181
equipment 31
ethics, walking 308
events, working for 188
expeditions 271

Index

F

farming, sheep 115
FATMAP 46
features, contour 41
features, linear 41
filter, water 291
fire pits 288
first aid 260
first aid kit 261, 263
fleece clothing 22
flooding 229
flowers, knowledge of 87
fogbows 83
food, camping 292
food, group 142
food, snacks 293
freelancing 194
fronts, weather 80

G

Gaelic, Irish 328
Gaelic, Scottish 324
gaiters 29
gas stoves 285
gender 165
gloves 29
gloves, belaying 251
gloves, spare 33
goggles 28
GPS (global positioning system) 32, 36
grid references 44, 45
group clothing 33
group, getting to know 152
group kit 33
group kit list 33
group pace 161
group shelters 267
groups, minority ethnic 166
group, splitting 163
grouse 111
grouse shooting 111
guardians 143

H

handrailing 41, 42
hard shell layer 23
Harvey maps 45
hats 27, 28

hats, spare 33
hazard management 213
hazards 212
hazards, animal 233, 239
hazards, atmospheric 223
hazards, environmental 216
hazards under foot 224
hazards, water 227
help, calling for 264
heuristic traps 242
high pressure 77
Hill and Moorland Leader 314
hoods 27
huts 299
hyperthermia 176
hypoglycaemia 182
hypothermia 175

I

improvised carries 265
incident, dealing with 257
informed consent 144
injuries, pre-existing 172
INSPIRE 198
Ireland, access 103
isobars 77, 80

J

jacket, belay 25
jacket, down 26
jacket, synthetic duvet 25
Jetboil stoves 286
John Muir Trust 129

K

karabiners 246
Keep Cairgorm Snow White 296
Kinder Trespass 307
kit, group 33
kit list, group 33
knots 248
knowledge, environmental 85

L

Land Reform Act 102
layer, base 21
layering (clothing) 20
layer, mid 22

layer, outer 23
leader's checklist 209
leadership 135
leadership models 198
leadership styles 197
leader's rucksack 34
Leave No Trace 107
Lemons Theory 201
lighters 287
lightning 224
linear features 41
line, Mountain Leader 11
litter 123
Local Nature Reserves 131
locate (your position) 36
Lowland Leader 315
low pressure 77, 79
Lyme disease 237, 239

M

map management 39
map orientation 47
mapping apps 36, 46
map-reading 44
maps, Harvey 45
maps, OS 45
matches 287
mats, sleeping 282
MBA (Mountain Bothy Association) 299
meadow pipit 97
medical conditions 178
medical matters 175
menopause 165
menstruation 159
mental health issues 167, 187
Met Office 71
micro-fibres, fleece 22
micro-route finding 218
midges 235
mid layer 22
mines 240
minority ethnic groups 166
moorland 110
Mountain Leader line, the 11
mountain rescue, calling for 264
Mountain Training 311
MTA (Mountain Training Association) 312
MWIS (Mountain Weather Information Service) 71

N

Naismith's rule 49
names, remembering 153
National Nature Reserves 131
National Parks 126
National Three Peaks Challenge 190
National Trust 127
Natural England 126
Natural Resources Wales / Cyfoeth Naturiol Cymru 126
nature, benefit of 88
Nature Reserves 131
NatureScot / Buidheann Nadair na h-Alba 126
navigation 35
navigation, coarse 57
navigation, good visibility 56
navigation, poor visibility 57
navigation, teaching 55, 64
navigation, toolbox 62
neck gaiter 28
Northern Ireland Department of Environment and Rural Affairs 126

O

off-road vehicles 122
Open Access Land 101
Open Spaces Society 129
orientation, map 47
OS maps 45
outer layer 23

P

pace, group 161
pacing 59
parents 143
participation statement (BMC) 144
phones, mapping apps 36, 46
physical literacy 160
planning, route 67
PLB (personal locator beacon) 32, 265
pockets, jacket 26
poles, walking 32
poo pots 296
pre-existing injuries 172
pre trip risk assessment 146
primary survey 258
public rights of way 100

Q

QMD (Quality Mountain Day) 335
quarries 240

R

rainbows 83
rainfall, in the hills 74
Ramblers, the 310
reflective practice 170
relocate, how to 36
remote supervision 183
repair kit 34
rescue, calling for 264
responsibilities, environmental 147
responsibilities, Mountain Leader 138
rewilding 120
rights of way 100
'right to roam' 102
risk assessment, dynamic 147, 214
risk assessment, pre trip 146
river crossing 229
rope, how to carry 247
rope, using 250
rope, which 245
ropework 243
route choice 216
route finding, micro 218
route planning 67
RSPB (Royal Society for the Protection of Birds) 128
rucksack, leader's 34
rucksacks 31
runners. leading 322

S

scale, maps 45
Scarf's variation 50
Scotland, access 102
Scottish Access Code 274
scrambling 220
scree 225
sea level 53
sheep farming 115
shooting estates 110
sleeping bags 279
sleeping bags, washing 280
sleeping mats 282
slings 246

slope, aspect of 63
snacks 293
snakes 233
snow 226
socks 18
South African abseil 253
spare clothes 30, 34
splitting the group 163
sponsored walks 189
spotting (scrambling) 222
sprains 183
SSSI (Site of Special Scientific Interest) 130
steep ground, managing 219
stiles 241
stoves 284
summer conditions 82
sun cream 32
sundew 98
sunglasses 32
survey, primary 258
survival bags 176
swimming, cold water 227
symbols, map 44
synoptic charts 76
synthetic duvet jacket 25

T, U

tarps 276
teaching and learning skills 318
temperature, in the hills 73
tents 276
Three Peaks Challenge 190
thunderstorms 224
tick removal 238
ticks 237
timing 48
timing cards 63
toileting 174, 296
trainees, notes for 335
Trangia stoves 286

V

vehicles, off-road 122
Venturi effect 75
vulnerable people, working with 169

Index

W, X

Wales, access 100
walking ethics 308
walking poles 32
walking skills 158
walks, sponsored 189
washing base layers 21
washing fleece 22
washing, personal 295
washing sleeping bags 280
washing waterproofs 24
water, drinking 289, 292
water hazards 227
waterproofs 23, 24
water, treating 291
waymarking 308
weather 69
weather forecasts 70
Welsh 332
What3words 45
wicking fabric 22
wicking layer 21
wild camping 273
Wildlife Trusts 128
wind, gusty 223
wind, in the hills 75
wind speed 81
winter conditions 82
Winter Mountain Leader 315
World Heritage Sites 132

Y

Yr Wyddfa timings 164

Z

zips, jacket 27